Peter Mörtenböck, Helge Mooshammer (eds.)
Space (Re)Solutions

Cultural and Media Studies

PETER MÖRTENBÖCK, HELGE MOOSHAMMER (EDS.)

Space (Re)Solutions

Intervention and Research in Visual Culture

[transcript]

**Bibliographic information published by
the Deutsche Nationalbibliothek**
The Deutsche Nationalbibliothek lists this publication in the
Deutsche Nationalbibliografie; detailed bibliographic data are available
in the Internet at http://dnb.d-nb.de

Cover illustration: © Peter Mörtenböck & Helge Mooshammer,
San Diego/Tijuana, 2009
Printed by Majuskel Medienproduktion GmbH, Wetzlar
ISBN 978-3-8376-1847-1

Global distribution outside Germany, Austria and Switzerland:

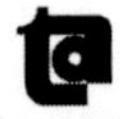

Transaction Publishers
New Brunswick (U.S.A.) and London (U.K.)

Transaction Publishers
Rutgers University
35 Berrue Circle
Piscataway, NJ 08854

Tel.: (732) 445-2280
Fax: (732) 445-3138
for orders (U.S. only):
toll free 888-999-6778

Contents

GEOGRAPHIES OF CIRCULATION

BOUNDARIES OF PRACTICE

Motions

PETER MÖRTENBÖCK AND HELGE MOOSHAMMER

When we take a closer look at the mutability of discourses, institutional practices and research approaches today, two phenomena stand out in particular: on the one hand the rapid changes in thinking relating to how we encounter the subjects of our experiential world, and, on the other, the rapid change in the subjects themselves that constitute the substance of these encounters. Together these phenomena account for the shifts in cultural boundaries that guide what we do. They alter the focus of our attention and the manner in which we critically process our environment, relate it to our own interests and thereby make it a matter of concern.

For more than two decades the process of engaging with this continuous reconfiguration has been a central focus of the various strands of enquiry grouped around the concept of Visual Culture. This field of critical thinking is not tied to a particular subject or methodological canon, and in the course of its development it has drawn a range of academic discourses, artistic currents and emancipatory interests into its orbit. The insistence on boundaries as sites of engagement within the field of Visual Culture has made it possible to absorb a range of different voices into a discursive field conceived as a process of permanent change. This field repeatedly coalesces around new terrain precisely because it is founded not on a fixed subject of interrogation but on an orientation to prevailing boundaries whose exigencies provide a basis for the development of a critical discourse and the creation of possibilities of intervention.

A look back at the development of the discourse of Visual Culture reveals not only the diversity of interests directed at this field but also the degree to which what is regarded as a boundary in Visual Culture has changed over the last ten, twenty or twenty-five years. Whereas in the 1990s the issue was still one of crossing the disciplinary boundaries between art history, photography, new media, cultural anthropology and the burgeoning projects of Cultural Studies and Queer and Postcolonial Studies, this situation has now changed significantly. The central concepts of gaze, vision and visuality and their convergence in the context of practices of looking continue to echo in the engagement with questions of technology, spectacle, surveillance, globalization and the role of art; but today the signs, institutions and subjects of visual culture are embedded in a growing complexity of geographies, apparatuses and participations. The geocultural instabilities of the present, political upheavals, worldwide economic crises, global migrations, technological changes, new forms of collective interaction and new forms of education mean that an improved instrument is required that can make sense of these developments and offer new perspectives. Some of the most important markers of the resonance of these changes in the discourse of visual culture are the incessant shifts of focus in Visual Culture as a field of study, the different reflections on the field's own journey in its attempts to narrate the history of Visual Culture, the various debates on the state of Visual Culture that have taken place in the *Journal of Visual Culture*,[1] perhaps the field's most notable journal, as well as recent initiatives within the academy that question the project of Visual Culture altogether vis-à-vis an enormous enthusiasm among new generations of researchers in different world regions and the current attempts to consolidate Visual Culture further through a global association of Visual Culture scholars.

However symptomatic these efforts may be, what has emerged over the last decade as one of the most enduring aspects of work in Visual Culture is a persistent desire for both a critical sensitivity toward its theoretical underpinnings and an experimental elasticity in its methodological approaches. Today, this drive is giving rise to a plethora of new investigative practices and multi-directional engagements, particularly with respect to matters of geopolitical urgency and their cultural and spatial implications. What has become evident in recent years, in particular, is that the established scenarios of visuality that we have been concerned with in Visual Culture over many years—the questions of who looks, who is being watched, who is part of a representation and who is given permission to voice their political concerns, etc—have turned into something far more volatile and unbounded: they have turned into radically new ways of being together, into new assemblages of people, apparatuses and governments, into new forms of global connectivities that demand a new relational sensibility based on spatial distribution rather than territorial belonging. Most importantly, we are now faced with a plethora of questions and demands that have to do with the changing realities we find ourselves immersed in, be it as academics, artists, writers, activists, or whatever role one may be willing to subscribe to.

An important question that arises from this increasing complexity of the cultural sphere is how to make this global change productive—how to deal with the erosion of numerous boundaries and with the ways in which we are now confronted with the manifestation of new and ever more sophisticated boundary and network structures. In other words, how to inhabit the current

---

1   See *Journal of Visual Culture* 2(1&2), April & August 2003, and 4(2), August 2005

cultural and political transformations both in terms of academic work and in terms of practice more generally. It is not by chance that practice has become such a buzz word in the academy and art education respectively. Practice has moved centre stage as an experimental mode of knowledge production, one that is often linked to an emerging research culture characterized by notions of collectivity, collaboration and intervention. Especially in recent years, these dynamics have brought to the fore a range of political and educational initiatives, transversal knowledge platforms, and activist networks that have begun to spearhead the debate about forms of critical engagement in processes of globalisation. As opposed to purely theoretical or conceptual speculation, practice seems to be much more attuned to the politics of intervention, and thus to hold the key to promoting unsolicited participations. Not least in light of this unruly potential for civic participation, it seems pertinent to call upon the rising interest in practical experimentation across a wide range of civic actors for in-depth reflections on acts of translation between the theoretical and the practical, artistic and pragmatic.

At the university and art academy level numerous practice-based Ph.D. programmes are now providing an important platform for this discussion, although they are more a symptom than the result of the changing relationship between theory and practice. These programmes clearly show how closely research and intervention parallel one another when we comprehend research not as a field of academic thought but as an open cultural practice and when we begin to plumb the different possibilities inherent in this practice. Probably one of the most significant potentials of this approach consists in the fluid transition from one practice to other practices and the associated contaminations and intertwinements between different spheres.

Such a focus on practice is therefore significant for Visual Culture research in several respects: one the one hand as a way of mobilizing contemporary critical discourse beyond the confines of disciplines and the separation of methods, roles and subjects they presuppose. However, on the other, this orientation to forms of practice also means that research interests are not only oriented to a structural analysis of the objective components of our experiential sphere but also to the question of what is being maintained and/or promoted by the institutions, discourses and actors under investigation, i.e. what type of practice the complex constellations of our environment themselves represent. Moreover, this orientation also entails not least a consideration of the potential of one's own practice with all its protocols, rules and procedures—of the significance of the prevailing tension between the abstraction and representation of research observations and one's own engagement in critical situations. Both tendencies—abstraction and intervention—work from different ends in the process of probing realities, of revealing aspects that are not part of our knowledge, that are possibly concealed or suppressed such that they do are not included in the scope of our claims and possibilities for action.

One radical point of departure of this type of practice-based research is thus the question of what it is that we do not know—the question of the apparatus we require to generate the knowledge that we have previously disregarded, either intentionally or unintentionally. This attitude not only assumes that parity of all knowledge in principle but also directs our attention to the actors involved and the factual environment in which these experiences can take place, i.e. the formation of conditions under which a certain type of material can be encountered and used. When, for example, the issue is one of learning experiences then the focus must be on the actual learning environment and the practice of learning rather than the transmission of knowledge from one person to another. The question of what knowledge can be produced is thus ultimately dependent on the spaces in which we deal with material, the relational structures we thereby enter into and the quality of our dialogues. Interventionist research therefore also entails the interrogation, manipulation and formation of the settings in which a certain question is pursued.

An important site of this critical engagement in the field of visual culture is constituted by the numerous approaches characterizing contemporary artistic practice with which collective processes of empowerment can be initiated in order to open up a new understanding of cultural participation. A parallel development can be observed in the recent emergence of many academic institutions, platforms and project groups devoted to the creation of new perspectives and new forms of practice in knowledge production around questions of social and spatial environments. Moreover, the many current aspirations detectable in the exhibition field, art pedagogy and practical processes of mediation to explore new ways of opening up, representing and communicating complex spatial and social processes also need to be seen as part of this development.

What we are aiming to trace through this volume of essays are the interactions of different forms of practice that critically address forces constitutive of our current moment: the coming together of phenomena such as border violations, wartime media coverage, circulation anxieties, live art events, counter-environments, dreaming economies, blogospheres, educational protest programmes and informal urbanism. All these phenomena have a critical impact on the ways we conceive and inhabit the spaces we share. They have themselves been affected by the different forces and movements that embrace, ignore or fight the growing instabilities of our urban, political and institutional fields. The restive dynamics of these phenomena are giving rise not least to an erratic concept of space itself—the space arising from the numerous theatres of war we are currently confronted with; the space traced by the labyrinthine routes of migrations; the all-encompassing phantasmagorical space of the War on Terror; but also the space of new collective experiences and transversal aggregations; the space of improvisation, invention and practical experimentation. Space is thereby shifting once again to the centre of engagement, a space whose authority does not primarily emerge in the context of reflective observation but in the moment of emergence itself. What is at issue here is thus a probing of the contours of a space, contours that cannot be anticipated either with the instruments of a strategic practice or a practice-oriented strategy.

In the light of such dynamics, this book brings together researchers and practitioners whose work is deeply embedded in the turbulent enmeshment of emergent spatial phenomena and new modes of theoretical inquiry. The assertion in this context of a combined concept of intervention and research brings spatial practice—one of the three points in Henri Lefebvre's spatial triad—together with Michel Foucault's use of the concept of the *dispositif* (apparatus). In Lefebvre's words, spatial practice embodies »a close association [...] between daily reality (daily routine) and urban reality (the routes and networks which link up the places set aside for work, ›private' life and leisure)« (Lefebvre 1991: 38). As examples of his concept of spatial practice, Lefebvre points to the everyday experience of renters in tenements, life on motorways and the politics of air traffic. Here spatial practice entails the linkage of localities with routine processes. But what is missing here is a strategic logic concerned with power and knowledge. And it is precisely this logic that forms part of what Michel Foucault characterizes as *dispositif.* Foucault's concept of the *dispositif* comprises a network of heterogeneous elements that can be discourses but equally also institutions, architectures, laws, administrative procedures, scholarly statements or moral principles, in short the strategic composition of the mechanisms deployed in the constitution of subjectivity. The strategic function of the *dispositif* involves clearly calculated interventions in power relations in order to destabilize, utilize or further develop them (Foucault 1980: 194–196). Whereas competence in the field of spatial practice consists in abidance and the generation of consistency and continuity, the strengths of *dispositifs* lie in the aspiration to change. However, both concepts relate to a fundamental point around which their action potential coalesces: their logic is oriented to the principle of networks, the site of exchange, distribution and multiplications. It is founded on the morphological openness of networks, an aspect that is crucial to the spontaneous unfolding of social processes and that facilitates an ongoing transfer of dissident meanings and values in the sphere of political action in the shadow of all attempts at regulation.

This shared orientation of spatial practice and *dispositifs* makes it possible for us also to think agency independently of strategic aspiration, i.e. to see a form of activism also in the ramifications and resistances that spatial practice always entails and not only in the mobilization of this practice as concerted political action. Conversely, it becomes clear that a strategic endeavour around the production of knowledge does not necessarily need to have political dimensions that promote self-determined action. Such an endeavour can also aspire to protect dominant systems, establish internal homogeneities and ward off dissenting behaviour. Both strands thus offer neither stabilities nor guarantees but rather a degree of the unknown from which something can emerge. It is the tension between the two logics, i.e. their fundamentally unpredictable interplay, which enables them to open up our knowledge to the uncertain. And it is through examining this tension that the essays in this volume hope to better grasp not only what kinds of spaces we collectively create, but also what the animating principles of the ever-changing field of Visual Culture are today and what they could be in the future.

BIBLIOGRAPHY

Foucault, Michel (1980): *Power/Knowledge: Selected Interviews and Other Writings, 1972–1977*, edited by C. Gordon, New York: Pantheon Books.
Journal of Visual Culture, London: Sage.
Lefebvre, Henri (1991): *The Production of Space*, Oxford: Blackwell.

Ecologies of Visibility

On the Ground

Media in Conflict Zones[1]

KRISTA GENEVIÈVE LYNES

In wrestling with the imagery of Abu Ghraib and Guantanamo, Anne McClintock posed the question, »How do we insist on seeing the violence that the imperial state attempts to render invisible, while also seeing the ordinary people afflicted by that violence?« (McClintock 2009: 52). What she identifies is a paradox of visual culture in conflict zones: that an exposure of the spectacle of wartime media coverage may render a more grounded perspective impossible, and—less obviously—that the converse might also be true. Grounded visions historically have sought to flesh out the cost of war, the immediacy of battle, and have played an important role in shattering the singular views of the war presented on either side of the conflict. Multiple and fragmentary visions on the ground of conflict zones may work to counter the consolidation of war-time power (which draws heavily on iconic images and mythical forms of speech), demonstrating acts of solidarity within nascent resistance movements and drawing transnational attention to local political actions. Such visions may also, however, confirm (and allegorize) the binary oppositions within the conflict zone and thus contribute either to a resurgent nationalism (on either side) or to the rendering of absolutist subject positions. The immediacy of grassroots media (and their distribution through the networks of new media platforms) may electrify distant (and differently located) publics just as they may repeat the mythical speech of top-down media forms. What critical tools exist, then, to parse the expanded field of visual culture and, particularly, its role in visualizing contemporary conflict zones?

---

1   I presented an early version of this article at a New Media Caucus panel at the College Art Association Annual Conference in Los Angeles, California in 2009, the proceeds of which were published in the online journal *media-N* 5(2), summer 2009. http://www.newmediacaucus.org/html/journal/issues.php?f=papers& time=2009_summer&page=kelley

Visual culture studies has drawn the connections between the spectacular violence of military campaigns (with names like *Operation Enduring Freedom* and *Shock and Awe*) and the spectacle of war-time media coverage—the ›liveness‹ of events unfolding on television screens and the destructive vision from the perspective of so-called ›smart bombs‹, the spectacle of light combined with the utter obscurity of the bombing campaign's effects on the civilian population. Robert Stam, for instance, has argued in relation to the first Gulf War that TV news gave viewers an »exhilarating sense of visual power,« combined both by the reach of cameras deployed around the world, the direct transmission of images and sounds through satellite transmission, and the apparatus of a military simulation and surveillant gaze (Stam 1992: 102). The iconic images at the onset of the US war in Iraq and Afghanistan contrasted the *visibility* of US power with the *invisibility* of the enemy, both the elusive nature of key figures (such as Saddam Hussein and Osama Bin Laden) and the iconoclasm of the Taliban.

Specifically, the binary of visibility and invisibility served to prop up the distinctions the US regime was making between ›freedom‹ (aligned with the West) and ›terrorism‹ (associated with various ›others‹ that crossed geographical, political, ethnic and religious lines). Thus, the Taliban's ›iconoclasm‹ was figured in Western media through, first, the images of women forced to wear the burqa under the Taliban regime, and second, the 1 March 2001 shelling of the Buddhist statues in the Bamiyan province. As compensation for these visual prohibitions, images of both the Bamiyan Buddhist sculptures and of Afghani women became icons in the Western imaginary for a country »out of time with Western modernity, by referencing an existing discourse in which image destruction indexed the inherently medieval nature of Islamic culture« (Flood 2002: 641). Since 11 September 2001, this particular imagery has been bolstered not only by the depictions of ›Islamic terrorism‹, but also by a re-codification of self and other across newly articulated racial, gendered and ethnic boundaries. Central to this was the attachment of discourses of ›freedom‹ to the specific image of Afghan women's unveiling.

The images of Afghani women come into view in the Western media through a quite striking mythological sleight of hand, one where they become transformed (and naturalized) as icons of Afghanistan's suffering at the hands of the Taliban. Cornelia Brink has unpacked the particular tropic value of the icon and finds that a) they are indexical (in religious terms, they imply a direct causal relationship between the copy and the original image); b) they are symbolic (in other words, they »condense complex phenomena and represent history in an exemplary form«); c) they rely on their reproducibility and the image becoming canonized; and d) they rely on separation. The effect, for Brink is that iconic images »make a moral claim to be accepted without questioning« (Brink 2000: 141–144). Top-down media thus *reveal* graphically to us (explicit in the doctrine of shock and awe), but also conceal and mediate our relation to war, providing what Brink calls a ›protective layer‹. These images thus inure us to violence, dehistoricizing and decontextualizing them, and distancing us from the events unfolding. Official media channels (on the left and the right) rely on a discourse of visibility—within an ideologically constrained channel—to present us with a kind of offer we can't refuse: the retributive might of the United States in avenging the wrongs of 9/11 embedded in the moral rectitude of a discourse of freedom and a civilizing narrative that has its roots in the mantra identified by Gayatri Spivak of ›white men saving brown women from brown men‹.

Such an analysis, however, has not yet dealt with the proliferation of images, tapes, and leaked documents that have constituted the expanded media culture of conflict in the twenty-first century. Images taken with cell phones, the work of embedded journalists, viral videos on the Internet, and independent reportage by journalists and NGOs have increased the visual rhetoric of the war, and supported both the war efforts and opposition movements around the world. Such new visions—relying on more grainy amateur production equipment, as well as alternative channels of distribution and reception—have also shifted the vantage points on the war from the spectacular heights of smart bombs or the iconic portraits of rescue, to the more grounded perspective of the desert road, the city street, the inside of an advancing tank, or a secret school.

Optimistic accounts of the expanded field of visual culture have emphasized the potential of these media forms to challenge the hegemony of cable media channels. The grounded perspective employed by soldiers, reporters, and civilians suggest a kind of democratizing of images of war, not only because the number of actors recording their experiences has multiplied, but because the images are channeled through not only traditional news media, but also blogs, email campaigns, YouTube and other viral avenues. This footage at times relies on representational conventions to indicate the immediacy of the action taking place (a shaky camera, for example, or the sudden disappearance of a recorded image), but such conventions also render certain subjects and certain forms of seeing impossible, even as they cloak themselves in the guises of a new form of objectivity.

There is a need to parse more carefully, however, the important structural connections between top-down and bottom-up media forms within a given image environment. How do media frame events and subjects? What are the thresholds of visibility? And how are these thresholds critical to the politics of representation? The key question here is whether new media *reflect* dominant iconographies across the field of visual culture, or whether they *diffract* such visions, implicating multiple perspectives, media and visual languages. Donna Haraway has argued that reflexivity might be an impoverished framework for critical practices because, in her terms, it »only displaces the same elsewhere« (Haraway 1997: 16). The transparency of certain figurations thus may take the place of various labours of communication across cultural, racial, gendered and class differences. Diffraction, on the other hand, contains the possibility of attending to the interference patterns that mediate our relation to the visible world—be these technological, economic, political or ethical. How might we parse the different forms of media and their interconnection? Attend to the processes of reflection and diffraction in representations of conflict zones?

In the service of examining this complex field of visual representations, I would like to propose a (perhaps limiting) schema, but one which may contribute to expanding the conceptual tools for analyzing the field of visual culture. This Greimasian ›semiotic square‹ takes as its central opposition the relation between visibility and invisibility in contemporary representations of the wars in Afghanistan and Iraq, and overlays this binary with the distinction between top-down and bottom-up media.

Figure 1.1: The expanded field of visual culture in conflict zones

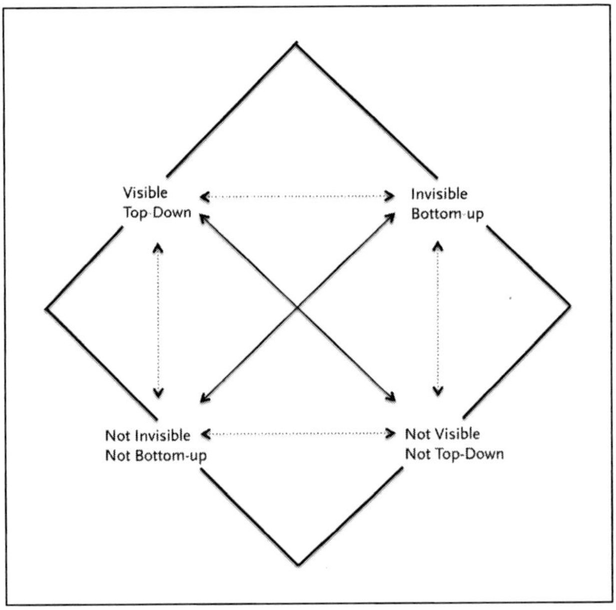

Visible
Top-Down

Invisible
Bottom-up

Not Invisible
Not Bottom-up

Not Visible
Not Top-Down

Greimasian Semiotic Square

INVISIBLE; BOTTOM UP

The top set of terms traces the relation between, for example, the ›frenzy of the visible‹ presented by *Operation Enduring Freedom* and the forms of new media taken with a grounded perspective of the conflict. While works taken on the ground seem to provide an immediate, first-hand account of the theatre of war, the experiences they reveal are often coded within the very terms of the iconic images of war, and thus confirm the governing logic of that conflict. Such works make use of the immediacy of a grounded perspective without the appeal to ›grassroots‹. An example of this form of media is a video recorded by a Canadian soldier serving in Afghanistan, Glen Villa. Villa shot footage of his base camp, the battlefield and his unit patrolling villages, all through a small camera attached to his helmet. The footage was picked up and edited in a longer reportage piece entitled *Fighting Ghosts*, which aired on CBC's *The National*.[2]

Figure 1.2: Glen Villa, Fighting Ghosts, *2009*

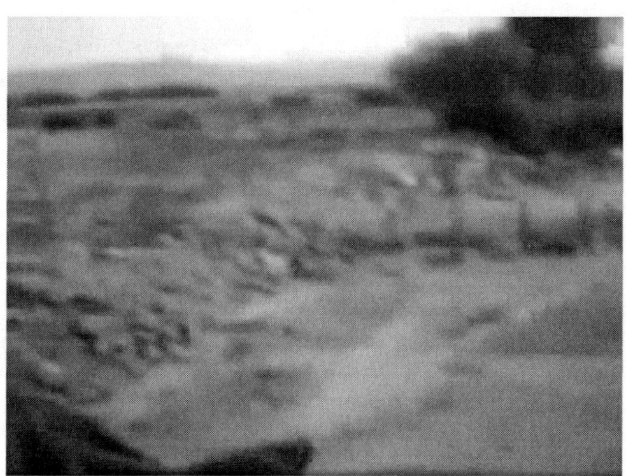

Source: Screenshot of broadcast by Canadian Broadcast
Corporation

The footage paradigmatically exemplifies the liveness of the war from the ground. The viewer feels the camera's moving and shaking as Villa repositions himself, sees the dust kicked up, the frenetic panning of the horizon, and the gunshots ringing out in space. The video thus participates in the extension of visions of the war, from the mainstream news media to amateur footage by inside sources. What is particularly interesting about this footage, and the title *Fighting Ghosts*, however, is how the perils of the war against the Taliban are particularly articulated as a failure to see the enemy, and hence the figuration of a ›shadowy enemy‹. In presenting the Taliban in this manner, such footage reinforces the tropes employed by the US administration, and serves to associate invisibility with a threat to security, the oppressive and secretive regime, and the abuses against women in Afghanistan and against American citizens on 9/11. The very vividness of the footage cap-

---

2   The video is available on CBC's website at http://www.cbc.ca/national/blog/ special_feature/fighting_ghosts/. It has also been posted on YouTube at http:// www.youtube.com/watch?v=BE7ANG2HS-w.

tured therefore lies in what it fails to represent: the Taliban fighters, the very human contact which should *ground* the experience of war on the ground.

This failure of seeing, however, is precisely what the footage represents as the vulnerability of war. Hence, the invisibility of the enemy guarantees in some ways the immediacy of this alternative media form. We might further think of the grainy aesthetic of night-video and of satellite reportage through cellphones by embedded journalists as a kind of aestheticization of grassroots imaging within the terms of the mainstream media. The form signifies a groundedness which masks the more normative channels of war's visual culture.

In Villa's footage, the struggle to identify the location from which he is being fired upon reconfirms the rhetoric of ghostly apparitions at play in official government statements—for example, George W. Bush's statement that »we do not know who the enemy is, but we know they are out there« or former Attorney General Gonzalez's statement that »we face an enemy that lies in the shadows« (McClintock 2009: 55–57). Thus, the prevalence of camera phones and video cameras, like the practice of embedding journalists with army units, might extend rather than challenge the iconicity of war, mobilizing a grounded vision to reinforce the indisputability of the events unfolding before the camera. It is worth noting also that the footage dehumanizes the enemy not only because it presents it as a target one cannot see, but also because the effect of the camera mounted on Villa's helmet reproduces in fact the figuration of identity in video games and—more importantly—in army training videos. Thus the reality effect is closer to the simulated energy of game culture than the complexity of combat on the ground.

NOT INVISIBLE; NOT BOTTOM UP

In using a Greimasian square to open up the binary of visibility/invisibility to its negations, the emergence of a more complex vision complicates the representation of conflict zones, if only through an exposure of the mechanisms of power in dominant visual culture. Thus, the forms of media characterized as ›not invisible‹ and ›not bottom up‹, for instance, might constitute an irruption into public view of what would have remained hidden, a return of the repressed—both in the sense of the bodies, desires and affects rendered invisible in the conflict zone and in the sense of the modes of disenfranchisement produced out of the occupation of a foreign country (and the institution of a weak governing structure). The photographs at Abu Ghraib testify not only to the desire to produce the enemy as a »legible enem[y],« but also to codify and represent a »phantasy of domination« (McClintock 2009: 62). Thus, the dazzling omnipotence of the Shock and Awe footage of air raids might reveal beneath—and co-extensive with—its logic the heterogeneous enactments of domination on the ground (forms of domination covered over with the discourse of ›bad apples‹).

A semiotic square might seem like a blunted instrument for prying open the field of new media, especially given its static and ahistorical appearance. It may, however, remain a useful tool for at least two reasons: first, there is a tendency to associate new media with new developments in technology, and thus to see the opening of new communications spaces in the light of narratives of progress (the promise of democracy, access, expansion, the freedom from hierarchy, and the absence of authoritarian or monopoly control). Saskia Sassen, however, insists that »electronic space is inscribed, and to some extent shaped, by power, concentration and contestation as well as by openness and decentralization,« and thus challenges the progress narratives that underwrite forms of technophilia (Sassen 1998: 177). Secondly, a structuralist model allows for an examination of the processes of *mediation* between levels or instances of visual culture, an understanding of the interdependencies in a larger structure, and most importantly a foregrounding of the sites of foreclosure or the aporias within that structure (heavily inflected by gender, race and ethnicity).

Fredric Jameson argues that Greimas's schema should be viewed as »a set of categories to be explored, rather than as a forecast of the shape of the results of analysis« (Jameson 1981: 46). What appears to be a static analytical scheme, then, organized around binary oppositions, can be reappropriated for criticism by, in his terms, »designating it as the very model of ideological closure« (ibid.: 47). Analyses of new media must accordingly pay particular attention to these sites of ideological closure, and to mechanisms through which certain figurations of gender, sexuality, ethnicity and/or class are upheld. The semiotic square proposed here thus not only maps the manner in which new media might support or critique normative models of difference, for example, but also presents methods for a critical media practice.

NOT VISIBLE; NOT TOP DOWN

The final quadrant in the schema outlined above points to a form of media that engages with the iconicity of the image without counter-posing it with the immediacy of a grounded vision. This final level of analysis also sheds light on the inadequacies of certain figurations of subjectivity within this field of visual culture, and specifically, the manner in which the mobilization of iconicity repeats the dehistoricizing gesture of top-down media. In this regard, the Afghani-American artist Lida Abdul's *The White House* (2005) serves as an interesting critical example.

The White House was produced while Abdul was an artist-in-residence in Kabul in 2005, and has circulated broadly in international contemporary art circuits.[3] In the work, Abdul approaches the ruins of a large Greco-Roman style building in Kabul that has been turned to rubble. Armed with a can of white paint and paintbrush, she endeavours to paint the entire ruin white, down to the smallest stone. At one point, a man emerges in the scene, and he too is painted with a broad brush-stroke across his back.

The work clearly engages the status of the icon (the iconic nature of the ruin, but also the reification of everyday life through the artistic process), and its relation to the artistic performance. Because the work presents a de-contextualized image of ruin, however, the ruin itself transcends the histori-cal and geopolitical specificity of contemporary Afghanistan. This is true not only of the excising of the contemporary history of the ruin in Afghani-stan (most of the bombed buildings in Kabul are a result of the war against Soviet occupation and point perhaps to the ongoing devastation of the coun-try, caught in the crosshairs of the Cold War) but also to the nostalgia of ruin, which Andreas Huyssen has identified as a nostalgia for modernity it-self. Further, the relation between Abdul and the man who steps into her sculptural tableau may refigure the art historical conventions of the mascu-line creative act and woman-as-image. But it does so only through a reversal that doesn't question the very structures of gender ideology at play across the US and Afghani context, as well as across the different sites of the work's display (the nationalist residual imaginaries of the Venice Biennale, or the appeals to a ›global feminism‹ in the exhibit at the Brooklyn Mu-seum).

This example serves not simply to elucidate the models of ideological closure within the structure of the semiotic square outlined above, but also to articulate how the structure itself works against multiplicity, difference and diffraction. Accordingly, strategies within media cannot simply expand their reach to those subjects that do not appear within the system, since the system itself guarantees their very invisibility (often by narrowly defining political subjectivity). Within existing media structures, the politics of rep-resentation often lead to largely metropolitan (and often Western) audiences being invited to witness abuses, which are always conceived as occurring elsewhere. These structures of visibility reinforce the terrain represented as a visible field, open for inspection or revelation. Attention, then, to the struc-ture of ideological closure by cultural producers opens the possibility of rup-turing received frameworks, attending to issues of cultural difference, as well as to the translation of images as they travel across contexts, classes, or historical realities. Centrally, such strategies at least hold open the possibil-ity of registering difference at the level of both the subjects invoked in me-dia, but also the viewing subject.

---

3   Most notably, it represented Afghanistan at the Venice Biennale in 2005 and was
     included in the Global Feminisms exhibit at the Brooklyn Museum in 2007.

THE EXPANDED FIELD OF VISUAL CULTURE

How then might these larger structures of ideological closure function in relation to grassroots media? A key example of grassroots feminist media in the case of Afghanistan is clearly the Revolutionary Association of the Women of Afghanistan (RAWA). RAWA was founded in 1977, and has acted as a public voice, first, for women's rights in Afghanistan, and following, against the Soviet occupation, the Taliban's rule, and the US-led war after 11 September 2001. They have been central in voicing social justice issues in Afghanistan, and organizing access points for basic human rights (creating hospitals and schools, teaching nursing courses and promoting literacy, and distributing basic food and medicine). Since 1992, they have recorded incidences of human rights abuse and provided them to human rights organizations, the news media, and—since 1997—have been posting footage on their website to disseminate records of abuses under the Taliban, by the Northern Alliance, and as a result of the US-led war. Most of the videos and photos posted on the site have been taken by RAWA activists with a hidden camera and have used the structure of invisibility imposed by the Taliban on women (specifically the mandatory requirement that women wear the burqa) to subvert the Taliban's ban on image-production more widely. The footage is largely unedited, recorded and posted to a YouTube gallery that overflows from page to page.

Figure 1.3: Public Execution of an Afghan Woman
(Zarmeena) by Taliban, 1999

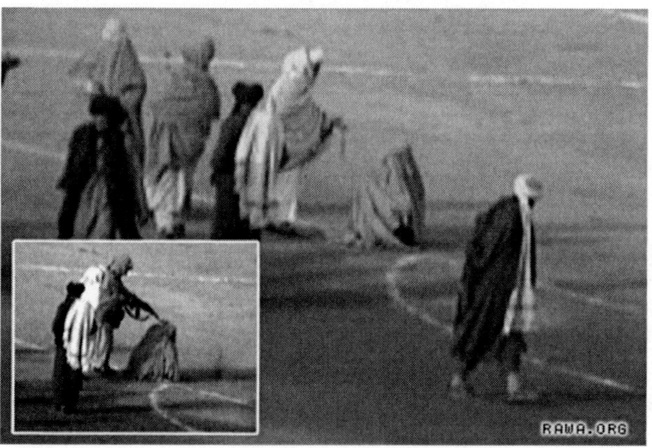

Source: Revolutionary Association of the Women of Afghanistan
(RAWA)

Perhaps the most well known video recorded by RAWA is the footage of the execution of a woman, known simply as Zarmeena, accused of murdering her husband. Brought to the national football stadium, she is publicly executed by a Taliban soldier in front of a cheering crowd. While the Associated Press reported the execution, cable and broadcast media outlets such as the BBC, CNN, and ABC refused to air the video. RAWA states, »We were told ›as the footage is very shocking, Western viewers can't bear it, so we are sorry that we can't air it‹ « (Rawi 2004: 118). After 9/11, however, these same media channels aired the footage repeatedly.[4]

What emerges, then, is the path of a piece of footage within the circuit of the visual culture of conflict zones, from the bottom-right hand corner of the semiotic square (not visible; not top-down) to its top right-hand corner (invisible; bottom-up). As it does so, the forms of visibility shift, from a form of invisibility sequestered from the mainstream media through censorship, to a form of invisibility that parallels both the vision of the Taliban as a ›shadowy enemy‹ and the violence of its purported iconoclasm. Although RAWA has made strong critical statements against the war, the US support for the Northern Alliance, and the diminishment of women's rights since the overthrow of the Taliban, their transnational interventions have had to negotiate the complex relation between their isolation from the Bonn Accords, for example, and their media presence on Oprah Winfrey and in *Glamour Magazine* (where they were named ›Women of the Year‹ in 2001). The debate surrounding RAWA's critique of the Feminist Majority Foundation (a Western feminist organization which has supported RAWA's fundraising efforts and helped put a stop to a secret oil pipeline deal between the Taliban and the US multinational Unocal) signals the complex emergence of RAWA in the Western press, and its efforts to resist its enclosure within the wartime field of visual culture.

Thus, it is important for critical media studies to trace a given media's function within the larger structure of media culture, to trace the mediation of the tropes of visibility and invisibility as objects move through the system. Specifically, such critical resources are tasked with highlighting the disjunctions between media platforms in the field of visual culture, and thus with mapping the diffraction—the interference patterns—within that system and between the actors they call upon and interpellate. This signals that it is not enough to ›make visible‹ as a rights-granting mechanism, since the terms of visibility are already predefined by a socio-cultural system and semiotic apparatus that only brings certain subjects into visibility, and only on specific terms. Cultural producers must, instead, examine *in media* the manner in which framing devices limit the rights-bearing subject herself, often in ways which disable not only differences between cultural systems but also differences *within* them.

Judith Butler has stressed that we conventionally think that gaining representation increases the likelihood that the subject will be humanized, but invites us to think more complexly about the processes of humanization and dehumanization—how certain forms of representation contribute to the de-

---

4   It is worth noting also that the US military appropriated images from RAWA for use in propaganda flyers dropped by US warplanes over Afghanistan.

humanization of subjects—and of the multiple ways in which violence can happen in and through representation. There is the possibility of violence in both visibility and invisibility, and this is especially true in media representations in times of political conflict and war. Butler states,

»The demand for a truer image, for more images, for images that convey the full horror and reality of the suffering has its place and importance. The erasure of that suffering through the prohibition of images and representations more generally circumscribes the sphere of appearance, what we can see and what we can know. But it would be a mistake to think that we only need to find the right and true images, and that a certain reality will then be conveyed. The reality is not conveyed by what is represented within the image, but through the challenge to representation that reality delivers« (Butler 2004: 146).

Although grassroots media have often stressed the importance of producing positive images, such a position risks producing boundary debates about what (formal, stylistic or thematic) markers point to a properly positive aesthetic. Diffraction (as a critical and creative methodology) serves to flesh out a politics which produces what Teresa de Lauretis calls »the feeling of internal distance, a contradiction, a space of silence, which is there alongside the imaginary pull of cultural and ideological representations without denying or obliterating them« (De Lauretis 1988: 181). Diffraction then is a practice that highlights how images might produce subjective and social contradictions as they engage individuals in articulating meanings. Historically, feminist critiques of representation have noted how images in the field of visual culture are placed within and read from the context of ideologies whose values and effects are »social and subjective, aesthetic and affective, and permeate the entire social fabric, and hence all social subjects, women as well as men« (De Lauretis 1984: 38–39). Analyses of media *on the ground* need therefore to consider who is made visible, how, and for whom, and what work might be achieved by documentary and artistic projects. In the contemporary moment, the promise of access and democratization in grassroots media has renewed the demand for analyses which critically appraise the new channels, patterns and forms of alternative media, art work and documentary, and assess the social relations mediated by new technologies. Visual culture studies are especially tasked with examining more carefully the channels of media communication, structures of visibility, genres of expression, modes of spectatorship, and social relations of production and display. What is brought into view by new media? Who is figured and for whom? How are the restrictive frameworks of mainstream representations challenged? What new forms of relationality and connectedness are produced? Which channels of identification and/or desire are allowed to flow or are dammed up? On the ground, yes, but whose ground? And on what grounds?

BIBLIOGRAPHY

Brink, Cornelia (2000): »Secular Icons: Looking at Photographs from Nazi Concentration Camps«. *History & Memory* 12(1), p. 135–150.

Butler, Judith (2004): *Precarious Life: The Powers of Mourning and Violence*, London: Verso.

De Lauretis, Teresa (1984): *Alice Doesn't: Feminism, Semiotics, Cinema*, Bloomington, IN: Indiana University Press.

——— (1988): »Aesthetics and Feminist Theory«. In: E. Deirdre Pribham (ed.), *Female Spectators: Looking at Film and Television*, London: Verso, p. 174–195.

Flood, Finbarr Barry (2002): »Between Cult and Culture: Bamiyan, Islamic Iconoclasm, and the Museum«. *Art Bulletin* 84(4), p. 641–659.

Haraway, Donna (1997): *Modest_Witness@Second_Millenium.FemaleMan ©_Meets_OncoMouse^{TM}*, New York: Routledge.

Jameson, Fredric (1981): *The Political Unconscious: Narrative as a Socially Symbolic Act*, Ithaca, NY: Cornell University Press.

McClintock, Anne (2009): »Paranoid Empire: Specters from Guantanamo and Abu Ghraib«. *Small Axe* 13(1), p. 50–74.

Rawi, Mariam (2004): »Betrayal«. *Reproductive Health Matters* 12(23), p. 116–119.

Sassen, Saskia (1998): *Globalization and its Discontents*, New York: New Press.

Stam, Robert (1992): »Mobilizing Fictions: The Gulf War, the Media, and the Recruitment of the Spectator«. *Public Culture* 4(2), p. 101–126.

Landscapeness as Social Primer and Ground

Visual and Spatial Processes between Biopolitics, Habitation and the Body

IRENE NIERHAUS

This text is concerned with the effects of landscapeness, with its ideational structure as a (putative) extension of the true, authentic and original and its ›friendly‹ visualization of the biopolitical in residential construction after 1945 as well as the interventions of visual media in this process.

We are currently seeing a reactualization of landscape as an image/space of reference for ›big‹ themes such as ›world‹ or society as a whole. In this context landscape seems to have the potential to render the contemporary structural changes in politics, the economy and morality emphatically visible. Between the conceptual markers of the catastrophic (environmental damage, climate change etc.) and the universal remedy (harmony between human beings and between human beings and nature), the kaleidoscopic figure of landscape unfolds and refracts into a wide spectrum of universal, futuristic and eschatological concepts.[1] And within this structural transfor-

---

1   On the meaning of landscape see the two large exhibitions on architecture (2010) and art (2009) at recent Venice Biennales, which refer to this theme in multiple ways. Under the motto of ›Making Worlds‹ the art biennale interconnected ideas of creation and the creative with the concept of the creatural—see, for example, the orchestration of the Corderie in the Arsenale with the shafts-of-light setting by Lygia Pape at the entrance, *Overgrowth*, a bonsai tree re-natured to its ›natural‹ size by Ceal Floyer at the exit, the swamp garden by Lara Favaretto, the conversion of the façade of the Giardini general exhibition pavilion into a beachscape by John Baldessari, the catastrophic *Garden of Eden* by Nathalie Djurbeg, and the fable-like super-saga landscapes by Pavel Pepperstein. Many contributions to the architecture biennale were characterized by an integration of landscapeness as a means of improving everyday life (US Pavilion; residential

mation, landscape is being renegotiated as a political and economic space and characterized by a surge of aggressive, pervasive capitalization, such as seen in speculation with agricultural property on financial markets, land-grabbing, and neocolonialist resource policies applied on a large scale. At the same time, ecologically and socially sustainable alternatives promoting, for example, biodiversity, fair trade and the valorization of the regional production of foodstuffs are being articulated. The relationship between these processes is one structured by inequality and power, as is clearly evident in the movements of labour (migration) and recreation (tourism). The kaleidoscopic figure of ›landscape‹ is thereby able to draw on an overflowing reservoir of ideas and imagery that since the Renaissance (and here I am speaking of occidental and in particular European traditions) have been developed and extended, for example, in landscape painting (including images of mountains and ocean and images of exotic and ›homeland‹ spaces as spaces in which the modern subject resonates) and landscape architecture (including landscape gardening and the planting of green spaces).

It is particularly with the advent of modernity (meaning the epoch beginning around 1800) that landscape as an aesthetic and social project literally becomes the ›primer‹ of the social, inasmuch as social processes and their demands for homogenization and difference (gender-race-class) become naturalized. An example is the role of landscape in the visualization of the nation state and associated notions of the homogeneity of its inhabitants as a ›people‹. Based on this spatially organizing political function, landscape can also be thought of here as a figure of the image-space relationship, one that in its kaleidoscopic character exhibits the spatial potential for dominance and intervention as well as the paradoxical—landscape as aesthetic and political display. Display here connotes aesthetically mediated social ascriptions, differences and omissions of the social subject and its affiliations. It refers to the ordering relations and ordering relationships that are configured at different levels of object relations, discursive processes and subjective positions and within which we are occupants and occupied. Displays are understood as a totality of meaningful constellations and groupings that are con- and defigured in situational terms and, in addition, are linguistically structured in representations and available media and media networks. This means that, on the one hand, displays are discursively structured and, on the other, that discourses are display-forming. Landscapeness connotes a dovetailing of display spaces within the framework of a motivic reproduction of landscape and is here a metonymic instance of relational spaces that ultimately appear unplanned or ›naturally‹ developing. Decisive for this concept is not the fact that it addresses a multitude of different landscapes by widening the traditional notion of landscape as garden, park or alpine scene to include ›vernacular‹ landscapes in everyday ›interim terrains‹

---

living as resource intersection point in Fray Foam House by Andrés Jaque Arquitectos). On the meaning of landscape see: Nierhaus/Hoenes/Urban 2010.

(Franzen/Krebs 2006: 12)[2] and urban peripheries, but the fact that it relates to different effects and strategies—the different directions and levels in the way landscape speaks, as it were. In this sense, the real question, as formulated by W.J.T. Mitchell, is: What does landscape do?[3] How does landscape operate when it comes to the constitution of the subject, the state or the nation? What sort of visibility is generated by landscape and what vanishes into it? For example, what are we to make of the fact that in landscape images of the lonely trekker and nature observer or travel images the beholders with their pointing, attention-drawing and knowledge-designative hands are so often male?[4] And what are the implications when an urban green space used by migrant groups for Sunday picnics is suddenly fenced in and rendered inaccessible by city authorities so that all it has to offer is the view of an empty lawn?[5] These examples alone already illustrate how landscape can be used to define affiliation and exclusion according to social, gender and ethnic positions. Landscape is an intentionally aesthetic and social entity and in this sense is certainly not a »weak power« (Mitchell 2002: VII).[6] The

---

2   These two authors are responsible for introducing the principles of cultural landscape studies to the study of the history of art and architecture in German-speaking countries and have thus made a decisive contribution to the discussion around an extended concept of landscape; see also Franzen/Krebs 2005 and Aigner 2004.

3   Mitchell describes the goal of the book he has edited in the following terms: »to change from a noun to a verb [...] not as an object to be seen or a text to be read, but as a process by which social and subjective identities are formed« (Mitchell 2002: 1).

4   This applies in particular to images of journeys to Italy and Rome, in which the landscape and its ancient elements are referred to by the pointing, measuring, drawing and marvelling hands of observers within the image. These hands often contrast with those of resting or working shepherds and farmers.

5   The example relates to a regulation introduced in Rome in 2007 regarding the area around the Via Marmorata, where migrants from Southeast Asia had been meeting. Similar measures have been taken for some time now with regard to the small park areas behind the Capitol—a popular meeting point for homosexuals—which have been increasingly fenced in and rendered inaccessible.

6   It is interesting that in the foreword to the second, expanded edition of the book Mitchell writes that if he had the opportunity to rename the book he would use ›space‹ and ›place‹ instead of ›power‹. This discursive shift is probably connected with the extensive discussion around the concept of space that has been going on since the 1990s. However, global political and economic changes are now giving a new urgency to the question of power and empowerment. While this political dimension of landscape is linked by American and French authors with questions of colonialism, the historical contamination of the concept and its close association with ideologies around blood and soil, homeland, conquest and racism is hardly being addressed in the German-language study of art history.

issue here is not merely what landscape does but also and above all *how* it does it. With what aesthetic tools does it operate? For example, in formal terms the occidental precisionist and hyper-detailed painting of the nineteenth century presented a descriptive »artlessness« (Nochlin 1989: 38) that characterized the represented not as art but as factuality and employed a reality affect to assert the truth of landscape and its inhabitants—aesthetic practices that persist in today's omnipresent television documentaries about nature and indigenous peoples.

Whether near or far, whether we perceive it in movement or as view, landscape is always an act of translation and an articulation—historically negotiated in particular in terms of gaze, image and movement. This means that landscape operates as a medium and as part of the machinations of representation, thereby generating meaning and allowing it to circulate. However, recognizing this does not mean we are in the happy position of being able to decode it entirely, but merely that we are cognizant of its representational relief, its densities, depths, ridges and flat expanses, its transversal reactions and specifics in terms of the relationship of the medium to the represented and the relationship between the media and media networks used for representation.

LANDSCAPENESS AND BIOPOLITICS I
On the display of the politics of residential building and the body

It is precisely through the sphere of the residential, which was already being related to ideas of social nature and naturalness at the beginning of modernity, that the principles of landscapification have been transmitted to society as a whole. After 1945 the green lawn, the green expanse, spread ›among‹ and around all types of architecture and, in ideal terms and together with the asphalt ribbons of traffic streams, formed the ground of the city. Greenery, which since the nineteenth century had been distributed across the city in insular expanses such as parks or cemeteries, was now envisioned as spreading and merging to become a shared ground within a society coordinated in terms of social ›naturalness‹ (figure 2.1).

The green expanse is a figure for the healed and ideal ground following the world war and at the same time a metonym for the biopolitical foundation of the population—in literal terms, a ›natural‹ biopolitical display of post-war society. Greenery can be understood as the membrane of an order in which social processes can be represented as ›naturalized‹. Describing

---

Exceptions include the overview provided by Warnke (Warnke 1992) and studies of garden and landscape design such as found in Gröning/Wolschke-Bulmahn 1993.

Figure 2.1: Vienna, public housing, self-portrayal of the Vienna municipality, photograph from the 1950s

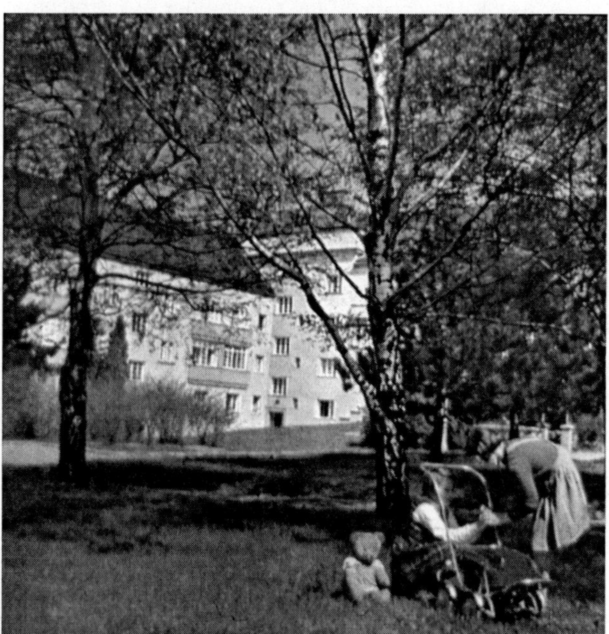

Source: author's archive

residential living in terms of ›countryside‹, Frank Lloyd Wright argued that the line of domesticity was horizontal, the earth line of human life. The green expanse common to all serves as a primer and ground for the foundational aspect of residing; it is a figure of a type of homogenizing *Seinslandschaft* (topology of being)—as Martin Heidegger put it in 1951 during the Darmstadt Symposium: »To be human means to be on the earth as a mortal, means: to reside« or »residing is the main feature of being« (Heidegger 1991: 90, 101) and precedes building.[7] With the landscapification of the city in the 1950s, residential life, which had been related to ideas of nature and naturalness since the beginning of modernity, was widely and comprehensively converted into a set of biopolitical principles. The metric order of the biopolitical becomes visible in the green expanse as spatial display, and the geometry of the plan operates between territory and inhabitants, between planning as biopolitical regulation and body-related discipline. The extent to

---

7   Heidegger, who bases everything on language and negates the promise of origin, nevertheless, in his linguistic performance and the iconography of his examples—Black Forest farmstead, childbed, *Totenbaum*—evokes a patriarchal, agrarian-romantic configuration that provided a tenuous (because apparently causal) topology for living and dwelling after 1945—particularly since the text became a central reference in the field of architecture.

which this biometrisizing and disciplining spatial expanse in the city of the twentieth century constitutes an exclusory, hermetically sealed zone or a permeable action space depends on the possibilities of intervention open to the inhabited and inhabitants. Since the 1970s the Kassel school of landscape design, for instance, has been directly addressing green-space planning in terms of the rights of residents (e.g. the inclusion of walking paths) versus regulated green-space use (prohibitions on games and access, zone planning etc.).

In sociopolitical terms, pragmatically oriented residential building after 1945 represents a cadastralization of a biopolitical mass, whose translations and discursive renderings around images of home, family and child were produced in image and text in an endless range of variations. The network of representations making up this interwoven image-regime around the themes of housing and residing wandered and roamed through the post-war reconstructionist mentality. The pictorial migrations of the ›nature‹ of the home and social naturalness produced social, colonizing and self-colonizing primers, as seen in discourses around the home/homeland and the exotic. Expressions of this in residential design range, for example, from the naked ›negro‹ girl as lamp stand and the ›gypsy woman‹ bedroom painting to the porcelain shepherd in the living room cabinet and the ›homeland‹ landscape painting. Such images are supplemented and modified, for example, in cinematic forms such as the sentimental-regional and exotic genres. In the years after 1945 and in the 1950s the (re)formulation of the populace was subject to an excessive discipline, which, in terms of residential living, not only affected the spatial organization of the populace but was also directly aimed at the bodies of the inhabitants. A comprehensive didactics of residential behaviour presented in texts and images (e.g. lifestyle guides, residential exhibitions, illustrated magazines, films) was incorporated into the body.[8] One of these teaching films, *The Well-Laid Table*, shows ideal settings (table, cutlery setting, colour selection for the tablecloth etc.) for breakfast, lunch and dinner. A partially visible female body follows the directions of a disembodied voice. It is a choreographically orchestrated relationship between objects and the body, the disciplinary character of which corresponds to the general outlines of the pictorial culture of residing prevailing in the 1950s. The process of adapting to a middle-class lifestyle is clearly labourious, and the representation of satisfaction and happiness illustrates—to the contemporary gaze—the strenuous nature of regulation. The allegories and didactic narratives of the ›per cent for art‹ approach to public housing also bore traces of this authoritative finger-wagging. The years from the late 1940s to the mid-1950s, i.e. the actual period of reconstruction, are visibly marked a disciplinary character, one which only changes gradually during the sixties.

Such image migrations and image mutations follow the development and branching of discourses and are active on a *medientransversal* (media-

---

8   On the didactic activities of the *Werkbund*, see Albrecht/Flagmeier 2008.

transversal) basis, i.e. they show up converted in the different media and their various genres, as well as in ways that are fragmented, contingent and paradoxical, and that do not correspond to any clear, large-scale plan. They are generated in the situational accumulation of ascriptions, media-localizations (architecture, visual culture, fine arts, film etc.) at concrete historical junctures. Thus the profile of ›mother‹ takes on a productive role in the debate around correct living, in feature films, and in images of the female body in ›per cent for art‹ projects and on the title pages of magazines.[9] Media-transversal image paths thus move within a multifaceted structure in which very different »linguistic—and thereby also visual and special, mimetic, gestural and cognitive acts« (Deleuze/Guattari 1997: 17) exist. That is to say that they do not form clearly delimitable areas and totalities but rather mutating compendia and heterogeneous links between readings and productive moments. We are not dealing here with a powerless play of images but with a historically dimensioned and hegemonic ›given-to-be-seen‹, a selection of representations in which not everything is presented in equal measure. Particularly since the sixties, social and cultural movements have intervened in this harmony and hegemony, objecting to concrete practices and functions of regulation via the cadastralization of the body and its transformation into a biopolitical knowledge corpus.

LANDSCAPENESS AND BIOPOLITICS II
Interventions in the display of the politics of residential building and the body

The social, political and feminist movements of the 1960s and 1970s involved interventions in biopolitical and disciplinary corporeality and the associated—in both a literal and metaphorical sense—*Ein-Richtung* (accommodation) of inhabitants. New concepts of residential living were formulated across a broad spectrum, from communards to designers, including the idea of ›de-furnishing‹ (in favour of what was regarded as the essential minimum such as mattresses or so-called *Liegewiesen*, or seating landscapes)—examples of such developments in the design area include Ferdinand Spindel's rubber foam cave and Verner Panton's organoid spatial designs. In order to illustrate the pictorially migratory *Medientransversalität* (media-transversality) of *Ein-Richten* (accommodation) processes, we will now turn to three examples of interventions from the field of visual culture.

The theme of the French film *Themroc* by Claude Faraldo (1972, figure 2.2) is the dissection of an essentialized corporeality that aims to counter the subjection of residing to discipline. The male protagonist tears a huge hole in the building he lives in, demolishes his apartment and tosses out his furni-

---

9   On residential living see Hartmann 2008; On *Kunst am Bau* (per centage for art) see Nierhaus 1993; on magazines: Angerer/Nierhaus/Schöbel/Smudits 1989.

ture and domestic appliances, decomposing the act of residing into one of primordial dwelling. It is as if the generation of 1968 is yelling, ›The private is political, we are destroying the entire cadastralization of life by (state) power and consumption‹ from this giant hole in the wall, through which we can see the residential surroundings and the deployment of police.

Figure 2.2: Themroc *(dir. Claude Faraldo), 1972*

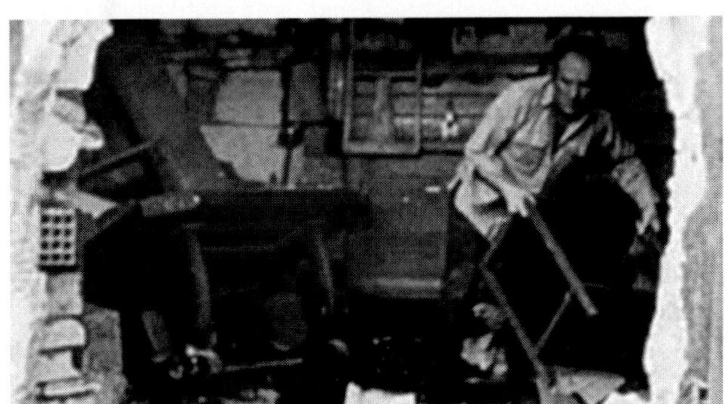

Source: author's archive

Through the act of destruction the male protagonist seeks to discard the social corpus in favour of ›an‹ elementized body. Language itself is also decomposed into wordless, sentenceless and grammarless babble, grunting and sighing. The half-naked body of the main figure (played by Michel Piccoli, who seems tailor-made for the role) is the real protagonist and is structured by the film in terms of the explicit presence of the corporeality and gestures of the acting body. This body reacts against residing as a locus of convention, and the power of the state, represented by the police, steps in to counter this attempt at liberation. In the film, an analogy is drawn between residing as the middle-class site of a dual *Ein-Richtung* (accommodation) and the living space of the mother, who represents convention (in her function of housewife and mother as educator, that has been biologically attributed to women since the nineteenth century) and from whom the protagonist separates himself with a wall in order to be able to realize his form of residing, understood primarily as corporal. Sexualization plays the key role here: the trigger for the separation and destruction of the residential space is the disturbance to the view of a naked female breast by the gaze of the (old and sighing) mother. From this point onwards the male protagonist happily copulates with women in his cave-like dwelling. However, this situation, which arouses the curiosity of the local neighbourhood, also attracts an ever increasing police presence and is finally *ein-gerichtet* (accommodated) again in the prescribed order, with the hole in the building wall being filled in under police protection. At the end of the film, a conspicuous analogy is drawn between the oppressive process of domestication in the apartment block and a prison when we see hands desperately reaching through the few openings left in the walled-in cave dwelling and the camera pans over the bar-like window grid of an apartment block. In the film the naturalized disciplining of residing is ruptured by sexuality, which operates as a sign for the actual body that is liberated by the male protagonist. Sexuality promises the emergence of a corporeality and carnality, which is always gendered. The naturalization of space and discourse is ruptured by a sexuality that is manifested in the ›wrong‹ place and is decoupled from the obligation to reproduce; this sexuality brings forth the (gendered) corporeality and carnality that appears to be sealed up, tamed and controlled in the conventional cityscape through the geometry of the urban plan. The transformation of the residential dwelling into a jagged rocky cave, which is visualized here as renaturalization, echoes the rediscovery at this time of ›troglodyte housing‹ (e.g. Matera, Cappadocia), which was seen by some as representing a type of ›anthropological alternative‹, a way out of civilizing domestication. The concept of such a release from the pressures of culture and civilization is anchored in the occidental display of primitivism and exoticism by the desire for an exteriority. *Themroc* intervenes in a societal spatial geometry and translates it into a new spatial landscape that is determined by the deformed, the presence of the material, the primacy of explicit corporeality and sexuality as the bearer of the liberatory act. An appropriate question at this juncture would be: What does the male author of the destruction of order uncover and what position is allotted to the female protagonists in this process? Where are they a desired interim space, where are they ›liberated‹ ground and where are they self-regulating residents? The artist Birgit Jürgenssen engages with the themes of residing and the body by way of a critique of gender roles. In her 1975 work, *Hausfrauen-Küchenschürze*/Housewives-Kitchen Apron (figure 2.3), she shows herself as a female body that has merged with a kitchen stove to form a new organism. The melding of female body, furniture and interior living space is a concept that has been part of different levels of discourse since the nineteenth century (e.g. social ascription of female functions, physio-psychological ascription of gender character, interior theory; see Nierhaus 1999). The stove body facilitates a double reproduction of the housewife and mother: the baking of bread and the incubation of offspring. It gives visible form to the female, biopoliticized body committed to birth rates and the hygiene of family and marriage as well as its localization in reproduction and residential living.

Particularly noteworthy in this connection is Pier Paolo Pasolini's confrontation of social rhetoric and discipline with a resistant real and his attempt to realize the body as »unremediated excrescence« and as »distance« (Nancy 2003: 33). His film *Mamma Roma* (1962, figure 2.4), which is set on the outskirts of Rome, speaks of the body—of the body of the city, flesh, the physical body, the bodies of the inhabitants, the corpus of capitalist bourgeois society, and deals with the power relations within these constellations. Pasolini seeks a body oriented to an outside and an externality and in

Figure 2.3: Birgit Jürgenssen: Hausfrauen-Küchenschürze, *photograph, 1975*

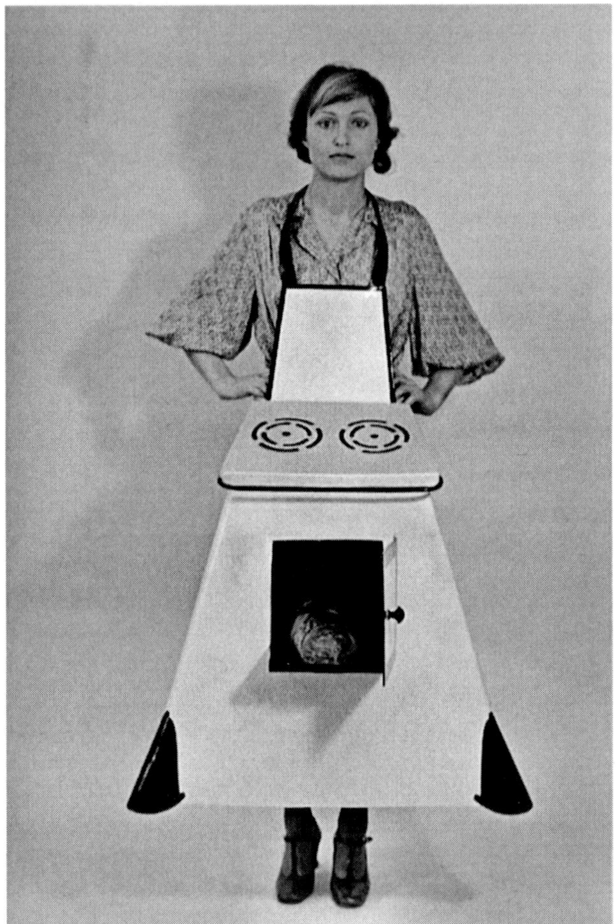

the process works with the dramaturgy of margins and urban peripheries on several levels. Mamma Roma (female figure of the city, mother, market-woman and prostitute) seeks social advancement for her son Ettore, a project that ultimately fails when he is imprisoned for stealing and dies as a feverish body tied down on an institutional table (which functions here as a kind of Foucauldian table that combines autopsy table, bier and altar). The disused periphery, with its overgrown meadows, ancient ruins, underground caves and trash, functions here as a counter-space to the residential city. This is where Ettore prefers to be, spending time with his friends and his first love Bruna, hiding and appearing among the ruins, walking, running, tussling, lazing and loving. This landscape of ruins echoes with baroque music, twittering and chirping, whereas the city is filled with the sound of sirens and car engines. In contrast to the uneven forms of the meadows the apartment blocks and asphalt surfaces of the city are portrayed as grids of (petty) bourgeois Catholic (family) order—Pasolini used the term camp. The girls from this petty bourgeois milieu are seen on this sealed surface or only in groups in the meadows, whereas the promiscuous Bruna crosses into the wasteland alone, sits on a road barrier running through space and image at the end of a wide asphalt street, behind which the meadows begin—the gaze is drawn to her décolleté, the boundary between dress and naked skin. The trash heaps, meadows and ruins denote a movement to an externality and an otherness. The long lines of the aqueduct ruins appear in the background as a spatial and temporal periphery—in historical visual culture, the area around the aqueducts was a central icon for the Roman Campagna. Pasolini takes his cue here from the images of the Roman pastoral with its crumbling walls, goats among the ruins and roaming shepherds—a melancholy symbol in high European culture of reflection on time and the yearning for a space far from culture and regulation—and populates it with symbols of proletarian urban everyday life as a mythic and primal source of vitality and resistance to Catholic bourgeois culture and capitalism. The filmic space is a

Figure 2.4: Mamma Roma *(dir. Pier Paolo Pasolini), 1962*

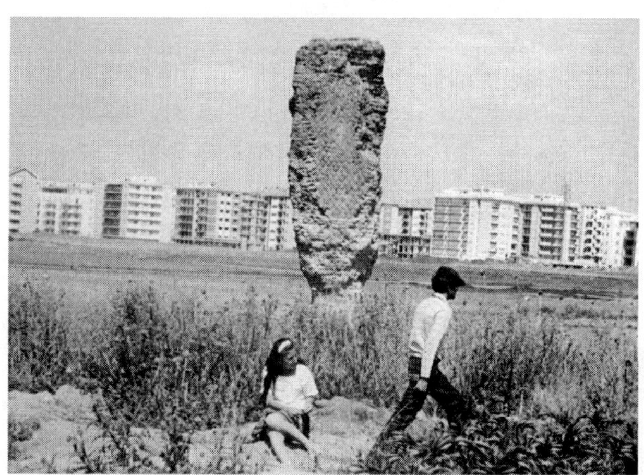

Source: author's archive

mesh of spatially and temporally multiplying margins (streets, paths, rows of houses, bends, street barriers, necklaces, ties, belts ...) with closed or open surfaces (asphalt, bare wall, meadow) in which territoriality and ex-territoriality are produced and in which the protagonists dwindle, rove and pulsate. Pasolini looks for the margins of and gaps in capitalism, increasingly detaching them from a fixed geographical and temporal locus, and pushing them into the mythical and the archaic, which signify the horizon of an externality. The space-time that is presented is not a vehicle for plot but is rather incorporated into city, landscape, bodies and »carnal fantasms«

(Cappabianca 2000: 33). The Roman city periphery and the protagonists become a sign for territorial play and struggle around the *Ein-Richtung* (accomodation) and housing of the inhabitants, of their sex and their body as »unremediated excrescence« and »as boundary: boundary—external margin, break and incision of the alien into the continuum of meaning, into the continuum of material« (Nancy 2003: 33, 20).

BIBLIOGRAPHY

Albrecht, Nicola von/Flagmeier, Renate (2008): »Sich einrichten, Die Wohnberatung des Deutschen Werkbundes«. In: Annette Maechtel and Kathrin Peters (eds.), *Die Stadt von morgen. Beiträge zu einer Archäologie des Hansaviertels Berlin*, Cologne: Walther König. p. 120–125.

Aigner, Anita (2004): *Landschaft vor Augen. Neutralisierung eines romantischen Gebildes*, Vienna, Sonderzahl.

Angerer, Marie Luise/Nierhaus, Irene/Schöbel, Judith/Smudits, Alfred (1989): Wandel medialer Körperbilder am Beispiel von Titelblättern zwischen 1955 und 1986«. In: Jeff Bernhard et al. (eds.) (1987), *Semiotik der Geschlechter*, Akten des 6. Symposiums der österreichischen Gesellschaft für Semiotik Salzburg. Stuttgart and Vienna: Heinz and ÖGS, p. 121–139.

Cappabianca, Alessandro (2000): »Pasolini a Roma. Dal Sogno all' Incubo«. In: Americo Sbardella (ed.), *Roma nel Cinema*, Roma: Semar.

Deleuze, Gilles/Guattari, Félix (1997): *Tausend Plateaus. Kapitalismus und Schizophrenie*, Berlin: Merve.

Franzen, Brigitte/Krebs, Stefanie (2005): *Landschaftstheorie: Texte der Cultural Landscape Studies*, Cologne: Walther König.

Franzen, Brigitte/Krebs, Stefanie (2006), *Mikrolandschaften: Landscape Culture on the Move*, Münster: Landschaftsverband Westfalen-Lippe/ Westfälisches Landesmuseum für Kunst und Kulturgeschichte.

Gröning, Gert/Wolschke-Bulmahn, Joachim (1993): »›Ganz Deutschland ein großer Garten‹. Landespflege und Stadtplanung im Nationalsozialismus«. *Kursbuch 1993* 112, »Städte bauen«, p. 29–46.

Hartmann, Johanna (2008): »Aber wenn die Frau aus ihren Grenzen tritt, ist es für sie noch viel gefährlicher. Geschlechtermodelle für die Stadt von morgen«. In: Annette Maechtel and Kathrin Peters (eds.), *Die Stadt von morgen*, Cologne: Walther König, p. 200–207.

Heidegger, Martin (1991): »Bauen, Wohnen, Denken«. In: Ulrich Conrads and Peter Neitzke (eds.), *Mensch und Raum*. Das Darmstädter Gespräch 1951 (Bauwelt Fundamente 94), Braunschweig: Vieweg.

Mitchell, W.J.T. (2002): *Landscape and Power*, second edition, Chicago, IL: Chicago University Press.

Nancy, Jean-Luc (2003): *Corpus*, Berlin: Diaphanes.

Nierhaus, Irene (1993): *Kunst-am-Bau im Wiener kommunalen Wohnbau*, Vienna: Böhlau.

Nierhaus, Irene (1999): »Text und Textil: Zur Geschlechterfigur von Material und Innenraum«. In: Irene Nierhaus, *Arch 6*, Sonderzahl, p. 115–139.

Nierhaus, Irene/Hoenes, Josch/Urban, Annette (2010): *Landschaftlichkeit: Forschungsansätze zwischen Kunst, Architektur und Theorie*, Berlin, Reimer.

Nochlin, Linda (1989): *The Politics of Vision. Essays on nineteenth century art society*, New York: Harper & Row.

Warnke, Martin (1992): *Politische Landschaft. Zur Kunstgeschichte der Natur*, Munich: Hanser.

Contemporary Art, ›Counter-Environmentalism‹, and the Politics of A-Signification[1]

JORELLA ANDREWS

WORDS FAIL ME

Figure 3.1: Sam Durant, We Are the People, *vinyl text on electric sign, 77 x 48 x 11 inches. Installation view at Project Row Houses, Houston, Texas, 2003*

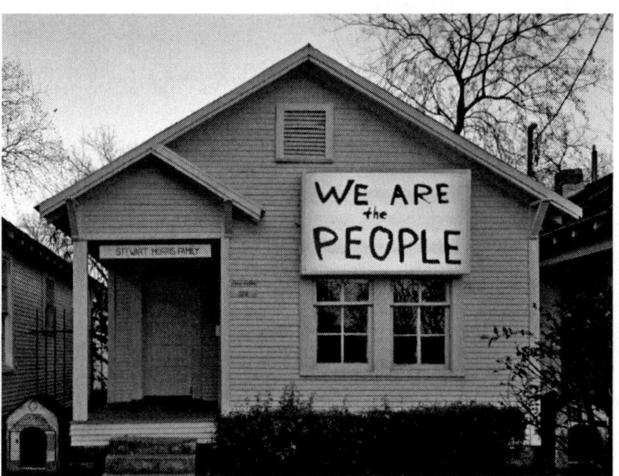

Photo: Thomas R. Dubrock. Image courtesy of the artist and Blum & Poe Gallery, Los Angeles, CA

---

1   An earlier version of this essay, using different visual sources and orientated more specifically towards questions of research in art, is available as follows: »How to be counter-environmental: art, research and the techniques of discovery«. In: José Quaresma et al. (eds.) (2010), *Research in Art: A Forest, Many Paths*, Edição CIEBA, Faculty of ›Fine Arts, University of Lisbon.

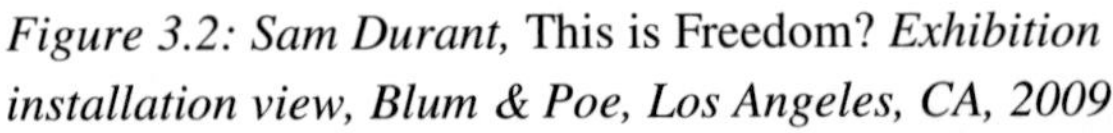

Figure 3.2: Sam Durant, This is Freedom? *Exhibition installation view, Blum & Poe, Los Angeles, CA, 2009*

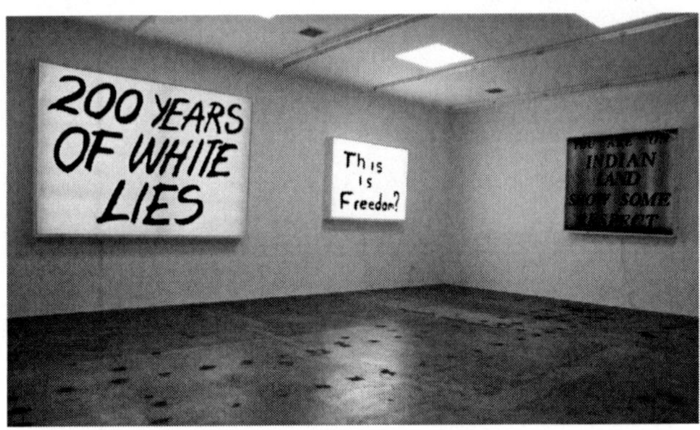

Photo: Joshua White. Image courtesy of the artist and Blum & Poe Gallery, Los Angeles, CA

Whether as an artist, a writer, or a curator—of the 2009 exhibition *Emory Douglas: Black Panther* at the New Museum, New York, for instance—Sam Durant's work asks questions about the changing languages, practices, spaces, and effects of twentieth-century and contemporary political activism. More broadly, it asks questions about the relationships, within culture, between rhetorics, aesthetics, and politics, or, put differently, between the realms of persuasion, sensibility, and governance or self-governance. These are of course relationships in constant need of renegotiation depending on the contexts in which we find ourselves.

It is this territory that I also want to address in this essay. My particular focus, however, will be on the often dismissed realm of the non-verbal as (or so I argue) the vital site for the creation of deep political motivation and agency. Perhaps surprisingly, a discussion of one of Durant's *text-based* works will serve as my starting-point.

Durant's *Electric Signs* series consists of large, boldly coloured pieces in which hand-written slogans sourced in photographs of mid twentieth-century political marches, sit-ins, and other forms of protest have been transposed into a new vernacular format: in his words that of »commercially produced outdoor illuminated display units [like those] found on the sides of small, local businesses such as convenience stores, restaurants, liquor stores and auto repair shops«.[2] Appropriately, some of his *Signs* have themselves been exhibited on the outside of buildings although not necessarily commercial ones. *We are the People* of 2003, for instance, was installed on one of the Houston Project Row Houses, the nonprofit communal art-and-life organization set up in 1993 by artist-activist Rick Lowe and others. Other

---

2   Sam Durant, *Electric Signs.* Source: http://www.samdurant.com/electric-signs [accessed 19 February 2011].

Signs have appeared in more conventional exhibition spaces including the 2007–08 group show, *Words Fail Me* at MOCAD (Museum of Contemporary Art Detroit), and Durant's 2009 show *This is Freedom?* at Blum and Poe in Los Angeles. When the *Signs* are exhibited, Durant aims, whenever possible, to include what he refers to as an ›index‹ consisting of documents (photographs, as noted, drawings or posters) that refer back to the concrete circumstances in which his now purposefully decontextualized and thus generalized,[3] reformated, and repositioned slogans first made their appearance.

Inevitably, the connections and contrasts that are summoned up between the activist politics of the past and present vary from site to site. In 2003, at Project Row Houses, the connections were particularly strong although clearly this is not an activist space of the kind associated with the mass public uprising. The atmosphere is not one of demand-making, exhoration, appeal or accusation. It is instead a specific, self-organized, long-term, living, working, hospitable, and collaborative community in which art, made by residents and by invited artists (like Durant), plays a core social, cultural and political role (Bless 2000: 33–39). Nonetheless, it has also grown out of certain, earlier aspirations. Certainly, a key, stated influence was the artistic and philosophical legacy of Joseph Beuys (1921–1986), and particularly his reconceptualized notion of sculpture from art object to social activity (›social sculpture‹). But Project Row Houses also recalls other important legacies: the diverse community programmes that were integral, for instance, to the Black Panther Party's activist agenda between 1962 and 1982, and the BPP's understanding of the vital relationship between successful communal transformation on the one hand and their capacity to create and disseminate powerful visual iconographies of their own on the other. Indeed, if we turn to Durant's ›index‹ for *We are the People*—a drawing of a photograph—we find an explicit reference to Black Power activism and to BPP terminology. The image shows a group of protesters. Several make the Black Power salute, and one also holds a placard on which the words that Durant has ›grabbed‹ are followed by: »All Power of the People. PIGS out of our Community.« Seen in this light, here in Houston, decades later, Durant's reproduction of the placard's first four words—›We are the people‹—with its scawled, sloping black letters now greatly enlarged against a luminous blue background gains particular resonance as it not only pays homage to a historical moment by reactivating it, but also announces and affirms the rather different actualities of Project Row Houses now.

We are the People was a temporary installation. Thus it now exists via its photographic record. What's notable, however, is the altered sensibility

---

3   In his words: »the text or message on the sign should be general in nature. The message should not refer to any specific event, cause, person or time…« Sam Durant, *Electric Signs*, http://samdurant.com/electric-signs/electric-signs-2/ [accessed 2 April 2011].

that seems to accompany this further transposition into photography. For rather than being justly celebratory, or conveying something of the collective energy of the place and the project that it represents, the photograph is profoundly melacholic (that is, it is melanchoic beyond the generalized sense in which all photographs might, by nature, be defined as such). The house with its sign is depicted in gloomy half-light and deep shadow. And the scene is utterly devoid of people.The house looks like an abandoned shell, its windows reflecting only the darkness of the immediately adjacent urban landscape. Presumably, given the ongoing contemporary impact of Project Row Houses, this melancholia is intended to be understood neither as a representation of, nor a comment on the realities of that place. What then might be at issue?

A similar sense of melancholy pervades the gallery installations of Durant's *Signs*. Despite the bold backdrop of colour that he has introduced to each one, and despite the powerful material presence of the *Signs* themselves as objects, the energy and sense of urgency of the original handwritten placards seem to have dissipated. What we have now are apparently obsolete and redundant artefacts,[4] museum pieces that seem to be memorializing the mid-twentieth-century political and social projects that they directly reference as largely unfulfilled in terms of their aspirations and long-term impact. As such, they also seem to signal a related failure: that of even the most powerful, pithy, truthful or well reasoned of words, in and of themselves, to activate deep constitutional change, change that is not merely a matter of external form (a matter or policy or legality) but is first and foremost personal, internalized, heartfelt, committed and lasting. This seems to be supported—perhaps even anticipated—by some of the *Signs'* battleworn words themselves: *This is freedom?*, *200 years of white lies*, and *Like, man, I'm tired (of waiting)*.

Notably, though, this melancholia is unable to erode the unmistakably powerful material, mediumistic, and visual insistence at play in these pieces. In the first place, to stand in front of them in the gallery or to view them in photographic form, paying particular attention to their non-textual qualities—that is, allowing the works' material character gradually to gain precedence over their more immediate linguistic status as statements—is to become suddenly redirected from the ›what‹ of communication to the ›how‹, in ways that expand, enrich and complicate issues already opened up at a textual level. For instance, when we reflect on Durant's *Signs* as material transpositions from hand-written, hand-made placards to fabricated electric signs, they inevitably highlight specific questions about the ways in which the utopic/dystopic rhetorics of industry, service industry, and commerce as manifested through everyday advertising and promotion may frame, contain,

---

4   Although I cannot discuss this here, themes of obsolescence and entropy are of longstanding interest to Durant, and are linked with his early interest in the work of Robert Smithson.

absorb, and neutralize, if not directly oppose our most passionate efforts, even where they may appear to affirm them. And here, a historically specific instance of engagement with this broad fact comes to mind: the views of the artist-activist already noted as being of interest to Durant, namely, Emory Douglas, who was the BPP's Minister of Culture and key iconographer from 1967 onwards. In his lecture ›Art for the People's Sake‹, delivered in 1972 to students at Fisk University, Douglas began by focusing on the Black community's need to contend against the prevalent, classical tradition in image-making if they were to find their own voice and values. He then went on to argue in a characteristically uncompromosing and oppositional way for a fundamental incompatibility between the aspirations of radical Black politics on the one hand, and those of commerce on the other:

»[...] we have a greater enemy in relationship to art. We have a greater enemy, I would say, in commercial art. What is commercial art? It is a method of persuasion, mind control; it oppresses Black people. If we look around our community, what do we see? We see billboards, with advertising, that tell us what to buy, how to buy. And we go out and buy [...] our own oppression« (Douglas 1972: 4).

In the second place—this is also implicit in Douglas's words and, as he indicates, knowingly exploited by the commercial world—the material, mediumistic, and visual impact of Durant's *Signs* underlines the understanding that human responsiveness and motivation are activated above all not by explicit, well-worded appeals to reason but, in effect, by less immediately discernable persuaders of a visceral and emotive nature, that is, by those rhetorical and aesthetic dimensions that are the proper realms of art. Indeed, when viewed from this perspective, Durant's works seem to go further. They seemingly question the propositional, word-based, and fundamentally rationalistic communicative strategies that are still conventionally prioritized both by activists and artist-activists—strategies that continue both to attract and disappoint us.

This questioning is difficult. Since it reveals the unspoken structures and systems in which we are embedded, their modes of operation, and their impact on us, it brings us face to face with those forces that insidiously shape and delimit us, as individuals and collectively. Thus one of the ways in which we often try to dispel these terrors, individually and collectively, is by turning quickly to some kind of counter-action or activism, drawing on an arsenal of already elaborated arguments and strategies that we hope will demolish their power. Arguably though, it is precisely this temptation and this tendency that is blocked when Durant's *Signs* are experienced in their full material and mediumistic force. Indeed, they seem to direct us elsewhere, towards less definable but potentially more enduring resources for actualizing social and political change. Which brings me closer to the particular claims I would like to try and make in this essay.

A SECRET SCIENCE

When Durant writes about his *Signs*, it is to their complex, multiple, ambiguous and context-dependent meanings and impact that he refers. They are intended to operate not as directives, but as provocations. Here, though, his discussions do seem to be primarily focused on their linguistic qualities. A particular alliance that he foregrounds, for instance, is with the enigmatic and strategically deceptive rhetorics of what African-American literary scholar Henry Louis Gates Jnr has called ›signifyin(g)‹, and with the poetics and politics of free indirect speech as explored particularly in Gates' 1988 book *The Signifying Monkey: a theory of African-American Literary Criticism.*

This is fascinating, fertile territory. But primarily, in this essay, I'd like to consider the value when approaching Durant's work (and art more generally), of at least provisionally setting aside linguistic considerations, including those, as here, of a highly open-ended nature. That is, the value of engaging with his work (and, again, with art more generally) at that moment, or in that register, when words seem to fail. For although the expression ›words fail me‹ expresses incapacity, the roots and nature of this incapacity have important positive dimensions that I think it is the particular calling of art to probe and make experientially explicit. Literally, these words refer to an inability to put thoughts or feelings into words, usually because of surprise or shock. But we know these thoughts or feelings to exist nonetheless; they make themselves felt in us. Indeed, their visceral density and force are announced precisely by those sudden irruptions of verbal incapacity. Thus, the physicality of Durant's *Signs*—works in which words are by no means the only medium at issue, and whose indexes inevitably provoke reflection on mediumistic change—has the additional effect of orientating us away from a primary concern with questions of representation, identity, and interpretation, the past, loss and gain, etc., towards a realm of presentation that is unfolding in the here and now in ways that are just as likely to defy as confirm expectation.

This type of response to Durant's text-based work may seem inadequate, relatively anomolous within contemporary art historical contexts that are still much dominated by semiotics and post-structuralism and in which visual art in general is primarily regarded as a kind of linguistic text to be decoded or otherwise deciphered. Arguably, though, as already noted, it is precisely on those other, still relatively disregarded a-signifying communicative registers that the deep motivational force of Durant's, and indeed all communicative acts, is to be found.

Admittedly, this territory can be difficult to think and write about sensibly. Nonetheless, various thinkers and writers have tried, and are worth turning to. One such was the French phenomenologist Maurice Merleau-Ponty. In his 1952 essay ›Indirect Language and the Voices of Silence‹, for instance—written during a period when he was trying to find a satisfactory way of articulating relationships between our perceptual and our linguistic modes of being in the world—he insisted on the philosophical urgency of prioritizing what he called »a second-order language« that is »hidden in empirical language« and in which »signs once again lead the vague life of colours ...« (Merleau-Ponty 1964b: 45). Vague, that is, in linguistic terms, since precise definitions are eluded. But irreducibly compelling and relational for exactly the same reasons, and therefore foundational for the development of his intersubjective, indeed intercorporeal, understanding of the nature of perception, thought, action, and meaning.[5]

Also useful in Merleau-Ponty's ›Indirect Language‹ and elsewhere, were his intimations about the political dimensions, the political agency, connected with, and generated by, this ›vague‹ communicative mode. These arguments are found, particularly, in his discussions of painting, and his claims that their particular capacity to provoke social and political transformation lies precisely outside of the realms of the conventionally linguistic, declarative, or representational. Art, he wrote, in his last completed work, ›Eye and Mind‹ of 1961, draws upon a »fabric of brute [that is embodied, situated and lived rather than already conceptualized] meaning which activism would prefer to ignore ...« (Merleau-Ponty 1964a: 161). And, although by activism Merleau-Ponty was referring to a problematically reductive interpretative strategy found in the sciences also known as operationalism, his words could apply just as easily to certain formulaic types of political response.[6] »From the writer and the philosopher,« he continued, »we want opinions and advice [...] they cannot waive the responsibilities of men who speak [... whereas the painter, by contrast, with] no other technique than

---

5   Merleau-Ponty's main legacy was his ongoing non-dualistic exploration of what, early on, he referred to as ›embodied thought‹. During the 1950s he explored this topic in relation to an increasing interest in semiotic theory, and its applications to broader aspects of cultural and philosophical interrogation and critique. The perspective cited here is also tied to certain earlier discussions in his *Phenomenology of Perception* (1945) concerning the synaesthetic nature of perception and the gestural nature of words: »If we consider only the conceptual and delimiting meaning of words, it is true that the verbal form—with the exception of endings—appears arbitrary. But it would no longer appear so if we took into account the emotional content of the word, which we have called above its ›gestural‹ sense, which is all-important in poetry, for example. It would then be found that the words, vowels and phonemes are so many ways of ›singing‹ the world, and that their function is to represent things not, as the naïve onomatopoeic theory had it, by reason of an objective resemblance, but because they extract, and literally express, their emotional content« (Merleau-Ponty 1962: 187).

6   In ›Eye and Mind‹, Merleau-Ponty contrasts this kind of perspective with an approach to knowledge that grounds itself, instead, in »the site, the soil of the sensible and opened world such as it is in our life and for our body« (Merleau-Ponty 1964a: 160).

what his eyes and hands discover in seeing and painting persists in drawing from this world, with its din of history's glories and scandals, *canvases which will hardly add to the angers or the hopes of man—and no one complains*« (ibid.). Nonetheless, Merleau-Ponty presents this compulsive transformation of the world into paintings as an interrogative project marked by the utmost urgency. »What, then, is this secret science which [the painter] has or which he seeks?« he asks. »That dimension which lets Van Gogh say he must go ›further on‹? What is this fundamental of painting, perhaps of all culture?« (ibid.).[7]

It is this dimension of questioning that I think is important to extend to Durant's *Signs*, and to other obviously text- or message-based works of art. Conversely, they are questions that also need to be brought to forms of contemporary art (ranging from the non-narrative film and video art of Rosalind Nashashibi, to Katarina Grosse's large-scale abstract work with pigment) that are often taken to operate at the opposite pole, to be actively resisting interpretation since, whether figurative or non-figurative, they seem to have ›nothing to say‹. Work, therefore, that may be regarded as primarily concerned with issues of a formal, art-for-art's-sake, nature, and thus judged to be culturally, socially and politically irrelevant. An interpretation that I believe must be strongly challenged—indeed, the broader context for this essay is my interest in forms of contemporary debate that (perhaps clumsily) have been coined ›post-linguistic‹, post-conceptual‹, or ›post-critical‹. Specifically, debates which far from designating such a-signifying works as socially and politically disengaged, point instead to the less articulate, but more deeply embodied and embedded orientations that are activated when, to reference another well known twentieth-century thinker, it is not message (with its often highly idealized and ideological maxims) but medium that is foregrounded.

And so it is that I now shift to the work of that other thinker, and to his claims about the important perceptual, behavioural and ethical changes that occur when, both in everyday life and in contexts of cultural critique, we stop automatically prioritizing questions of ›content‹ (representational and narrative material) over questions of medium (issues of presentation, communication and transmission) where meaning is concerned. I am referring, of course, to the Canadian media theorist Marshall McLuhan (1911–1980), famed for his aphorism ›the medium is the message‹ as well as for his (some would say prophetic, others misguided) vision of the interconnected and involved ›global village‹ he believed was being opened up as people were increasingly transformed, neurologically and behaviourally, by the ever escalating mediumistic shift that had been occurring since the mid-nineteenth century from print-based communication cultures to those animated and

---

7   This is a topic I have written about in »Painterly Transubstantiations/Political Change« in A.-T. Tymieniecka (ed.) (2004), *Analecta Husserliana LXXXI*, Kluwer Academic Publishers, Dordrecht, Boston, London, p. 141–151.

empowered by ›electric circuitry‹—first via the telegraph and radio and, more recently what he called the new television culture. (McLuhan died before the emergence of the mass internet age.) The key source to which I will refer is an essay from 1968, ›The Emperor's New Clothes‹, written collaboratively by McLuhan and the artist, designer, and scholar Harley Parker and published as part of their aphoristically constructed book *Through the Vanishing Point: Space in Poetry and Painting*.[8]

ENVIRONMENTS AND COUNTER-ENVIRONMENTS

A key argument in ›The Emperor's New Clothes‹ is that part of our condition, as humans, is that we are immersed in, and to a large degree controlled by, situations that are perceptually unavailable to us—not in and of themselves, but because we are culturally predisposed not to perceive them. Due to their pervasiveness, McLuhan and Parker referred to these situations as ›environments‹. And they proposed that the urgent work of the cultural critic or investigator is to break into this realm of non-availability, bringing it into awareness through the creation of ›counter-environments‹ that attend, above all, to the workings and effects of medium and process where perception and communication are concerned. Here, the main dispositional barrier to be overcome is that of ›rear view mirror‹ perception, in which the actualities of the here and now are mis-perceived, or missed altogether, because they are approached via the paradigms and expectations of the past, including the recent past.

The best way to get a sense of what McLuhan and Parker meant not only by ›environment‹ but also by the problem of rear-view mirror perception is to focus on their discussions of television. This medium, they argued, despite its near ubiquitous presence within Western domestic life by 1968, was nonetheless by no means understood. This was because television was consistently perceived (or misperceived) by its viewers, and indeed by programme makers and producers, predominantly in terms of its content (the earlier environments of the photograph and the movie in particular) rather than as a new kind of medium. As such, it was imperceptible except in terms of its content: »all that is seen or noticed is the old environment, the movie ... even the effects of TV on the movie go unnoticed, and the effects of the

---

8   There would be a second collaborative project: the typographically experimental *Counterblast* (1970), London, Rapp and Whiting. Worth noting here that Parker (1915–1992), a graduate of Ontario College of Art, also attended the influential Black Mountain Collage in Virginia in 1946. There he studied under Jozef Albers, a key figure, for many years, at the Bauhaus in Germany, where again attention to medium and materiality was foregrounded as key to the creation of new, non-alienated inter-relationships between art, life, and modern industrialized mass culture.

TV environment in altering the entire character of human sensibility and sensory ratio are completely ignored« (McLuhan/Parker 1968: 241).

For McLuhan and Parker, the aim of cultural investigation is to discover points of divergence from, not continuity with the familiar old environments in which we remain inappropriately embedded, and to pursue the new possibilities that our current environments are in fact actively opening up. Thus (remaining with the topic of television), one of their important (and refreshingly counter-intuitive) assertions was that neither black and white nor colour television should be regarded as a fundamentally pictorial medium. On the contrary, »totally different from photographs and movies, the TV image is discontinuous and flat. That is, it is a world of intervals. It is extremely tactile and participant« (ibid.: 266). Their argument, in other words (the inverse of that being formulated at the same time by Guy Debord in his *Society of the Spectacle*) was that from a finely grained mediumistic point of view what television actually provokes is not passive consumption but interaction (thus, there are unexpected affinities here with Beuys' rethinking of sculpture as social sculpture, referred to earlier). Rather than encase us within the realms of the superficial, McLuhan and Parker referred instead to the capacity of the televisual to initiate involvements that they described as being »in-depth«. As noted, these capacities are generally missed however, because:

»Ordinary human instinct causes people to recoil from these new environments and to rely on the rear-view mirror as a kind of repeat or *ricorso* of the preceding environment, thus insuring total disorientation at all times. It is not that there is anything wrong with the old environment, but it simply will not serve as a navigational guide to the new one« (ibid.: xxiii).

By way of further elaboration, amongst the several errors caused by the ›rear-view mirror perception‹ affecting not only television but also movies, McLuhan and Parker cited the continued dominance of paradigms inherited from the Western obsession with linear perspective. The movie industry made a mistake, they insisted, when »it pushed toward photographic realism rather than realism of process« (ibid.: 266).[9] And this conventional, perspectival logic was now also being applied to the televisual. What this amounted to therefore was yet another lost opportunity for our perceptual capacities to be challenged and extended as a consequence of our involvement with technological innovation. And today, arguably, the same is true of our varied involvements with digitization. In 1995, for instance, the architect and writer Sarah Chaplin observed that cyberspace, which could in principle be activated to create radically unfamiliar spatial experiences, was instead being

---

9   For instance, the reality of its actual, discontinuous nature that a new generation of structuralist film-makers were also identifying and foregrounding in their work.

steadily colonized by the determination of most soft- and hardware designers to »produce virtual photo-realism in real time« (Chaplin 1995: 33). What this content-driven, rear-view mirror perception clearly testifies to is not just an apparently constitutional human unwillingness to adapt. More seriously, the false continuities it proposes between the past and the present embeds us in situations of radical, but unacknowledged, disorientation. Situations, then, in which adequate and effective politics cannot emerge.

COUNTER-ENVIRONMENTS, ART AND POLITICS

It is at this point that we turn to the realm and roles of artistic activity which, for McLuhan and Parker, »includes the preparing of an environment for human attention« (McLuhan/Parker 1968: 238). At issue here is the artistic creation not of autonomous works of art but of ›counter-environments‹ in which, to repeat, the workings of medium and process are the main point of focus. For McLuhan and Parker, it was principally via such engagements with the ›how‹ of communication that the real political potential of art-making and art-viewing was evident.

This again may seem counter-intuitive, and at odds with then- and now-dominant understandings of the nature of political art as message-based. However, worth noting is that McLuhan's media orientation and his understanding of its cultural and political implications, was significantly influenced by the work of fellow Canadian communication theorist Harold Adam Innes. Key was Innis's paper ›The Bias of Communication‹ delivered at the University of Michigan in 1949 and published in 1951, and his book *Empire and Communication* published a year earlier in 1950, in which he forged persuasive arguments for the crucial, politically inflected understandings of culture that could be opened up by media research. As Innis put it in the beginning of his 1949 paper, here using temporal versus spatial paradigms in order to analyse media types and their relative historical and political impact:

»A medium of communication has an important influence on the dissemination of knowledge over space and over time and it becomes necessary to study its characteristics in order to appraise its influence in its cultural setting. According to its characteristics it may be better suited to the dissemination of knowledge over time than over space, particularly if the medium is heavy and durable and not suited to transportation, or to the dissemination of knowledge over space than over time, particularly if the medium is light and easily transported. The relative emphasis on time or space will imply a bias of significance to the culture in which it is imbedded« (Innis 1968: 33).

He then supported his argument with a sweeping historical and cultural survey, beginning with the moment when the »monopoly of knowledge centring around stone and hieroglyphics was exposed to competition from papyrus as a new and more efficient medium« and ending with the moment when »the bias of communication in paper and the printing press was destined to be offset by the bias of the radio« (ibid.: 60). For Innis, radio, as a light, easily transportable, and thus spatially biased medium, was particularly associated with modern cultures that had by such technological means themselves become wide-ranging—empires of one kind or another. And which, for the sake of uniformity and stability—and, I would add, despite the democratic and participatory rhetorics often accompanying them—tended to be centrally administered and controlled.

Seen from this perspective, the emphasis and the value of McLuhan and Parker's ideas is that it is never enough for specific issues (of injustice, for instance) merely to be brought to awareness and protested. Above all, questions about the means and media by which information of different kinds is disseminated must be addressed. Indeed more recently the political theorist Jacques Rancière has also drawn our attention to these matters with his discussions of what he has called »the distribution of the sensible«. By this he means the ways in which societies assign what may be seen, and what remains unseen, what can be said and what can't, what can be heard, and what remains inaudible. It also refers to the alliances that are set up between different kinds of information or content, and the ways in which they are characteristically communicated. As Rancière put it in a recent interview published in *Art Review*: »What is important for me is to shift from the question ›is it possible to make this or that image?‹ to the question ›what does it imply, more generally, about the distribution of the sensible, how people are located in a certain universe, in a certain interrelation of words and images?‹« (Charlesworth/Rancière 2010: 73). By way of explication he referred to Godard's joke »that epic is for the Israelis and documentary is for the Palestinians. The idea that there are certain situations where only reality can be taken into account—there is no place for fiction« (ibid.: 75).

For Rancière, as for McLuhan and Parker earlier, art is particularly well-orientated towards carrying out such detailed, media specific investigations. To cite him again: »... a work, the practice of art, the practice of exhibition, it's always addressing a specific form of visibility and what I call a dissensus. It's not a general form. It's always a relation to a given form—an attempt at displacing that given form« (ibid.: 74–75). This implies that the most politically potent forms of art-making are those that evade embedded alignments between certain kinds of subject and subject-matter on the one hand, and certain forms, styles, and we might add technologies, of communication on the other.

THE POLITICS OF A-SIGNIFICATION

Clearly, art-historical and art-theoretical attention to the workings of materiality and medium challenges and extends our understanding of, and engagement with, the realms of representation and signification. But this is only part of the story. Such attention can also transition us into what are best described as a-signifying spaces of presentation in the here and now. Arguably, this transition—which can only be made at the point where words fail (without this failure our habits of perception, thought and action remain fundamentally unchallenged and unchanged)—is particularly vital, indeed foundational, for the emergence of deep political agency founded in internal, constitutional change. More on what I mean by this shortly.

This notion, then, of a politics of a-signification—as foundational for any politics, and as inevitably also extending the parameters of how political agency is generally understood—can perhaps best be exemplified by returning to, and extrapolating from, McLuhan and Parker's discussions of television bearing in mind the broader political contexts that surrounded their writing during this period: the widespread, grassroots activism that had been erupting around the globe in and around 1968. In North America, this included the anti-Vietnam War protests that had been proliferating alongside civil liberties activism. Of course, there were philosophical and theological bases to these varied revolts. Particularly influential, for instance, was a new wave of largely (neo)-Marxist and existentialist-inspired ideas and counter-ideologies proposed by such thinkers as Jean-Paul Sartre, Adorno and Horkheimer, and Guy Debord. But also worth considering, following McLuhan's logic, is the degree to which that ubiquitous environmental shift towards the televisual may also have played a crucial role.

One impact of the new TV environment was that images of global conflict, disorder and injustice were now being broadcast into the heart of the Western home on a more-than daily basis. The existential consequences of this, and other increasingly relentless media disseminations of violence and despair, was much discussed during this period, not least in Simone de Beauvoir's powerful novel *Les Belles Images* of 1966. And the Vietnam War in which the USA had been embroiled since 1955, was known from the mid 1960s onwards as the first »television« or »living-room« war.[10] But as artists like Martha Rosler had insisted, and attempted to disrupt with such works as *Bringing the War Home: House Beautiful* (1962–1972), while the content of these electronic image-invasions raised social and political awareness, arguably its repetition also had an inevitable (and perhaps intended?) normalizing effect. A rather different dimension of television's impact on activism emerges, however, if we follow instead the material and

---

10 These were the words of Michael J. Arlen, an American author and former television critic of *The New Yorker*, who went on to publish a book, *Living-Room War*, in 1969.

mediumistic logics of McLuhan and Parker. This was principally associated not with what it conveyed (content), but, as already noted, with its non-pictorial, tactile and participant qualities. In other words, we are asked to consider the relationship between the rise and character of 1960s activism in the west and—as McLuhan and Parker saw it—the deep, medium-driven constitutional changes that were occurring simultaneously at micro and at macro levels due to increasingly intensive human exposure to the workings of this particular manifestation of electric circuitry.

Yet again this is a provocation that seems deeply counter-intuitive. And certainly, since it has remained largely unexamined at broader intellectual, social and cultural levels, its existential potential has barely been pursued. To repeat, McLuhan believed that the technological changes advanced by electric circuitry were also bringing about evolutionary change at human neurological and behavioural levels, as noted, and in the domains of communal and cosmic interaction. And that it was only extensive constitutional change of this kind that would bring about lasting, actual change in our everyday ways of living and relating. Thus also at issue was the necessity of breaking out of rear-view mirror perception where our conceptions of ourselves and our place in the world were concerned. And here another key influence on McLuhan's thought is worth noting: the controversial work of the French palaeontologist and Jesuit priest Pierre Teilhard de Chardin (1881–1955) who, in such works as *The Divine Milieu: An Essay on the Interior Life*, written in 1929, and in his memoir, *The Heart of Matter* written in 1950, presented a view of material, technological and spiritual evolution as existing hand in hand. Indeed, as early as 1927, in an essay on the phenomenon of man, he had elaborated a notion of ›noosphere‹ or »earth's thinking envelope« (Teilhard de Chardin 1978: 31) in this regard. This was in effect an evolving thought environment which he took to cover the biosphere, in which the intelligent, conscious qualities normatively associated with the human were being increasingly extended to incorporate the realms of the organic and the artificial.

What also followed from this was a reconfigured notion of internality since the internal could no longer be understood as a realm separated from the material, collective, relational and cosmic. Rather, each was the other's counterpart, dependent on, emerging from, and becoming explicit in relation to those others. (Interestingly, an analogously non-autonomous and relational understanding of human interiority was also to be found in the writing of Merleau-Ponty. In his claim, for instance, in the preface to the *Phenomenology of Perception*, that »Truth does not ›inhabit‹ only ›the inner man‹, or more accurately, there is no inner man, man is in the world, and only in the world does he know himself« (Merleau-Ponty 1962: xi)).

This in turn opened up a new alliance between an intimate—because deeply and constitutionally embedded—sense of involvement with and in the world, and a sense of inevitable relocation into a radically enlarged realm, in which conventionally subjective, subject-centred or identity-based positions could no longer take pride of place; a realm that was actively characterized by various non-personal or organic agencies, and by what Merleau-Ponty called ›anonymous‹ modes of being. The counter-environmental challenge, therefore—that is, the properly political challenge thus understood—was first of all to enter this relatively opaque and inevitably controversial territory. Indeed, perhaps it is precisely this territory that would open up were we to take a non-melancholic, mediumistically-aware route into the semi-dark and depopulated photographic record of Durant's *We are the People*, discussed earlier.

BIBLIOGRAPHY

Andrews, Jorella (2004): »Painterly Transubstantiations/Political Change«. In: A.-T. Tymieniecka (ed.), *Analecta Husserliana* LXXXI, Dordrecht, Boston and London: Kluwer Academic Publishers, p. 141–151.

Bless, Nancy (2000): »Welcome Home: Project Row Houses«. *Sculpture* 19(5), June 2000, p. 33–39.

Chaplin, Sarah (1995): »Cyberspace: Lingering on the Threshold«. *A.D. Architectural Design* 65(11/12) (*Architects in Cyberspace*), London: Academy Editions, p. 32–35.

Charlesworth, JJ (2010): Interview with Jacques Rancière. *Art Review* 40, April 2010, p. 72–75.

Douglas, Emory (1972): »Art for the People's Sake: Emory Douglas Speaks at Fisk University«. *The Black Panther*, Saturday, 21 October 1972, p. 4.

Innis, Harold A. (1968 [1951]): »The Bias of Communication‹. In: *The Bias of Communication*, Toronto: University of Toronto Press, p 33–60.

Merleau-Ponty, Maurice (1962 [1945]): *Phenomenology of Perception*, trans. Colin Smith, London: Routledge and Kegan Paul Ltd.

——— (1964a): »Eye and Mind« [1961]. In: James M. Edie (ed.), *The Primacy of Perception*, Evanston, IL: Northwestern University Press, p. 159–190.

——— (1964b): »Indirect Language and the Voices of Silence« [1952]. In: John Wild (ed.), *Signs*, Evanston, IL: Northwestern University Press, p. 39–83.

McLuhan, Marshall/Parker, Harley (1968): *Through the Vanishing Point: Space in Poetry and Painting*, New York: Harper Colophon Books.

Teilhard de Chardin, Pierre (1978): *The Heart of Matter*, New York: Harcourt Brace Jovanovich.

The *Mise en abyme* Effect

Politics and the Fantasy of Total Visibility

MARGOT BOUMAN

As the following description of an instant replay clip from a televised football match between Japan and Denmark demonstrates, multiple narrative devices are used to tell a story. The match took place late last June in the group stage of the 2010 FIFA (Fédération Internationale de Football Association) World Cup, staged in South Africa. In a six-second instant replay, the Japanese goalkeeper Eiji Kawashima is shouting orders at the rest of the team after a near-goal by Denmark. Shown in extreme slow motion, over the duration of the instant replay his body slowly dips down and drifts across the screen from audience left to right, and then back again. At the beginning, Kawashima's mouth forms a distended oval; as his lower jaw thrusts out the oval compresses slightly, and the angle formed by his jaw shifts upward. In the slow motion sequence, Kawashima evokes the furious, melodramatic intensity of a kabuki samurai. His hair bristles, the chords in his neck stand out, his shoulders are squared back, and his arms rigidly flexed. As his jaw angle changes Kawashima exhales, issuing a trail of steam like a dragon's breath into the crisp, African winter (figure 4.1).

This instant replay clip is complete. Quite brief, it produces the sensation of looking at something that transcends the longer narrative sequence out of which it was extracted. Additionally, it is part of a longer sequence of instant replay clips, which are in turn excerpted from the live flow of the football match. These sets of instant replays repeat an event, or series of events that the television producers decide to extract and emphasize. Here is an example of a complete sequence: a brilliant goal by the Japanese striker, Keisuke Honda (figure 4.2). The goal has already been scored in the game's ›real‹ time, and, over approximately thirty seconds it is replayed from five different angles. Now, a few elements of this instant replay bear emphasis. First, this sequence of clips is framed on either side by the FIFA logo. The frame signals to the television audience a beginning and end to a narrative that is both nested in and interrupts the game's ›live‹ flow. Second, each re-

Figure 4.1: The Japanese goalkeeper Eiji Kawashima

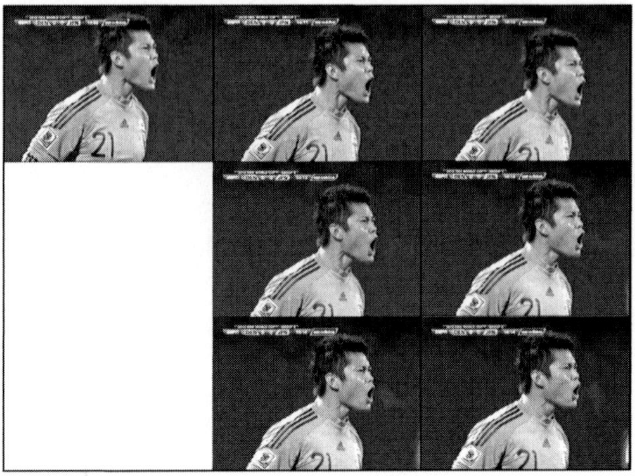

Source: ESPN

play provides a fresh angle of the goal being scored, allowing the television audience to see one more detail that was missing in both the previous replays and the live match. Third, within the television narrative, the replays provide progressively greater detail. Not just because the simple act of repetition produces a new relationship between the viewer and the event, but also because the action in each successive replay is incrementally slowed down.

The first two replays are shown at regular speed. The second two are somewhat slower. In the fifth and final replay of the goal, the audience is treated to the minute details, shown in extreme slow motion, of the Danish goalkeeper Thomas Sorensen's agonized attempt to prevent Honda's goal that are missing from the four previous replays. Sorenson's face is creased and folded into a study of effort and concentration. The excess fabric of his uniform, stretched taut against his straining torso, flutters in the wake of his leap's velocity. His body is fully outstretched, and at the end of the sequence it extends parallel to the ground as he appears to fly toward the ball, which inexorably hurtles past his splayed fingers and ricochets off the back of the net. No detail, it seems, is too small to go unnoticed by the television camera's eye.

When shown in extreme slow motion, these instant replays of the longer match show a rich texture of affect that usually occurs below our normal visual threshold, flickering past faster than the eye can see. Here emotions visibly seize hold of, shape, and reshape the players' bodies and faces. These bodies are not real, of course: rather, they are digital reproductions manipulated in post-production. Yet however distorted the images may

*Figure 4.2: Football match between Japan and Denmark
in the 2010 World Cup: goal against Denmark*

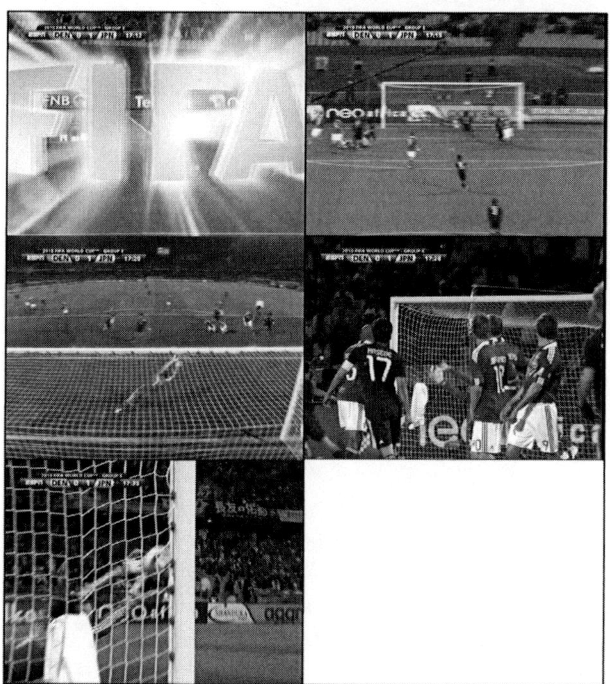

Source: ESPN

seem, the kinaesthetic movement they represent is not a digital invention created out of whole cloth. Kawashima and Sorenson did scream, exhale, gesticulate, flex and leap in ways that are only visible to the observer when their movements' execution has been dramatically slowed down. As Mark Hansen observed, new media technologies can expose to sight ›affectivity‹, or elements of being alive, of liveness, which are performed without conscious volition (Hansen 2004: 589).

Through this exposure to sight, micro-expressions that are already kinesthetically available to subjects through haptic regimes enter into visual representation and consequently acquire a new form of cultural meaning. And while these very brief video clips overflow with newly produced meaning, this article's subject, rather, is the framing mechanism that makes these instant replays possible, or, the narrative structure of *mise en abyme*. Textual and visual *mise en abyme* narrative structures include flashbacks, a story within the story, a telescoping inward of recessionary space, and the emplacement of a self-contained image within an image. In addition to the visual discourse produced by the television coverage of the 2010 South Africa World Cup, the case for war on Iraq made to the UN Security Council in

Figure 4.3: The final replay of the goal against Denmark

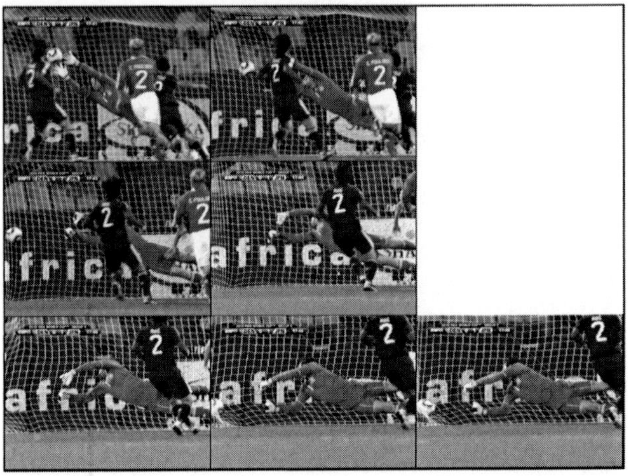

Source: ESPN

2003 by the US Secretary of State Colin Powell also assumes that by progressively telescoping inward on and fragmenting visual evidence, the technological gaze can access a more reliable truth. In these examples from sportscasting and international diplomacy, visual *mise en abyme* produces a fantasy that both draws attention to itself and embodies the ideal form of an argumentative structure through a synedochic relationship to the overall narrative. The broader implications of the success and failure of this rhetorical choice will form the conclusion of this article.

Mise en abyme was first identified by André Gide in an 1893 diary entry, in which he wrote that in a work of art he liked to find »transposed, on the scale of the characters, the very subject of the work. Nothing throws a clearer light upon it or more surely establishes the proportions of the whole« (Gide 1956: 17). Gide draws on heraldry for descriptive reference; in particular, the image nested within an image that is frequently found in escutcheons. Of special importance to Gide was the discrete nature of these heraldic images. Gide expands on the relevance of the characteristics found in escutcheons to literature when observing that »the retroaction of the subject on itself has always interested me [...]. An angry man tells a story; there is the subject of a book [...] it must be an angry man and there must be a constant connection between his anger and the story he tells« (ibid.: 17–18). The connection between a self-contained element and the overall narrative needs to be reciprocal: Anger is essential to and enriches the story and vice versa.

Not only does *mise en abyme* need to be both discrete from and integral to the broader narrative, Lucien Dallenbäch asserts that it describes »any aspect enclosed within a work that shows a similarity with the work that contains it« (Dallenbäch [1977] 1989: 8). Pictorial examples of the *mise en abyme* referred to by both Gide and Dallenbäch include Quentin Metsys' *The Money Changer and His Wife* (1514) and Diego Velázquez' *Las Meniñas* (ca. 1656). In both paintings, mirrors are used to expand on the narratives available to the viewer within the pictorial frame. In Metsys' *Money Changer*, a convex mirror included in the objects scattered on the table on which the couple is working expands the visual field beyond the painting's frame. The mirror's reflection allows the viewer to see a figure standing in front of a window, through which the street outside the interior is visible. In Velázquez' painting, the young princess Infanta Margarita stands in foreground centre, surrounded by her retinue and flanked on the left by the artist standing in front of a canvas. A mirror hung on the rear wall of the room reflects the artist's subject—the royal couple—who stand in the same position as the painting's audience. While Metsys' and Velázquez' *mise en abyme* consist of self-contained elements on a smaller scale that are crucial to the paintings' narrative, according to Dallenbäch they fail to embody *mise en abyme*, given that the elements reflected in the mirror are not found elsewhere in the painting. Rather, through reflection they create elements that exist fictitiously outside of the frame: »[…] a flawed approximation of the structure Gide had in mind« (ibid. [1977] 1989: 12). Given that a pictorial *mise en abyme* is restricted in these instances by the limitations of a still image, therefore, he concludes, it can only reflect, not repeat and provide increasingly abundant detail drawn from the primary narrative. Mieke Bal repeats this argument when she concludes that visual *mise en abyme* are limited to reflections, not repetition, in still images (Bal [1980] 2009: 62). Bal, and previously Dallenbäch, conflate the restrictions posed by painting with the failure of rhetorical possibility held out by visual culture more broadly. Because paintings can only represent reflection, Bal and Dallenbäch conclude, so it goes for the rest of visual culture.

However the World Cup's television broadcast and, as will be shown later in this article, PowerPoint presentations answer the formal and affective demands of the *mise en abyme* laid out by Gide, and then Bal and Dallenbäch. A story is told within a story that is both self-contained—or independent from the framing narrative—and repeats and expands on elements that are contained within this framing narrative. The FIFA logo both frames and separates the instant replay clips from the live play of the game. The iterative nature of the instant replays drawn from the narrative is reinforced by the extreme slow motion, which, in turn provides progressively more detail until, sometimes, movement stops. Most importantly, through these formal shifts, clips nested *mise en abyme* expand on elements that are absolutely essential to the larger story of the football match. For Dallenbäch, *mise en abyme* »brings out the meaning and form of the work« (Dallenbäch [1977] 1989: 8). For Bal, »the double interpretation of the relationship between primary and embedded text is a matter of life and death« (Bal [1985] 2009: 64). In the football match, *mise en abyme* both moves the story forward and provides a structure of visualization by emphasizing certain plays, or set pieces, or fouls. These repeated, slow-motion replays are necessary to our interpretation of the match's story. Kawashima's jaw clenched in anger, Sorenson's uniform fluttering under the pressure of his movement through air, create aspects of the game—furious involvement, competitive spirit, intense disappointment—that shape our understanding, by repeating and slowing down elements that are crucial to it. This provides, as Ron Moshe observed, a »pattern at an intradiegetic level [that is] capable of suggesting a generalization about the work« (Moshe 1987: 424–425). Not only does the clip provide a generalization about the match—the physical and emotional demands of football are enormous—it also makes it expand exponentially. Watching Kawashima shout orders in close up and in extreme slow motion creates a much more durable impression than it would if his involvement was shown at regular speed during the game's flow.

Not only are certain affective moments that occur in the football match valorized through *mise en abyme*, but, thanks to its role as an essential component in a narrative's causal structure, justice meted out by an expert witness inside the television announcer's booth is privileged by the game's broader audience over justice served by the referees on the field. In these instances the televisual *mise en abyme* promises that total visibility is total knowability. The ideological potential of this embedded narrative form is enormous. For example, in the World Cup, when a linesman allowed a goal scored by the Argentinean player Carlos Tévez in a knockout round match against Mexico, replays nested *mise en abyme* show that the goal resulted from an offside play between another Argentinean player, Lionel Messi and Tévez, and should have been disallowed. In this instant replay, a new element is introduced into the visual narrative that does not appear in the clips whose descriptions begin this article. At the critical moment the action is frozen, and an imaginary line is drawn across the field. The area between the imaginary line and the end of the field is darkened to conclusively demonstrate Tévez' offside position. In the replay, the announcers present the offside call as irrefutable. Also presumed is their superior ability to assess the play on the field. Thanks to *mise en abyme* structure made possible by video technology, through instant replay the television commentators assume a fuller and more just understanding of the match than the game's referees and linesmen. Here, the narrative is not merely reinforced visually through *mise en abyme*, but also ideologically. The narrative describes a triumph of potentially infinite technological visibility over the fallibility of human sight, a triumph that is performed through replays, and also through the way in which the visual narrative progressively slows down the athlete's body as the story-within-a-story progresses. As the action slows, the amount of information that emerges increases. The action is then frozen so that outside commentators, or the ›expert witnesses‹ in the television announcer's booth can conclusively assert their interpretation of the on-field play, which is supplemented through graphic overlays designed to provide the television audience with greater clarity. The synecdochic relationship between *mise en abyme* and the broader narrative lifts these excerpts into a fantasy relationship between the empirical devices it employs and the non-televised game, by promising justice served through technology.

The US government used a similarly painstaking process of telescoping in to and freezing visual evidence in order to advocate for war. On 5 February 2003 Secretary of State Colin Powell appeared before the United Nations Security Council to argue the Bush administration's case for invading Iraq. With the support of a PowerPoint presentation, Powell spoke before a skeptical Council, on behalf of an administration that had already decided to invade, with or without the UN's blessing. While Powell's presentation showed images that telescoped inward on what was presented as otherwise-inaccessible territory and referred outward to expert witness testimony, unlike *mise en abyme* footage in a televised football match, his presentation failed to provide more detail. This ruptured the fantasy of total visibility held out by *mise en abyme*. Notwithstanding, the presentation demonstrates the formal, ideological and synecdochic elements of *mise en abyme*.

Figure 4.4: PowerPoint slide of a satellite photograph shown by Secretary of State Colin Powell to the United Nations Security Council on 5 February 2003

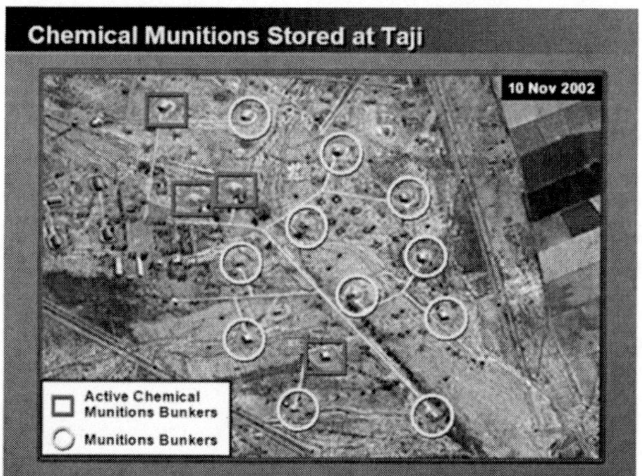

Source: The National Security Archive, George Washington University

Multiple accounts have recently been published that address various aspects of the failure of Powell's presentation, in particular his PowerPoint. David Zarefsky singles out the evidence presented in the PowerPoint as the weakest element in Powell's rhetorical arsenal (Zarefsky 2007). In the presentation, Powell showed a number of carefully annotated, high resolution satellite photographs of what he asserted was evidence of WMD activity in Iraq. Nate Kreuter laid the presentation's failure at the feet of the unclear nature of satellite imagery in general (Kreuter 2009). Jonathan Finn, on the other hand, singles out the satellite images as the strongest element in the PowerPoint and argues, rather, that multiple categories of images were suppressed under the rubric of the PowerPoint, conflating different regimes of images such as photographs, diagrams and satellite photographs (Finn 2010). Each account drew attention to the presentation's dependence on outside experts for interpretation as either a condition of evidence, a failing, or a strength.

Powell's presentation of the satellite images in particular draws out these arguments. After showing a transcript of an intercepted radio exchange, and slides successively labeled »Iraqi Declaration Documents« and »Documents Found in Home of Iraqi Scientist,« Powell showed a PowerPoint slide of a satellite photograph labeled »Chemical Munitions Stored at Taji,« and dated 10 November 2002. As the noun implies, a satellite photograph is taken using a still camera mounted on a satellite that orbits the earth. From this distance, the earth's surface is hyper-magnified. In the slide, an off-white line intersects a landscape from bottom right to the centre and then forks left. Toward the bottom, this off-white line is bordered by a dark grey gash. Off this central line multiple lines fork off, and then split off into more lines. At the end of each line and scattered through the image are small, off-white irregularly shaped rectangles, delineated by a dark grey edge. The ground against which these shapes are etched is a variegated light to medium grey. On the right side of the image is a patchwork of larger irregularly shaped rectangles, which are in turn bordered by a mottled grey verge that is distinct from the rest of the mottled grey background.

Powell's case did not depend on the legibility of the photographs: As he was careful to explain they are, indeed, illegible. »Let me say a word about satellite images before I show a couple,« Powell began, »The painstaking work of [satellite] photo analysis takes experts with years and years of experience, poring for hours and hours over light tables.« In other words, the satellite photograph can only be read through »expert witnesses,« just as the commentators of a football match provide conclusive interpretation of the instant replay nested *mise en abyme*. »As I show you these images, I will try to capture and explain what they mean [...] to our imagery specialists« (Powell 2003). The satellite photograph was further overlaid by red squares and yellow circles, and framed in a blue background. A legend in the bottom right indicates that red squares highlight active chemical munitions bunkers, and the yellow circles munitions bunkers. »Here,« Powell told the Security Council, »... you see 15 munitions bunkers in yellow and red outlines. The four that are in red squares represent active chemical munitions bunkers. How do I know that? How can I say that? Let me give you a closer look [Powell moves on to the next slide]. Look at the image on the left. On the left is a close-up of one of the four chemical bunkers. The two arrows indicate the presence of sure signs that the bunkers are storing chemical munitions« (ibid.).

Figure 4.5: PowerPoint slide showing a detail of the previous satellite photograph

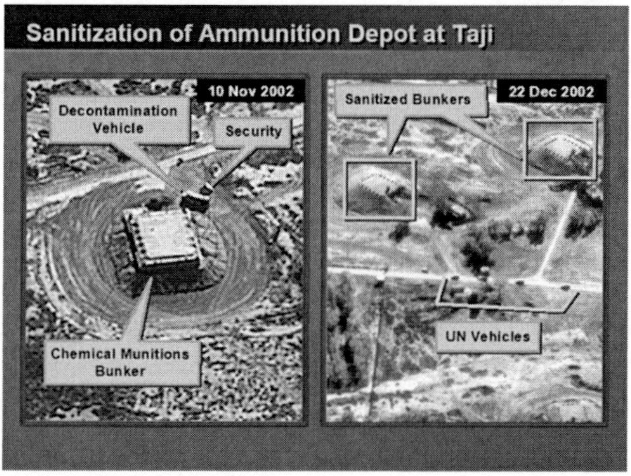

Source: The National Security Archive, George Washington University

Powell invoked the professionalism of his imagery specialists and used digital markers, close-ups and colour-coded visual aids to assure the UN Security Council that the images were proof of the existence of WMDs. The above quote is notable in that Powell uses the outlines, arrows and squares as avatars of the absent expert witness necessary to rendering the satellite image legible. Through this coding, as Finn points out, »UN Security Council members are encouraged to see what Powell purports to see in the images: an active programme of weapons storage and their sanitation in advance of inspections« (Finn 2010: 33). And while his argument depended on the expert eye, Powell never identifies them. Not only did his descriptions of the images refer repeatedly to external witnesses, but Powell's speech also made constant reference to external corroboration: »These are not assertions. These are facts, corroborated by many sources« (Powell 2003). Or, »This is evidence, not conjecture. This is true. This is all well documented« (ibid. 2003).

Moshe insists that »the originality and specificity of *mise en abyme*« lies in its peculiar habitat within the narrative, and the relative importance of this habitat to the narrative (Moshe 1987: 422). Like the extreme slow-motion clips began this article, the satellite photograph brought into existence a part of the world that was otherwise presumed unavailable, this time for political reasons. In Powell's presentation the satellite photograph, like the replays in football matches, depends on and are necessary to a framing narrative. For Kreuter, »making meaning from remotely sensed images [such as satellite photographs] is still fundamentally a rhetorical enterprise, governed by established rhetorical principles (Kreuter 2009: 217). Or as Zarefsky observed,

»The appearance of evidence often counts as evidence. The credibility of the source will outweigh internal deficiencies in the evidence« (Zarefsky 2007: 298). But as Kreuter observed, Powell »never explained what those sure signs were« (Kreuter 2009: 216). What links Powell's PowerPoint presentation to the World Cup instant replays is its implicit dependence on multiple framing narratives: the speech (in the World Cup, the game); the expert witness (in the World Cup, the television commentator); and the Bush administration's desire to go to war (in the World Cup, the broader context of professional football). Thus, believing Powell's evidence meant believing the Bush administration, an act of faith the Security Council was not ready to make.

Ostensibly, the Bush administration's desire to invade Iraq was premised on the threat it posed to the US in a post-9/11 environment. However Powell's February 2003 appearance in front of the UN Security Council set out to provide a veneer of respectability for a desire to topple Saddam Hussein that reached back decades prior to both 9/11 and the then-current Bush administration (Dizard 2004; Lang 2004). In the immediate aftermath of the attacks on the World Trade Center and the Pentagon on 11 September 2001 by the terrorist organization al-Qaeda, there was a rush by the Bush administration to connect these attacks to Hussein (Woodward 2002: 60; 9/11 Commission Report 2004: 334; *The Guardian* 26 November 2009). However after multiple reports from the intelligence community proved no reliable link between al-Qaeda and Hussein, the Bush administration shifted its focus to another claim: that Hussein's regime was violating UN agreements by manufacturing and stockpiling weapons of mass destruction (WMD). This argument also predated 9/11 (Waas 2005: 1, 2; Suskind 2006: 23; Pillar 2006). This was the argument that Powell brought to the Security Council. The trigger for military action preferred by the British government, other allies, and some segments of the Bush administration—specifically Powell—was a second UN resolution that would authorize an armed response.

What distinguishes the World Cup television broadcast from Powell's PowerPoint presentation is its ability to fully represent a fantasy of visibility that underwrites both examples of *mise en abyme*. The discrepancies between these non-fictional accounts and their shared base assumptions help draw out the fantasy elements that they have in common. Both the televised football match and Powell's presentation to the Security Council are structurally predicated on the assumption that looking deeper, harder, and longer at an image will necessarily provide a more accurate understanding of it, an assumption made possible through *mise en abyme* that privileges prolonged looking, and the introduction of outside experts. The rhetorical strategy of *mise en abyme* used by football commentators to contradict calls made by the referee changes perception of the football match. The Bush administration (and a portion of the US public) believed that the digitally enhanced satellite imagery provided plausible enough evidence of WMDs to include it in their official rhetorical arsenal before the international community. Powell's presentation began and ended with an unconvinced Security Council. Just over a week after Powell's presentation counter-experts from the United Nations (Hans Blix) and the International Atomic Energy Agency (Mohamed ElBaradei) contradicted many of Powell's claims (2003). The attempt by the US and the United Kingdom to obtain a UN Security Council resolution authorizing an invasion of Iraq was withdrawn before a vote when France, Russia, and then China indicated that they would use their Council veto power against any resolution allowing the use of force against Iraq. However Powell's fiction was partially successful at the time, because it increased US popular support for war (Morin/Deane 2003). Unlike Powell, televised football matches succeeds in leading and educating the untrained eye—the average television viewer—by adhering scrupulously to the narrative conventions of *mise en abyme*. The limits to the factual claims to truth attainable through the visual rhetoric used by Powell's presentation are self-evident, not least because the Bush administration has since admitted that there were no weapons of mass destruction in Iraq. Notwithstanding, the underlying rhetorical claim in both these cases—visual experts can train the otherwise-uneducated eye by slowing down, stopping and magnifying evidence through visualization technologies—defines both.

Finally, a *mise en abyme* becomes a meme. Because of its self-contained nature it can be removed from its original context and inserted into new contexts. For example when a controversial call by the Mali referee disallowed a goal between the US and Slovenia in the South Africa World Cup, the extreme slow motion replays disproving the referee's call were lifted out of their original context—the live flow of the game—and inserted into an array of other media contexts such as the postgame wrapup, the pregame and half-time shows in following matches, and past the televised World Cup to the Internet, the US televised news media and points beyond. Because of its historic nature, Powell's PowerPoint presentation, as well as the transcript of his speech has been archived and is freely available from multiple sources. In a similar fashion, the afterlife of Powell's PowerPoint has spread far beyond its original context, reappearing and then disappearing, meme-like, in the Department of State website, and in fragments in a variety of scholarly articles, and again in its entirety in the George Washington University Archive. At each point in its propagation beyond its original context, synecdochic relationships are re-fashioned between the *mise en abyme* and each new context that it is deposited in.

BIBLIOGRAPHY

Bal, Mieke ([1985] 2009): *Narratology: Introduction to the Theory of Narrative*, third edition, trans. Christine Van Boheeman, Toronto: Toronto University Press.

Blix, Hans (2003): Briefing of the Security Council, 14 February 2003. Archived in: http://www.gwu.edu/~nsarchiv/NSAEBB/NSAEBB80/ [accessed 14 March 2011].

Dallenbäch, Lucien ([1977] 1989): *The Mirror in the Text*, trans. Jeremy Whiteley with Emma Hughes, Chicago, IL: Chicago University Press.

Dizard, John (2004): »How Ahmed Chalabi Conned the Neocons«. *Salon*, 4 May 2004; http://dir.salon.com/story/news/feature/204/05/04/chalabi; *Christian Science Monitor*, 15 June 2004.

El Baradei, Mohammed (2003): »The Status of Nuclear Inspections in Iraq«, 14 February 2003. Archived in: http://www.gwu.edu/~nsarchiv/NSAEBB/NSAEBB80/ [accessed 14 March 2011].

Finn, Jonathan (2010): »Powell's Point: ›Denial and Deception‹ at the UN«. *Visual Communication* 9, p. 25–49.

Gide, André (1956): *The Journals of André Gide, Vol. 1: 1889–1946*, edited, translated, abridged and with an introduction by Justin O'Brien, New York: Vintage Books.

The Guardian, 26 November 2009. http://www.guardian.co.uk/politics/blog /2009/nov/26/iraq-iraq [accessed 19 January 2011].

Hansen, Mark (2004): »The Time of Affect, or Bearing Witness to Life«. *Critical Inquiry* 30, p. 584–626.

Kreuter, Nate (2009): »The Subjectivity of Eyes in the Sky: Understanding Remote Sensing through the Cuban Missile Crisis and the 2002 Build-Up to War in Iraq«. *Journal of Visual Literacy* 27(2), p. 209–218.

Lang, Patrick W. (2004): »Drinking the Kool-Aid«. *Middle East Policy Council Journal* XI(2).

Moshe, Ron (1987): »The Restricted Abyss: Nine Problems in the Theory of *Mise en Abyme*«. *Poetics Today* 8, p. 417–438.

Morin, Richard/Deane, Claudia (2003): »Most Support Attack On Iraq, With Allies: Poll Finds Renewed Backing for War«. *Washington Post*, Tuesday, 11 February 2003, p. A14.

National Commission on Terrorist Attacks upon the United States (2004): *The 9/11 Commission Report: Final Report of the National Commission on Terrorist Attacks Upon the United States*, New York: Norton.

Pillar, Paul R. (2006): »Intelligence, Policy, and the War in Iraq«. *Foreign Affairs* 85(2), p. 15–27.

Powell, Colin L. (2003): Remarks to The United Nations Security Council February 5, 2003 New York, New York (10:30 a.m. EST). Statement released by the Office of the Spokesman of the US Department of State. Archived in: http://www.gwu.edu/~nsarchiv/NSAEBB/NSAEBB80/new /doc%2023/Remarks%20to%20the%20United%20Nations%20Security %20Council.htm [accessed 4 January 2011].

Suskind, Ron (2006): *The One Percent Doctrine*. New York: Simon & Schuster.

Waas, Murray (2005): »Key Bush Intelligence Briefing Kept from Hill Panel«. *National Journal*, 22 November 2005.

Woodward, Bob (2002): *Bush at War*. New York: Simon & Schuster.

Zarefsky, David (2007): »Making the Case for War: Colin Powell at the United Nations«. *Rhetoric & Public Affairs* 10(2), summer 2007, p. 275–302.

Of Lights, Flesh, Glitter and Soil

Notes towards a Complex Ecology of Live Art

João Florêncio

> Toto, I've a feeling we're not in Kansas anymore. (Dorothy in *The Wizard of Oz*)

Scene 1: Newtown, Johannesburg, 2001

In a shack settlement under the M1, amidst all the trash, both human and non-human, biological and inorganic, amongst all the decaying ephemeral structures some people called *home*, there is a pair of giant black high heeled shoes that struggle to keep the balance of the white, queer, Jewish bionic body of Steven Cohen, the South African artist-cum-chandelier.

Around his strongly marked white abject body-cum-source of light, black squatters gather in awe, rage or religious devotion while unexpectedly council workers in red overalls turn up to destroy the illegal settlement and allow for the construction of the largest cable-stayed bridge of Southern Africa, the Nelson Mandela Bridge, eventually inaugurated a couple of years after on 20 July 2003.

Faced with the sight of Steven Cohen's almost naked body covered in make-up and wearing nothing but a Victorian chandelier as if it was a tutu, tights, and giant high-heels, some men react angrily and insult the artist, while others seem to want to fuck and/or kill him. The women, on the other hand, appear to have a very different reaction to the presence of such body with some referring to the artist as ›Angel‹ or ›Jesus‹ and, along with the only albino man present at the scene, offering themselves as human shields against the men who push them trying to reach the artist. In the meantime, the workers, armed with crowbars, take down the walls of what once were the squatters' houses, opening up their territory for the layering of steel, concrete and speed.

Figure 5.1: Steven Cohen, Chandelier, *2001*

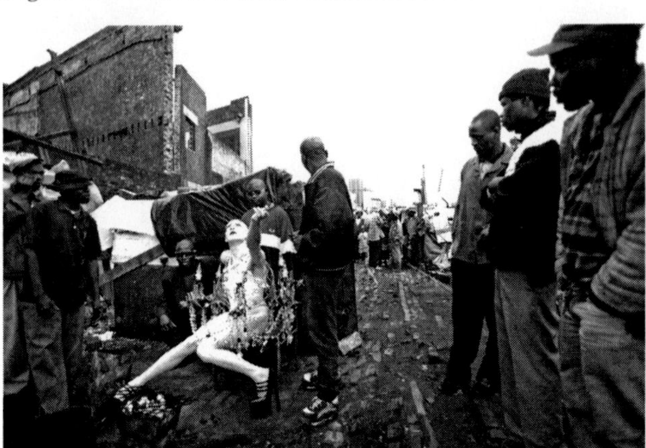

Photo: John Hogg, courtesy of the artist

The question concerning the above scene is not so much *what* happened in Newtown in 2001 but, rather, *how* did it happen? *How* did it come to be whatever it is now, whatever it meant to the squatters, to the artist, to its environment, to the performance or the art scholar?

The histories of art, its journeys from its beginning to wherever it can go, have started, according to Deleuze and Guattari, not with ›prehistorical‹ human beings learning how to represent the absent on cold stone walls but rather with animals building their habitats, their houses, their *oikoi*. Towards the end of their book *What is Philosophy?*, Deleuze and Guattari tell the story of the *Scenopoetes dentirostris*, an animal also known as the Tooth-billed Catbird or Stagemaker Bowerbird, and they tell it like this:

»Every morning the *Scenopoetes dentirostris*, a bird of the Australian rain forests, cuts leaves, makes them fall on the ground, and turns them over so that the paler, internal side contrasts with the earth. In this way it constructs a stage for itself like a ready-made; and directly above, on a creeper or a branch, while fluffing out the feathers beneath its beak to reveal their yellow roots, it sings a complex song made up from its own notes and, at intervals, those of other birds that it imitates: it is a complete artist« (Deleuze/Guattari 1994: 184).

Following this tale of great skill and bird exhibitionism, the two thinkers go on to conclude that art begins with the animal and with its house, but only on the condition that this house, this *oikos*, will open itself up and allow itself to *communicate* with other houses, to be intersected by other habits and habitats so that it will launch itself in a movement of deterritorialization, »a kind of *deframing* following lines of flight that pass through the territory only in order to open it onto the universe, that go from house-territory to town-cosmos« (ibid.: 187), that allow the event happening on stage—on the bird's stage—to receive inputs from other territories, that render possible the contamination of the bird's song with the signature-melodies of its neighbours.

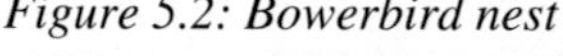

Figure 5.2: Bowerbird nest

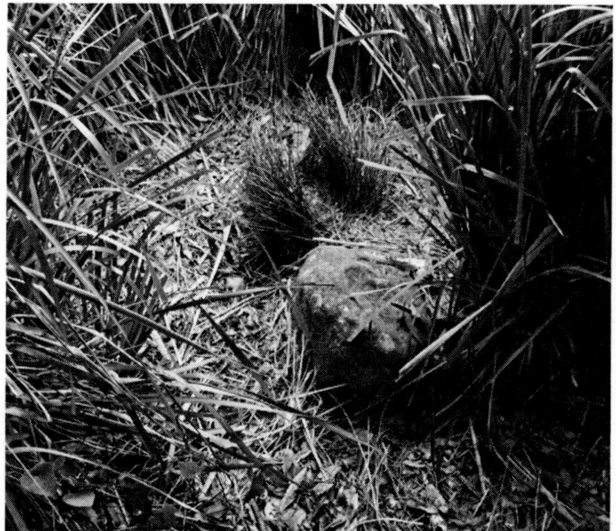

Source: http://www.flickr.com/photos/1234abcd/4717190370/
CC by thinboyfatter

Three points seem to stand out from Deleuze and Guattari's account of the artistic skills of the Stagemaker Bowerbird. First, for them art seems to precede the human. Second, art is a doing rather than a being, and it is a doing that must be shown. It is the crafting of a habitat, the performance of a personal architecture, the public display of one's own *house-territory*. Finally, art is one's house being built on groundless grounds, on a »mad vector« (ibid.: 185) of deterritorialization, like Dorothy has realized in *The Wizard of Oz* when, after leaving her house, she was hit by the fact that her house was not where she was expecting it to be. Like it was the case in Wagner's first use of what is now known as the Tristan Chord, it only takes a small step out the door and suddenly ›we're not in Kansas anymore‹, Wagner becoming Dorothy, the archetype of the artist who jumps on a line of flight without ever leaving the house, who takes part in the kind of inhuman performance-flight that, like a black hole, pulls reality towards the singularity of a posthuman time.

If art is for Deleuze and Guattari the being of sensation that results from the crafting of a house [*oikos*] that is opened up onto the cosmos, I would like to suggest that the way to understand the behaviour of a live artwork seen as the building of a fleeting habitat should pass through complex ecology, the study of one's house or dwelling place understood as a complex system. But what defines a complex system and how can such notion contribute for the study of live artworks?

According to engineer and philosopher of science Paul Cilliers, *complex systems* should not be confused with *complicated systems*:

»If a system—despite the fact that it may consist of a huge number of components—can be given a complete description in terms of its individual constituents, such a system is merely complicated. [...] In a *complex system*, on the other hand, the interaction among constituents of the system, and the interaction between the system and its environment, are of such a nature that the system as a whole cannot be fully understood simply by analysing its components« (Cilliers 1998: viii).

Cilliers goes on to define a complex system as an assemblage consisting of large number of elements in which complexity arises from the dynamic nonlinear interactions of its constituting elements, interactions which include processes known as positive (i.e. enhancing) and negative (i.e. inhibiting) feedback loops. Furthermore, complex systems are usually open systems, that is, systems that interact with their environment at conditions far from equilibrium and in which there has to be a constant flow of energy coming in from the environment in order to maintain the system, and another flow of energy and matter going out of the system and being dispersed in its environment as waste. Finally, the behaviour of the system depends not only on its present conditions but also on its history as complex systems have memory and the ability to learn. Nonetheless, each element of the system is always ignorant of the behaviour of the system as a totality and can only react to inputs reaching it from its direct vicinity.[1] Following ecological thermodynamicist Eric Schneider and ecological systems engineer James Kay, examples of open complex systems are to be found in both nonliving organized systems such as tornados or lasers, and in living systems such as cells and ecosystems.[2] Further to that I would like to propose that any artwork and particularly any live artwork is another example of a complex system. The live artwork, as the complex system it is, meets all the characteristics that according to Cilliers are necessary for the classification of a system as complex. In the case of Steven Cohen's piece *Chandelier* described above, the complex system is constituted by a large number of elements: performer and members of the audience (in this case the squatters and the council workers), but also the sounds, images, temperatures, props, make-up, high-heels, movements, crowbars, the Christian doctrine, the city lights on the horizon, the political power, the bridge to be built, the debris on the floor, etc., all elements that interact with each other either physically

---

1   For a detailed description of the characteristics of complex systems see Cilliers 1998: 3–4; for an in-depth account of the system's memory and capacity for learning see Wiener 1965: 116–129.

2   See Schneider/Kay 1995.

or through transference of information and thus influence and potentially change themselves and each other. As these interactions are, by definition, nonlinear, a small cause must be able to produce a big effect and as such the presence of the council workers, Cohen's costume and make-up or the white colour of his skin can have large consequences such as triggering fear, disgust, or religious hope in the locals. Finally as all other open systems, the live event also demands an input of energy from its environment, which in the given example can be seen in the decisions of the political power, on the electricity that keeps the chandelier's lights on, on the latest meal of the performer, the religious faith of the squatters, or on the irregularities of the pavement that, along with the high-heels, difficult the movement of the artist. And it too produces waste which can assume the form of semiotic sacrifices, debris on the floor, or energy consumed with no utility, with no

Figure 5.3: Steven Cohen, Chandelier, *2001*

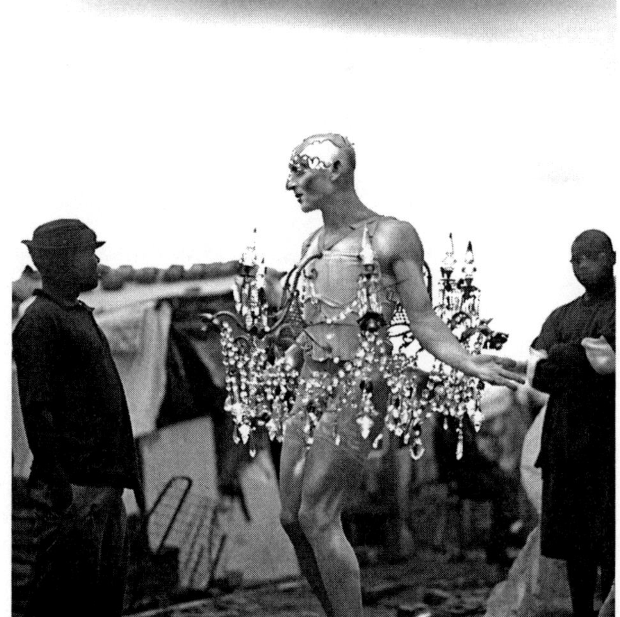

Photo: John Hogg, courtesy of the artist

production of useful and thus valuable commodities. Furthermore it is often this production of waste, this production of something in excess of what our contemporary apparatuses of knowledge production can capture, it is this semiotic loss common to all genres of live art that is often responsible for the creation of something other and totally unexpected such as affective or libidinal attachments, joy, hope, or the recycled subjectivities made out of the debris of the hegemonic capitalist means of production.

The analogy established between live art events and complex systems such as ecosystems, tornados, or lasers is not as surprising as it may seem as notions of complexity have already entered the domain of academic disciplines such as philosophy, anthropology or sociology some years ago and can be said to be one of their research avenues currently more en vogue. This awareness of the complexity of the real has been noted, for instance, by ethnomusicologist Timothy Rice in his seminal essay »Time, Place, and Metaphor in Musical Experience and Ethnography« in which the author asks »if we now understand our world as not so simple, but rather as a complex of unbounded, interacting cultures and as consisting crucially of the rapid movement of people, ideas, images, and music over vast distances, then what sort of questions arise?« (Rice 2003: 151). However, the social theorist who is perhaps most famously indebted to complexity theory is philosopher Manuel DeLanda who, in his book *A New Philosophy of Society*, makes use of theories borrowed from ecology and biology in order to propose an understanding of social structures not as closed totalities but, rather, as dynamic open system or *assemblages*. In it, the author writes:

»[I]n both the biological and the social realms there are processes of *decoding*, yielding assemblages which do not conform to the organismic metaphor. In biology such decoding is illustrated by animal behaviour which has ceased to be rigidly programmed by genes to be learned from experience in a more flexible way. [...] A social example of the result of a process of decoding would be informal conversations between friends. [...] But they involve rules, such as those governing turn-taking. The more formal and rigid the rules, the more these social encounters may be said to be coded. But in some circumstances these rules may be weakened giving rise to assemblages in which the participants have more room to express their convictions and their own personal styles« (DeLanda 2006: 15–16).

The idea that the properties manifested by an artwork at any given time are contingent and the resultant of a complex interaction of factors allows us to understand such artwork as a *living* system always-already open for unexpected changes of behaviour and unpredictable rearrangements of its structure or *meaning*, that is, always-already open for suffering what Deleuze and Guattari have elsewhere named *deterritorialization* or *becoming*, a movement of flight away from the capturing power of the organism, the structure »which life sets against itself to limit itself« (Deleuze/Guattari 2004: 554).

But what are the mechanics of creativity in a complex system, what triggers the system's flight, or what makes the house-territory of the artwork or performance event open itself up onto the cosmos allowing for the *emergence of new meanings*? What turns an object or an action into a work of art?

According to the literature, the capacity of complex systems for self-organization is characterized by the tendency they manifest for evolving to critical states in which their organization and behaviour changes. This principle of *self-organized criticality* is responsible for directing the systems away from their meta-stable states and into a threshold or state of crisis that will cause them to enter into processes of differentiation and adopt new patterns of behaviour.[3] If one considers state-space to be the n-dimensional space characterized by having one dimension for each of the n variables of the system,[4] the n-dimensional points of state-space in which the system starts moving away from its previous state and towards a new meta-stable state are called *bifurcators*.[5] Conversely, each point of state-space towards which the system will direct itself is called an *attractor*.[6] The movement away from a particular state-space and towards a new configuration where the system will manifest new features or express emergent properties is caused by what scientists know as *symmetry-breaking events*, events triggered by changes in the environment of by the non-linear nature of the interactions happening within the system,[7] and which, Bonta and Protevi write, »occur in ›zones of sensitivity‹ where bifurcators cluster and amplify each other's effects so that a new set of attractors and bifurcators is produced (such events are opportunities for ›creativity‹ in response to ›crisis‹ in the history of the system)« (Bonta/Protevi 2004: 20). It is, in my view, a symmetry-breaking event of this kind that is responsible for making a given assemblage reach a bifurcation point and suffer the deterritorialization responsible for turning it into a work of art.

Now given that (i) a complex system can move into areas of state-space previously unseen and (ii) any successful attempt to model (i.e. to *know*) a complex system can only occur if a model as complex as the system it tries to model is used,[8] then the problem for the live art scholar seems to be a lack of methodological tools in either art theory or performance studies that will allow him/her to study the dynamics of a live art system and its relationship with its environment from the point of view of complexity theory.

In other words, the understanding of live artworks as complex systems calls for a new methodological approach in performance studies and art the-

---

3   See Cilliers 1998: 86 and Bonta/Protevi 2004: 19.

4   See Cilliers 1998: 97.

5   See Bonta/Protevi 2004: 19.

6   See Cilliers 1998: 97 and Bonta/Protevi 2004: 20.

7   See Cilliers 1998: 95.

8   See ibid.: x.

ory away from pre-established interpretational grids and hermeneutical strategies and towards a focus on the processes of permanent de- and re-coding which are endogenous to the system. This methodological shift necessary for inaugurating the possibility of an understanding of live art according to the complexity paradigm must then follow what Deleuze and Guattari defined as *cartography* and which I shall *ecology*, i.e. an approach to the art object that starts by mapping the extensive and intensive properties of a system (including its attractors, bifurcators, patterns of emergent behaviour, thresholds, etc.) in order to understand the live artwork not as a system whose meaning is capable of being institutionalized and frozen in time but instead as a living being whose life is characterized by never-ending processes of change and creativity, i.e. by the constant emergence of new, provisional and contingent structures of meaning. As Deleuze and Guattari write:

»A body is not defined by the form that determines it nor as a determinate substance or subject nor by the organs it possesses or the functions it fulfills. On the plane of consistency, *a body is defined only by a longitude and a latitude*: in other words the sum total of the material elements belonging to it under given relations of movement and rest, speed and slowness (longitude); the sum total of the intensive affects it is capable of at a given power or degree of potential (latitude). Nothing but affects and local movements, differential speeds. [...] Latitude and longitude are the two elements of a cartography« (Deleuze/Guattari 2004: 287).

This cartographic methodology has a strong connection with the diagrammatic work of the scientific discipline known as ecology for ecology, defined as the study of ecosystems, is not only characterized by its use of tools for mapping ecosystemic dynamics such as migrations or fluxes of energy and matter but has also adopted as its own concepts first established within the domains of complexity theory and cybernetics. An example of those notions which migrated from complexity theory into ecology is the principle of emergent properties. As Eugene Odum and Gary Barrett write in *Fundamentals of Ecology*:

»An important consequence of [the] hierarchical organization [of nature] is that as components, or subsets, are combined to produce larger functional wholes, new properties emerge that were not present at the level below. Accordingly, an emergent property of an ecological level or unit cannot be predicted from the [analytical or structural] study of the components of that level or unit. Another way to express the same concept is nonreducible property—that is, a property of the whole not reducible to the sum of the properties of the parts« (Odum/Barrett 2004: 7).

Now, if the properties of a complex system emerge from the interaction of all its component parts and not as the direct result of the will of a great designer or of the genius of an artist, a final step needs to be taken, a step aimed at expanding the notion of authorship in live artworks.

In his 2002 book *Performance Studies: An Introduction*, Richard Schechner sketched a very simple but nonetheless extremely useful notion of *performing* in its relation to *being*:

»›Being‹ is existence itself. ›Doing‹ is the activity of all that exists, from quarks to sentient beings to super galactic strings. ›Showing doing‹ is performing: pointing to, underlining, and displaying doing« (Schechner 2002: 22).

Despite this simplistic formulation which comes with no surprise from a book aimed at being an introduction to performance studies, Schechner's definition of performance as the activity of a (living) being that displays his/her/its doings is exceptionally helpful in the context of the present argument. For if doing is condition *sine qua non* for the existence of all beings, then it is strongly plausible that everything that *is* might at any point in its existence display its actions regardless of possessing the capacity for self-reflexivity, i.e. conscience, or not. Such is the case, as it was seen above, with the Stagemaker Bowerbird but also with less obvious beings such as some species of flowers existent in Eurasia, South America, and Australia which mimic or *perform* female insects in order to be pollinated by the males that arrive to pseudocopulate with them.[9]

The idea that performing animals can influence the development of a live artwork and thus be responsible for its outcome by taking an active role in the production of its meaning has for long been firmly established in the minds of both theatre practitioners and scholars. »Children and animals bring uncertainty to the threatre,« notes Lourdes Orozco (Orozco 2010: 84), and so, as the theatrical maxim goes, one should never work with them. Such piece of advice, which according to Nicholas Ridout is usually accredited to American comedian W. C. Fields,[10] serves only to point out the perceived dangers of risking having animals on stage. Ridout writes:

»The theatre [...] is all about humans coming face to face with other humans and either liking it or not liking it. The animal clearly has no place in such a communication. Thus when it does appear on stage, untethered from framings as a pet within the dramatic fiction, the animal seems [...] out of place« (Ridout 2006: 97–98).

Further to this *being-there-when-it-shouldn't* of the animal on stage, it is also obvious that the presence of living animals in artworks will only serve to diffuse the agency over the shape of the work and such can be a very risky decision to take as the artist will often have to hand in to (or at least share with) the animals the responsibility over the outcome of the art piece. Such was the case, for instance, of the electric rock symphony that Céleste

---

9   For more examples of both animal and vegetal mimicry in plants, see Dafni 1984.

10 See Ridout 2006: 98.

Boursier-Mougenot installed in The Curve gallery of the Barbican Centre in London in early 2010. In it, the artist furnished the gallery with electric guitars, amplifiers, and a flock of zebra finches which, by landing on the instruments while going about their daily activities, created a live piece of post-(human)-rock.

But it is not just the presence of nonhuman beings that might affect the outcome of a live artwork as also the presence (and participation) of (human) audiences is known to influence the meaning of a work. As Richard Schechner writes, »without audience's collaboration no performance is possible« (Schechner 1971: 74).

Now as ecology ›proper‹ is, following Ernest Haeckel's 1869 coinage of the term, defined as the »scientific study of the interactions between organisms and their environment« (Begon et al. 2006: xi), also an ecology of live art will have to take into consideration all the bodies, human and nonhuman, taking part in a work alongside all the interactions amongst them in the particular social, cultural and institutional environment of the event. Such is also a consequence of considering live art as a social formation. One of the features of complex systems that seems to point out to the importance of taking into consideration all the components of the system regardless of their human, nonhuman, biological or inorganic character when trying to understand its dynamics is the fact that, as it was seen above, because the elements of the system have no knowledge of the functioning of the system as a whole and only react to stimulation received from their direct vicinity, the responsibility for the emergent properties of the system is distributed amongst all its elements rather than being the direct outcome of a centralized consciousness. In the work mentioned above, Steven Cohen's piece *Chandelier*, it would be impossible to argue that the artist is the sole agent or the great designer of the overall event that took place in that squatter camp of Johannesburg. In the study of such work, one must distribute the responsibility for the event amongst the artist, the local body politic, the squatters, the religious doctrine brought by the colonial power centuries ago, the particular characteristics of the soil, its irregularities, the debris covering it, etc., making the art event a »never-ending building-site« with »no overall architect to guide it, and no design, however unreflected« (Callon/Latour 1981: 295).

Hence, an ecological approach like the one I am proposing resonates with Bruno Latour's definition of *actor-network*. For Latour, an actor or *actant* is a composite body that can be made up of human and/or nonhuman elements and that is at the origin of an action exercised upon another body in a determinate context or environment. »[O]f actors it can only be said they act,« he writes (Latour 2004: 237). Latour's *actor* or *actant* can then be seen as a cluster of different elements which occupy a lower level of the system and cooperate with each other, acquiring a kind of identity as a collective within the larger complex assemblage: »The actors can bond together in a block comprising millions of individuals, they can enter alliances with iron, with grains of sand, neurons, words, opinions and affections« (Callon/Latour 1981: 292).

As Paul Cilliers writes regarding macroeconomic systems:

»If we want to shift the discussion to more complex economic phenomena (gross national product, stock-market indexes, the gold price, etc.), nothing extra needs to be added; the phenomena mentioned emerge as a result of nothing more than the interactions between the various elements which co-operate with each other, and also compete with other clusters. A bank, for example, is nothing more than a number of individuals grouped together to perform specific functions. The components of the complex economic system do not consist of different *types* of things (banks, the state, corporations *and* individuals); they consist of individual agents clustered together to form the larger-scale phenomena« (Cilliers 1998: 7).

Figure 5.4: Luis Lazaro Matos, Waterfall House for a Skateboarder I, *charcoal on paper, 2010*

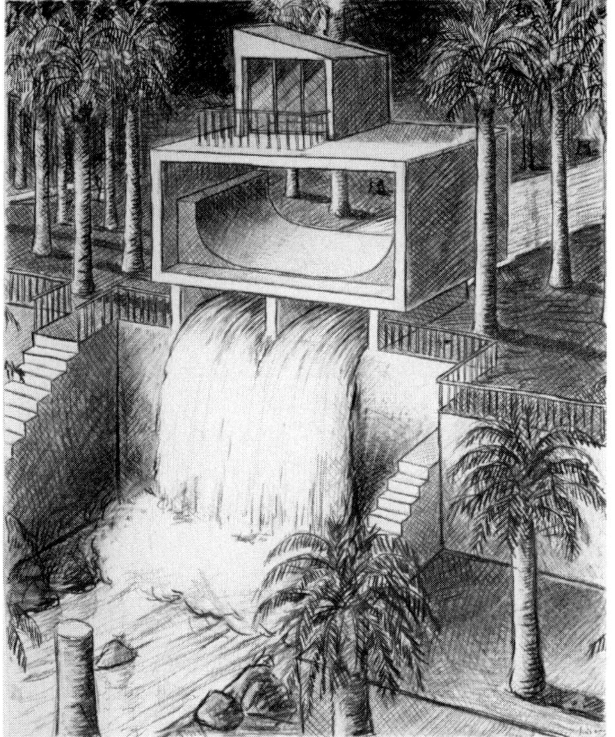

Courtesy of Luis Lazaro Matos, reproduced with permission of the artist

The fact that Latour decided to appropriate the word *actor* and remove it from its original theatrical context should just serve as another argument supporting the present thesis. For as Latour writes following performance theorist Irwin Goffman:

»To use the word ›actor‹ means that it's never clear who and what is acting when we act since an actor on stage is never alone in acting. Play-*acting* puts us immediately into a thick imbroglio where the question of who is carrying out the action has become unfathomable. As soon as the play starts, as Irwin Goffman has so often showed, nothing is certain [...]. If we accept to unfold the metaphor, the very word actor directs our attention to a complete dislocation of the action, warning us that it is not a coherent, controlled, well-rounded, and clean-edged affair. By definition, action is dislocated. Action is borrowed, distributed, suggested, influenced, dominated, betrayed, translated. If an actor is said to be an actor-network, it is first of all to underline that it represents the major source of uncertainty about the origin of action« (Latour 2005: 46).

In conclusion, if live art, as Félix Guattari writes in *Chaosmosis*, »delivers the instant to the vertigo of the emergence of Universes that are simultaneously strange and familiar,« if it has the power to »extract [...] intensive, a-temporal, a-spatial, a-signifying dimensions from the semiotic net of quotidianity« (Guattari 1995: 90), it is because it functions in a complex ecosystemic way that cannot be captured by pre-established codes or practices of knowing or have its meaning fully understood if taken simply as the direct outcome of the actions of its human participants. Rather, live art events are complex ecosystems, sets of bodies, both human and nonhuman, which are open to the environment despite the operative closure necessary for their survival as beings, and the elements of which work by interacting with their neighbours in a nonlinear fashion. The realization of this fact will allow theorists to understand live artworks as machinic assemblages that due to their complexity and refusal of equilibrium, contribute for the emergence of new configurations of the real and clusters of agency under the form of new subjectivities and existential territories, new modes of embodiment of oneself, new affective and libidinal attachments, new forms of political struggle, new communities, new hopes.

BIBLIOGRAPHY

Begon, Mike/Townsend, Colin/Harper, John (2006): *Ecology: From Individuals to Ecosystems*, Oxford and Malden, MA: Blackwell Publishing.
Bonta, Mark/Protevi, John (2004): *Deleuze and Geophilosophy: A Guide and Glossary*, Edinburgh: Edinburgh University Press.
Callon, Michael/Latour, Bruno (1981): »Unscrewing the big Leviathan – how actors macro-structure reality and how sociologists help them to do so«. In: Karin Knorr-Cetina and Aaron Victor Cicourel (eds.), *Advances*

in Social Theory and Methodology: Towards an Integration of Micro-and Macro-Sociologies, London: Routledge & Kegan Paul, p. 277–303.

Cilliers, Paul (1998): *Complexity and Postmodernism: Understanding Complex Systems*, London: Routledge.

Dafni, Amots (1984): »Mimicry and Deception in Pollination«. *Annual Review of Ecology and Systematics* 15, p. 259–278.

DeLanda, Manuel (2006): *A New Philosophy of Society: Assemblage Theory and Social Complexity*, London and New York: Continuum.

Deleuze, Gilles/Guattari, Félix (1994): *What is Philosophy?*, London and New York: Verso.

—— (2004): *A Thousand Plateaus*, London and New York: Continuum.

Guattari, Félix (1995): *Chaosmosis: An Ethico-Aesthetic Paradigm*, Sydney: Power Publications.

Latour, Bruno (2004): *Politics of Nature: How to Bring the Sciences into Democracy*, Cambridge, MA and London: Harvard University Press.

—— (2005): *Reassembling the Social: An Introduction to Actor-Network-Theory*, Oxford: Oxford University Press.

Odum, Eugene/Barrett, Gary (2004): *Fundamentals of Ecology*, Pacific Grove, CA: Brooks/Cole.

Orozco, Lourdes (2010): »Never Work With Children and Animals – mistake and the real in performance«. *Performance Research* 15(2), p. 80–85.

Rice, Timothy (2003): »Time, Place, and Metaphor in Musical Experience and Ethnography«. *Ethnomusicology* 47(2), p. 151–179.

Ridout, Nicholas (2006): *Stage Fright, Animals, and Other Theatrical Problems*, Cambridge: Cambridge University Press.

Schechner, Richard (1971): »Audience Participation«. *TDR: The Drama Review* 15(3), p. 72–89.

—— (2002): *Performance Studies: An Introduction*, London and New York: Routledge.

Schneider, Eric/Kay, James (1995): »Order from Disorder: The Thermodynamics of Complexity in Biology«. In: Michael Murphy and Luke O'Neill (eds.), *What is Life – The Next Fifty Years: Reflections on the Future of Biology*, Cambridge: Cambridge University Press, p. 161–172.

Wiener, Norbert (1965): *Cybernetics – or Control and Communication in the Animal and the Machine*, Cambridge, MA: MIT Press.

Queering Colonialism or Queer Imperialism?

Migrating Images and Methodologies of Spatial Transgression

Ernst van der Wal

Contemporary South African visual culture facilitates a complex process of renegotiation through which various issues regarding sexual identity are grappled with. In a post-apartheid context, convolution and ambivalence underscore the local visualization of lesbian, bisexual, gay, transgendered, and/or intersex identities (hence referred to as *lbgti* identities)—for the most part, this is evident in the domain of visual culture where diverse sexual identities are mobilized as reactions to the normative authority of South Africa and even the larger African arena. In studying these visual responses, the local transformation of the sexual topography can be traced in various changes that have occurred in the perception of homosexuality since the fall of apartheid.

Additionally, this investigation reveals South Africa to be caught up in continuing processes of discrimination and marginalization. This is evident in the rise of heteronormative discourses that question the purported authenticity of black South African homosexual identities, and that are largely shaped in response to other African countries where this is an issue of great dispute. In this regard, South African visual culture and media spaces present a platform for the mobilization of multiple *lbgti* identities, yet they also bear testimony to racial and sexual identities that are conspicuous in their radical absence and distortion.

I am interested in *re-membering*[1] those narratives and visualizations of sexuality that have been *dismembered*[2] by normative practices. Such a prac-

---

1   I use the term *re-membering* as an act of critical remembrance or awareness, and
    a socio-political reorganization of identity. My use of *re-membering* implies a re-

tice of *re-membering* can be regarded as an anamnesic equivalent to the queer project as it involves a questioning of memory and visualization devices, a blurring of delineations of sexual membership, and a transgression of the authority of both heteronormative and homonormative categorizations. My *re-membering* of peripheral narratives and visualizations of identity draws upon queer as a *troublant*, a way to *twist* (Sedgwick 1993: xii), and a means of *torturing* lines of demarcation (Hall 2003: 14). A queer methodology is thus concerned with spaces of intersection between (instead of absolute delineations of) the various discourses that shape the reading and expression of sexuality. My own queering of the South African sexual topography entails an investigation of those images, particularly photographs, which are inscribed in and partially erased from this country's visual and spatial palimpsest. Queer is not deployed for providing a resolution to the problematics surrounding the visualization of sexual identity—in fact, it is very sceptical of a dialectic framework with a ›final outcome‹ to the questioning of norms and boundaries. Rather, this essay emphasizes the power of images in troubling (instead of necessarily surmounting) hierarchical categorizations; thus bringing the complexity surrounding South African identity constructions to the fore.

Queer Methodologies, Heteronormative Censure and the South African Sexual Landscape

Various ideological structures have diminished (or increased) their normative stronghold over local discourses of alternative selfhood—that is points of reference that are not necessarily marked as heterosexual, male and/or white. One of the major transformations in the perception of alternative sexual identities was initiated by the South African Constitution that was adopted on 8 May 1996 after the first democratic elections.[3] By providing a

---

    thinking of the practices and discourses that govern a person or member as a social organ (or body) and a constituent within a particular context.

2   The term *dismembering* is employed as a practice that involves the forceful amnesia by which identities are discursively and visually silenced and repeatedly ›forgotten‹ in visual culture and spaces of identity formation.

3   This is the first constitution in the world to prohibit discrimination against people on the basis of their sexuality. The legal position of the South African *lbgti* population changed dramatically after the first democratic election and the adoption of the new Bill of Rights, according to which: »everyone is equal before the law [... and] the state may not unfairly discriminate directly or indirectly against anyone on one or more grounds, including race, gender, sex, pregnancy, marital status, ethnic or social origin, colour, *sexual orientation*, age, disability, religion, con-

space for people who identify as *lbgti* within a discourse of national belonging (Van Zyl 2005: 27), this constitution signifies a major shift in the expression and imagining of sexuality in contemporary South Africa. Yet, for all the legitimacy that the South African Constitution might bestow on *lbgti* identities, complex processes that simultaneously enunciate and disavow homosexuality's African heritage and political currency shape the local embodiment of sexuality. This is manifested in South African visual culture that is still marred by repressive, heteronormative discourses that deny certain identities space for renegotiation and expression. As a challenge to the myopic nature of apartheid visual culture and the sexual identities elided in its formation, histories and visual narratives of homosexuality are important for strengthening the case for the legitimacy of African *lbgti* identities.

The need for such visual narratives of sexuality is accentuated by postcolonial renegotiations of identity within the African arena, many of which have led to critical enquiries into those discursive and material structures that are somehow reminiscent of Western hegemony. By drawing into disrepute those products, cultures and identities that were brought into and enforced upon the local population (Spurlin 2001: 189), colonialism and its discursive or embodied traces are still under critical scrutiny in African countries. One such structure that is often interpreted as a vestige of colonial imposition is homosexuality. To a certain degree, this can be attributed to the notion that Western sexual discourses were imposed on the African population, and that the general autocracy and dissoluteness of Western colonialism is indicative of homosexuality's purported immorality.

As a result, homophobic discourses pervade the African continent as homosexuality is viewed by various influential political figures (such as Yahya Jammeh, Robert Mugabe, Yoweri Museveni, Sam Nujoma, Jacob Zuma, and others) as a colonial identity that was imposed on, and therefore assimilated by, black Africans.[4] The contentious issue of homosexuality being a supposedly foreign imposition has also recently been brought to the fore by Ugandan politician David Bahati, who proposed legislation that would impose the death penalty for some homosexual acts.[5] Bahati and his

---

science, belief, culture, language and birth [my emphasis]« (*Constitution of the Republic of South Africa* 1996).

4   The notion of homosexuality as a perverted, bourgeois Western phenomenon is found, for instance, in Zimbabwean President Robert Mugabe's much publicised condemnation of homosexuality in 1995 during the International Book Fair where he stated that homosexuals were »worse than pigs and dogs« and had no civil rights in Zimbabwe (cited in McNeal 1998). Even though Mugabe received worldwide criticism, his sentiments are echoed by various African leaders who regard homosexuality as an unAfrican identity category that entails the ›perverted‹ activities practiced predominantly by whites.

5   David Bahati, the MP from the ruling *National Resistance Movement* who proposed the bill, argues that homosexuals should be rehabilitated—an opinion that

supporters argue that the anti-homosexuality bill is meant to safeguard Uganda's cultural heritage by prohibiting the »promotion or recognition of homosexuality and ... protect[ing] children and the youth who are vulnerable to deviation« (cited in Mmali 2009). Homosexuality is thus often made the scapegoat for issues ranging from colonial oppression and racial discrimination, to fears of moral degeneracy and national insecurity. The persecution of the *lbgti* population in contemporary Africa is made all the more incongruous by the fact that the judgement of homosexuality as unAfrican is often based on the very standards that were intrinsically imposed through colonial rule.[6] The condemnation of homosexuality in Africa on the basis of its alleged colonial imposition reflects a deeply grounded heteronormative, colonial structure of prejudice and persecution that is still prevalent in contemporary African discourses (see Desai 2001 and Herdt 1997).

Recent studies on African sexualities challenge these strains of homophobia by contesting the notion of Africa as an authentic heterosexual territory. Research on homosexuality in Africa is used to recover historical material that can vouch for a homosexual heritage. For instance, Will Roscoe and Stephen Murray (1998) document same-sex practices in fifty societies found in most regions of the African continent, thereby providing a substantial account of same-sex practices and patterns that are not only found in contemporary societies, but also in traditional practices that predate colonial contact.[7]

Such discursive accounts may offer important material for fighting homophobia. In addition, the domain of visual culture is integral to the transgression of hegemonic, heterosexual regulations as media spaces are increasingly used to reconstruct sexually marginalized identities against the grain of heteronormative discourses. Images of homosexuality play an integral part in mobilizing queer visibility and countering heteronormative censure, and are often employed as vehicles for promoting *lbgti* acceptance. The notion of homosexuality having a liberated, discernable character is central to the system of visualization that is endorsed by certain media spaces. This drive towards visibility was manifested in the recent front-page coverage by a South African newspaper of two males kissing at an annual university event—see figure 6.1. With participants attempting to break the South African record for the most people kissing simultaneously in one

---

is shared by certain Ugandan religious organizations who call for homosexual sinners to repent and be rehabilitated (see Mmali 2009; Mujuzi 2009).

6   Sodomy and other homosexual acts were often considered by colonial rulers to be typical of the ›immoral‹ (African) inhabitants of colonised lands, and homosexuality was regarded by European colonists as characteristically African and »unEuropean« (Bleys 1996: 32). With homosexuality often considered deviant by colonial rulers, the actual persecution of homosexuals in contemporary Africa has its roots in the continent's previous colonial institutions.

7   See also Dunbar Moodie (1988) and Judith Gay (1985).

space, *Soen in die Laan* (or *Kissing in the Avenue*) has been an exclusively heterosexual affair to date. However, in 2010 members from the local *lbgti* population decided to use the opportunity to stage their own kiss-in to promote queer visibility. Ironically, most of the heterosexual kissing-pairs hardly took notice of the queer couples and only after this photograph appeared in a student newspaper did the presence of the homosexual participants come to light.

Figure 6.1: Vanessa Smeets, Soen in die Laan, *2010*

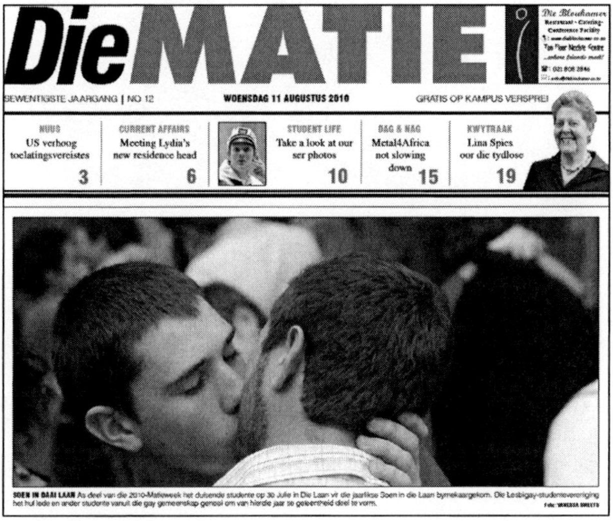

Source: *Die Matie*, 11 August 2010

The image sparked fierce debate—while the local *lbgti* population largely met the image with praise, many South Africans reacted with horror and scorn. Copies of *Die Matie* newspaper where the image was first published were defaced and slashed, with the picture torn out, the couple crossed out with a marker or their identities visually manipulated—see figure 6.2. Subsequently, the image has been circulated by various local and international newspapers, on the internet and even on television.[8] The public's reaction to the image ranged from the two students being hailed as »gay heroes« (*Queerlife* 2010) to the condemnation of the picture as an explicit and immoral ploy to enforce diversity (*Rapport* 2010). These responses reflect the various conflicting discourses that simultaneously disavow and enunciate homosexuality's place in South Africa. It is also a sign of the contemporary renegotiation of apartheid's heteronormative legacy and the hegemonic discourses that fuelled its obsession with moral and racial ›purity‹.

---

8   See Booi (2010), Jones (2010) and Kgatle (2010) for examples of the media's reaction to the photograph.

Figure 6.2: Defaced newspaper, 2010

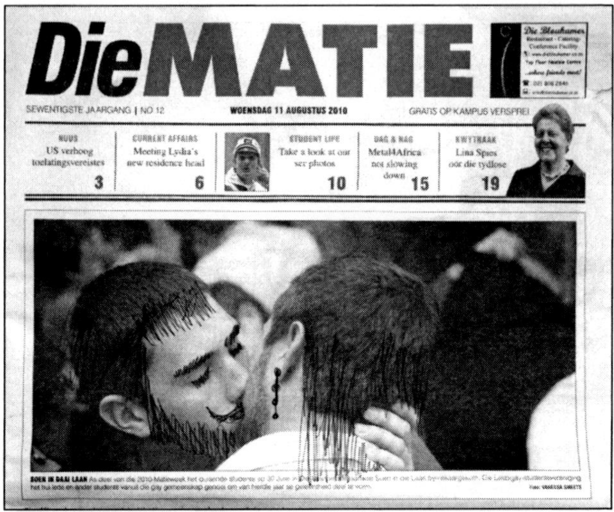

Source: author's archive

The fact that conflicting discourses intersect on the visualization of identity is made evident in the various reactions to this photograph, as well as the narrations of sexuality that are erased from its surface of homosexual intimacy. For this image is significant not only for the identities that it gives exposure to, but also for the identities that are elided in its construction and public circulation. The particular image that was chosen for the newspaper's cover is but one of a series of photographs that were taken at the event and that were considered as possible alternatives. Knowing that a queer image might prove to be contentious, the newspaper's editor settled on what she considered to be the least controversial photograph (Vanessa Smeets, personal interview, Stellenbosch, 11 October 2010)—in this case, it was decided that an image of two white males kissing would be less shocking to a South African audience than an image of an interracial couple, as seen in figure 6.3.

Even though the publication of homosexual imagery in media spaces may appear to be important vehicles for mobilizing *lbgti* identities as tactical points of resistance, they also draw upon pre-existing discursive frameworks for their visual constitution, with the presentation of a supposedly liberated gay identity playing a very important role in the local embodiment of homosexuality. Problematically, the imaging and imagining of homosexuality in visual spaces often perpetuate the notion that a gay and/or queer identity is necessarily white and male. The latter two categories are often conceived as the logical or safer—that is the more acceptable and less controversial—embodiments of homosexuality, with other identity narrations receiving less visual exposure.[9] The validity of the media for mobilizing queer transgression is therefore debatable, particularly as the media's call for gay visibility within the South African arena may actually undermine the complexity that pervade the local representation of sexual identity.

Figure 6.3: Vanessa Smeets, Untitled Image, 2010

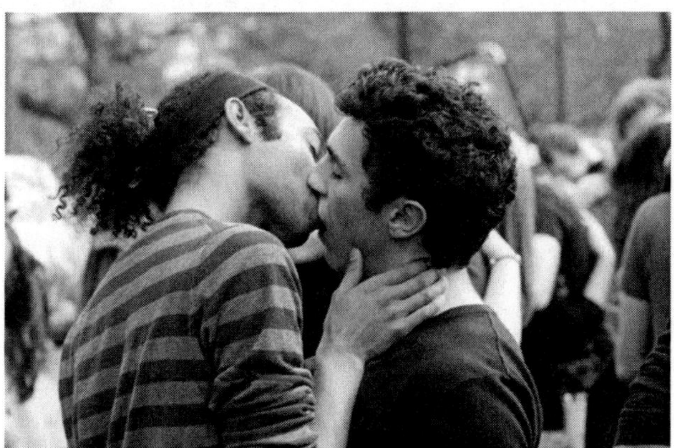

Courtesy of Vanessa Smeets

GAY PRIDE, QUEER TRANSGRESSION, AND IN-BETWEEN SPATIALITIES

Certain Eurocentric universalisms, such as Stonewall-inspired accounts of liberation,[10] have tremendous bearing on South African conceptions of homosexuality. Such accounts are frequently seen as narratives around which images of gay identity can be constructed. With visibility considered essen-

---

9   See Sonnekus (2007), Tucker (2009), Van der Wal (2009) and Visser (2003) for more information on the effect of apartheid's racial legacies on homosexual visibility in contemporary South Africa.

10 One global event that arguably played a definitive role in the construction of South African *lbgti* identities, is the New York Stonewall Riots of 1969—an event which marked the launch of the gay-rights movements in America and is still regarded as playing a key part in gay-rights struggles on an international level (De Waal/Manion 2006: 9). The global symbolism of the Stonewall Riots and »the configurations of Stonewall as a moment of universal gay and lesbian liberation and as a construction of ›liberation‹ itself« are questioned by Martin Manalansan, who regards it as extremely problematic to take for granted the legitimacy of Stonewall as the origin of international gay resistance. In this manner, Eurocentric universalisms are globally circulated as ›authentic‹ narrations of liberation that have significant bearing on gay phenomena around the world (Manalansan 2003: 208–209).

tial for raising gay consciousness, the visual images that encode homosexual identities are carefully selected as »sites of struggle« that can be mobilized for both celebration and protest (De Waal/Manion 2006: 9). The visibility of an autonomous gay community is often read as a visual antidote to homosexual oppression and censure. The notion of ›gay pride‹, which is used in contemporary media to galvanize homosexual acceptance, often underscores essentialism and prejudice as it allows for the visualization of homosexuality in terms of sameness at the cost of sexual multiplicity. Additionally, narrations of a liberated, visible homosexual subject run the danger of stripping local identities of their contingency by forcing them to claim their legitimacy with Western discourses of gay liberation. In this manner, the local imagining of a gay subject as white and male allows for the perpetuation of apartheid delineations of race and gender.

These problematic delineations that dictate the expression of gay subjectivity have drawn critical attention within the domain of visual culture. The questioning of gayness and its racial margins has recently taken the form of an art exhibition—appropriately entitled *Swallow My Pride*—that aimed to address the real life diversity of local queer culture where issues of race, poverty, religion and discrimination still have bearing on the visualization of sexual identity. This exhibition was envisioned as a visceral response to the commodification of gay culture in South Africa, with the title consciously subverting the concept of ›gay pride‹ which was once an urgent call to march and make visible the diversity and difference of local queer identities (*Swallow My Pride* 2010).[11]

One of the most prominent images that haunted the viewer at this exhibition was Lindsay Nel's photograph of Anelisa Mfo, a lesbian mother who was raped at gunpoint to ›cure‹ her of her sexuality—refer to figure 6.4. This horrific experience, coupled with her then five-year-old daughter also being raped, later drove Mfo to try and take her own life by setting herself on fire. With the scars from this incident still visible on her body, this image bears testimony to homophobic violence that is rife in township areas, but largely ignored by the South African government. South African lesbians are subjected to ›corrective rape‹ by men allegedly trying to ›cure‹ them of their sexual orientation—a crime that is for the most part going unrecognized by the state and unpunished by the legal system.[12] A rising tide of

---

11 This exhibition, which was held at *blank projects* in Cape Town in 2010, investigated the experience of commodified gayness, and the manner in which it is predicated upon acceptance from heteronormative capitalist society. This exhibition was presented as a general critique of gay stereotypes that are constructed around the notion of ›gay pride‹—typecast categories of sexual identity that are often imagined as white, Western and male in mainstream visual culture.

12 The subjection of lesbians to ›corrective rape‹ has gained public attention after the brutal rape and murder of Eudy Simelane in 2008 in Kwa Thema, a township

Figure 6.4: Lindsay Nel, Raped as a ›cure‹ to my sexuality, *2009*

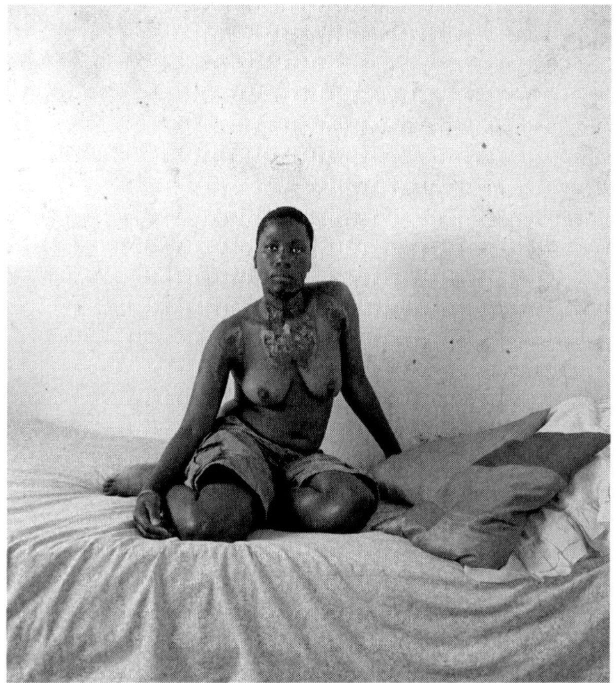

Courtesy of Lindsay Nel & Stellenbosch Academy of Design and Photography

on the outskirts of Johannesburg where she lived openly as a lesbian. Simelane was gang-raped and brutally beaten before being stabbed twenty-five times in the face, chest and legs. This event was covered extensively by the local and global media (see for example Harrison 2009; Kelly 2009; *The Telegraph* 2009), and gave rise to the publication of a report by the international NGO ActionAid that called on the South African legal system not to allow cases of ›corrective rape‹ to go unpunished (*ActionAid* 2009). This report found that 31 lesbians have been reported murdered in homophobic attacks from 1998 till 2009, and of these cases there has been only one conviction. *Triangle Project*, a local gay rights organization based in Cape Town, commented on the gravity of this issue by stating that it deals with up to ten new cases of ›corrective rape‹ every week (cited in Kelly 2009). From this report it became evident that local lesbians are increasingly at risk of rape and murder, particularly in townships where homosexuals are largely prone to persecution. Non-profit organizations, such as Luleki Sizwe in Gugulethu, provide shelter and support for women in townships, such as Analisa Mfo, who have suffered from ›corrective rape‹ (Luleki Sizwe 2010).

violence against the local homosexual population reveals an increasingly hostile political environment and a culture of impunity that allow for these hate crimes to go unpunished. These cases of ›corrective rape‹ are also brutal embodiments of the sentiment that homosexuality is unAfrican—that it should be exterminated with vehemence for its supposed deviance from heterosexual, African norms. However, what transpires when looking at this image of Mfo is not the deviance of homosexuality that is professed by heteronormative discourses, but rather the intolerance and inhumanity that still saturate heterosexual myths of normality.

In contrast to the notion of liberated gayness that is so glibly perpetuated in visual and textual spaces, this image clearly shows the suffering and discrimination that pervade the local experience of homosexuality. In the face of heteronormative oppression, the local *lbgti* population not only has to deal with hate speech and allegations of homosexuality being unAfrican, but with physical violence—an issue that is repeatedly obscured by the imagining of homosexuality as a white, Western identity formation.

CONCLUSION

By assimilating and visualizing previously marginalized identities within a national framework that is still burdened by colonial and apartheid discourses, media spaces—and particularly photographic practices—act as disruptive impetus for the visual mobilization of queer transgression. Yet, since heterosexual patriarchy is the dominant sexuality in most environments and the majority of interactions between people take place within heterosexual discourse (Valentine 1993: 241), gay and/or queer narrations of sexuality inevitably draw on the repertoire of heteronormative languages. In the same manner, a postcolonial queer project runs the danger of perpetuating the various discriminatory practices enforced during colonialism.[13]

Contradiction seems to rule the visualization of homosexuality in contemporary South Africa. From one point of view, media spaces contest notions of the unAfricanness of homosexuality by visualizing black *lbgti* identities to counter those homophobic discourses that still pervade the African arena. However, these spaces also promote homonormative discourses, and some critics are uncomfortable with the discursive limitations and uncritical consumption of ›gay pride‹, as well as its ignorance of the intricacies and problems that pertain to local experiences of sexuality. Occurrences of ›corrective rape‹ reminds one how easy it is to mistake the Western discourses of gay liberation and queer transgression that circulate on a global

---

13 The term ›queer‹ has been prone to critique from postcolonial writers for its perpetuation of whiteness as normative category in mainstream Western culture and its insensitivity towards racial inequalities—see for example Muños (1999) and Hayes (2000).

level for the brutal homophobia that many homosexuals still have to endure. For those homosexual South Africans who live in a township, gayness may not necessarily be a discourse of liberation, but can point to white ignorance and the manner in which only those who have the resources can buy into the notion of a united, free gay citizenship. Meanwhile, a queer project and its suspicion of normative identity politics may reveal the sexual topography to be an undemocratic and discriminatory space, yet its transgression of those homophobic discourses that pervade the African arena may be severely restricted. As long as the notion of ›homosexuality‹ remains settled in the public consciousness as a ›foreign imposition‹—as a bourgeois, Western phenomenon—terms such as ›gay‹ and ›queer‹ may prove to have limited currency for negotiating spaces of sexual tolerance.

BIBLIOGRAPHY

ActionAid (2009): »Hate Crimes: The Rise of ›Corrective‹ Rape in South Africa«. London: Hamlyn House. Available from: http://www.actionaid. org.uk/doc_lib/correctiveraperep_final.pdf [accessed 2 August 2010].

Bleys, Rudi (1996): *The Geography of Perversion: Male-to-male Sexual Behaviour Outside the West and the Ethnographic Imagination 1750–1918*. London: Cassell.

Booi, Malungelo (2010): »›Gay kiss‹ photo furore«. *iAfrica*. 16 August 2010. Available from: http://news.iafrica.com/sa/2593980.htm [accessed 10 October 2010].

Brent Ingram, Gordon/Bouthillette, Anne-Marie (eds.) (1997): *Queers in Space: Communities, Public Places, Sites of Resistance*. Seattle, WA: Bay Press.

Constitution of the Republic of South Africa (1996): Available from: http://www.info.gov.za/documents/constitution/1996/a108-96.pdf [accessed 2 August 2010].

Chimhavi, Dominic (2009) »Uganda Urged to Reject New Anti-Gay Bill«. *City Press*, 1 November 2009, p. 9.

Desai, Gustav (2001): »Out in Africa«. In Hawley, John Charles (ed.), *Post-colonial, Queer: Theoretical Intersection*, New York: University of New York Press, p. 139–157.

De Waal, Shaun/Manion, Anthony (eds.) (2006): *Pride: Protest and Celebration*, Johannesburg: Fanele.

Die Matie (2010): Wednesday, 11 August 2010, 70(12), p. 1–24.

Foucault, Michel (1980): *The History of Sexuality. An Introduction*, New York: Vintage Books.

Gay, Judith (1985): »›Mummies and Babies‹ and Friends and Lovers in Lesotho«. In: Blackwood, Evelyn (ed.), *The Many Faces of Homosexuality: Anthropological Approaches to Homosexual Behaviour*, New York: Harrington Press, p. 97–116.

Hall, Donald (2003): *Queer Theories*, Basingstoke: Palgrave Macmillan.

Harrison, Rebecca (2009): »South African Gangs Use Rape to ›Cure‹ Lesbians«. *Reuters*, 13 March 2009. Available from: http://www.reuters.com/article/idUSTRE52C3MN20090313 [accessed 2 August 2010].

Hayes, Jarrod (2000): *Queer Nations: Marginal Sexualities in the Maghreb*, Chicago, IL: University of Chicago Press.

Herdt, Gilbert (1997): *Same Sex, Different Cultures: Gays and Lesbians Across Cultures*, Oxford: Westview.

Jones, Michelle (2010): »Tongues wagging after Stellenbosch kiss« In: *IOL News*, 17 August. Available from: http://www.iol.co.za/news/south-africa/tongues-wagging-after-stellenbosch-kiss-1.673196 [accessed 10 October 2010].

Johnson, Patrick/Henderson, Mae (eds.) (2005): »Introduction: Queering Black Studies, ›Quaring‹ Queer Studies«. In: *Black Queer Studies: A Critical Anthology*, Durham, NC and London: Duke University Press, p. 1–20.

Kelly, Annie (2009): »Raped and Killed for Being a Lesbian: South Africa Ignores ›Corrective‹ Attacks«. *The Guardian*, 12 March 2009. Available from: http://www.guardian.co.uk/world/2009/mar/12/eudy-simelane-corrective-rape-south-africa [accessed 19 April 2010].

Kgatle, Moipone (2010): »The picture that shook the campus«. *Financial Mail*. Available from: http://fmcampus.co.za/the-picture-that-shook-the-campus/ [accessed 10 October 2010].

Leylah, Ndinda (2009): »Death Penalty for Love«. *City Press*, 20 December 2009, p. 17.

Luleki Sizwe (2010): »Supporting Victims of ›Corrective Rape‹ in South African Townships«. Available from: http://www.lulekisizwe.com [accessed 2 August 2010].

Manalansan, Martin (2003): »In the Shadows of Stonewall: Examining Gay Transnational Politics and the Diasporic Dilemma«. In: Jana Braziel Evans and Anita Mannur (eds.), *Theorizing Diaspora: A Reader*, Oxford: Blackwell Publishing, p. 207–270.

McNeil, Donald (1998): »Harare Journal; Mugabe Attacks, and Gay Zimbabweans Fight Back«. *New York Times*, 14 July 1998. Available from: http://query.nytimes.com/gst/fullpage.html?res=9B0DE3DD1031F937A25754C0A96E958260 [accessed 12 July 2010].

Mmali, Joshua (2009): »Uganda Fear Over Gay Death-Penalty Plans«. *BBC News*. Available from: http://news.bbc.co.uk/2/mobile/africa/8412962.stm [accessed 19 April 2010].

Moodie, Dunbar (1988): »Migrancy and Male Sexuality on the South African Gold Mines«. *The Journal of African Studies* 14(2), January 1988, p. 228–256.

Morton, Donald (1995): »Birth of the Cyberqueer«. *PMLA* 110(3), p. 370.

Mujuzi, Jamil (2009): »The Absolute Prohibition of Same-Sex Marriages in Uganda«. *International Journal of Law, Policy and the Family* 23, p. 277–288.

Muñoz, Jose (1999): *Disidentifications: Queers of Color and the Performance of Politics*, Minneapolis, MN: University of Minnesota Press.

Nicholson, Linda/Seidman, Steven (1995): *Social Postmodernism: Beyond Identity Politics*, Cambridge: Cambridge University Press.

Queerlife (2010): »Stellenbosch Gay Hero Tragedy«. Available from: http://www.queerlife.co.za/test/news/september2010/5701-gay-stellenbosch-hero-tragedy.html [accessed 08 October 2010].

Rapport (2010): »Spoeg Spat op Maties«. Available from: http://www.rapport.co.za/Suid-Afrika/Nuus/Spoeg-spat-op-Maties-20100814 [accessed 8 October 2010].

Roscoe, Will/Murray, Stephen (1998). *Boy-Wives and Female-Husbands: Studies in African Homosexualities*, Basingstoke: Palgrave Macmillan.

Sedgwick, Eve Kosofsky (1993): Tendencies, Durham, NC and London: Duke University Press.

Sonnekus, Theo (2007): »The Queering of Space: Investigating Spatial Manifestations of Homosexuality in De Waterkant, Cape Town«. *De Arte* 75, p. 42–57.

Spurlin, William (2001): »Broadening Postcolonial studies«. In Hawley, John (ed.), *Postcolonial, Queer: Theoretical Intersection*, New York: University of New York Press, p. 185–205.

Swallow My Pride (2010): »Press Release«. Cape Town: Blank Projects, p. 1–2.

The Telegraph (2009): »Lesbian Subjected to ›Corrective Rape‹ in South Africa«. In: *The Telegraph*, 13 March 2009. Available from: http://www.telegraph.co.uk/news/worldnews/africaandindianocean/southafrica/4982520/Lesbians-subjected-to-corrective-rape-in-South-Africa.html [accessed 2 August 2010].

Tucker, Andrew (2009): *Queer Visibilities: Space, Identity and Interaction in Cape Town*, Oxford: Wiley Blackwell.

Valentine, Gill (1993): »Negotiating and Managing Multiple Sexual Identities: Lesbian Time-Space Strategies«. *Transactions of the Institute of British Geographers* 18(2), p. 241.

Van der Wal, Ruurd Willem Ernst (2009): *Flaunting Difference: Carnival and the Queering of City Space in Post-Apartheid Cape Town*, Saarbrücken: Lambert Academic Press.

Van Zyl, Mikki (2005): »Shaping Sexualities—Per(trans)forming queer«. In Mikki Van Zyl/Melissa Steyn (eds.), *Performing Queer*, Pretoria: Kwela Books, p. 19–38.

Visser, Gustav (2003): »Gay Men, Leisure Space and South African Cities: The Case of Cape Town«. *Geoforum* 34, p. 123–137.

The Reciprocal Relationship between Art and Visual Culture in the Balkans

SUZANA MILEVSKA

Recently, several debates addressing various significant visual culture phenomena have been initiated in the realm of the blogosphere and online social networks in Macedonia. It is easy to deride these reactions for their amateurish tone, but on the other hand they can also be seen as filling a void. In Macedonia there is no one single academic programme that could be seen as thoroughly encompassing and theorizing visual culture or as taking an interdisciplinary approach to this field of study and the pictorial turn (Mitchell 1995).[1] The autonomously initiated visual culture blogs, Facebook profiles, posts, comments, mash-ups, user-generated images and other uses of social media and networks evidently represent a leap in the awareness of local communities and individuals regarding the importance of the omnipresence of art and non-art images in the visual field—not only because of their direct influence on everyday perception but also because of their long term influence on the cultural, social, political and economic realms.

Before bloggers started reacting to the uncritical use of imagery in billboard advertising and magazines and the effect of newly built public sculptures and historical monuments as well as changes to other visual landmarks in Skopje, it seems that the Macedonian public more or less took for granted whatever entered its visual horizon on a daily basis. This text addresses the urgent need in this context to ponder the theoretical and practical entanglements and contradictions between art and visual culture today. I want to explore and question the conceptual and visual implications of their reciprocal relations in public space and in the public sphere in general. I would first like to attempt a brief introduction to the historical and political reasons be-

---

1 At universities in Macedonia and other universities in the Balkans Visual Culture is only taught sporadically in the form of a few isolated subjects spread across different academic departments and mostly as an elective.

hind such contradictions within the concrete cultural and geopolitical space of the Balkan region during the period of socialist modernism.

By way of a comparative critical analysis of several more recent examples from the region (and particularly from Skopje) I intend to look at the ways in which art projects and neoliberal cultural policies are isolated from or influence one another. The lack of academic curricula devoted to visual culture in fine arts faculties and other theoretical and research programmes, I would argue, means that the complex reciprocal relations between art and visual culture are being all but ignored, which may in turn be preventing a better understanding of art itself. At the same time I want to look at how this situation underscores the importance of the nexus between the accessibility of public space and political and professional hierarchies and power relations. Approaches to the relationship between art and society, whether complicitous or conflictual, oppositional or even subversive, often rest on the paradoxical notion that art somehow operates outside, above or beyond society.

This essay also explores the role that new social networks and media such as Facebook profiles and groups and other personal and collective blogs and mash-ups have played in expressing individual criticism and, in some cases, more organized articulations of public objections to the reactionary visual culture developed by political power-holders in Macedonia.[2] The idea to write the essay was actually triggered by an event now known as the *First Architectural Insurgence*, which took place on 28 March 2009 in the main city square in Skopje. This event, which can in a very real sense be seen as an *indisciplinary* turn in the sphere of visual culture (Mitchell 1986: 9), began as a protest against the announcement of plans for the construction of a new Orthodox church in the main square of Skopje and later continued as a conduit of opposition to other public art and architectural projects supported by Macedonia's ruling parties.[3]

---

2   For some ironical responses including parodies and mockumentaries of *Skopje 2014* that went as far as to compare the project with fascist megalomania see: http://www.youtube.com/watch?v=2b1dsO8xsi4&feature=related, http://www.youtube.com/watch?v=wLsRnH62M_s&playnext=1&list=PL470DC490E66DDF9A

3   Protests have also targeted the *Skopje 2014* politico-architectural programme that approached the urban planning of Skopje as if it was a *five year plan* from socialist times and that was introduced to citizens only after the construction of some buildings had already begun. A similar programme was developed for public sculptures, mostly realist and often amateurish representations of historic figures. The political opposition estimates that this programme is costing around 200 million euros. See: Macedonia Timeless Capital Skopje 2014, http://www.youtube.com/watch?v=iybmt-iLysU

Skopje: The Heterotopia of Socialist Modernism

Skopje, similar to Foucault's renowned definition of the space of the mirror, is both *utopic* and *heterotopic* (Foucault 1986: 22–27). As an imagined space it was conceived as an ideal of modernist beauty but in reality has turned into a kind of uncanny beast. The centre of Skopje was developed from scratch from 1963 onwards after being largely destroyed by a catastrophic earthquake. This devastation gave rise to the idea of rebuilding the city centre based on an international design competition. The competition, which was held in 1965 and financed by the UN as a result of an unprecedented level of international solidarity, was won by the Japanese modernist architect Kenzo Tange. His design of a master plan for the reconstruction of earthquake-stricken Skopje was, in his own words, inspired by the city's similarity to the fortified villages of medieval Japan.

Tange imagined a dramatic *City Wall*, a continuous housing block reminiscent of a medieval fort that would redefine Skopje's existing city centre. However, the result offered little that could engage with the city's existing structures. While its shape certainly resembled the remains of a medieval city wall, this twentieth century version took what was once conceived as a form of protection from the enemy and a clear division between the *outside* and *inside* of the city and collapsed into an all-embracing and closed structure that actually left outside its own citizens. The *City Gate* tower blocks still define the pedestrian gateway to Skopje's city centre, as if the centre were the only element in the landscape that counted. Tange's project, which was both praised and criticized, was highly influenced by Le Corbusier's ideas of central planning and his autocratic top-down approach. However, the proposed design was never completely realized. Moreover, the elements of it that were built were in fact based on a draft version that left many spaces undefined in aesthetic and functional terms.

Today the empty and undeveloped spaces in the city centre act as a metaphor for the social gaps and conflicts besetting Macedonian society. The architectural difference between the left and right banks of the River Vardar is amplified by the different ethnic and religious backgrounds of their majority inhabitants. Thus, it underlines the elitist monstrosity of the uncritical application of international modernism in an underdeveloped city such as pre-earthquake Skopje. Unfortunately, the aesthetisation of the political that is characteristic of the kind of architectural programmatic manifestos proclaimed by Le Corbusier and Tange tended to render invisible the alienation it inevitably led to.

In Skopje it also resulted in a re-enforcement of the difference between political, social and cultural elites living within the *City Wall* and the socially and ethnically marginalized subjects (poor workers and ethnic minorities) left outside the *City Gate*. It also resulted in an extreme gap between art and society, unless we are talking about the official art of socialist realism.

In contrast to socialist realism, socialist modernist art was conceived as art that is beyond any societal and political interests, art that speaks for itself and only about itself, without entailing any reference to the outer world or offering any narrative of it. It follows that it represented no significant threat to the established *order* (or at least to the ruling order in the Yugoslav version of communism).

Figure 7.1: Unveiling of a sculpture as part of the government project Skopje 2014

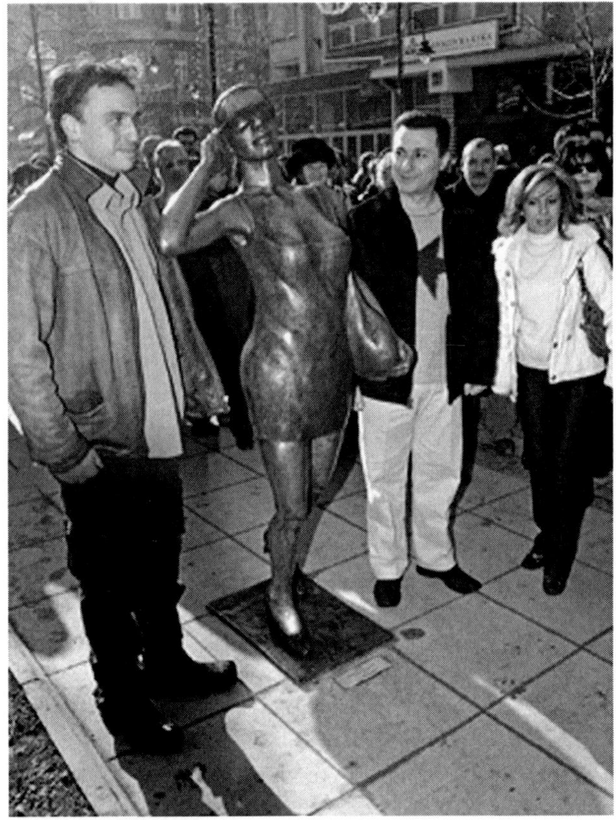

Photo: Sašo Stanojkovik

In order to clarify the phenomenon of this formalist distance or even abjection from political reality among intellectuals and artists, it is necessary to define the *political abject*. According to Julia Kristeva the term *abject* has religious roots and mainly refers to *primal repression* and *transgression:* »Discomfort, unease, dizziness, stemming from an ambiguity that through the violence of a revolt against, demarcates a space out of which signs and objects arise« (Kristeva 1982: 10). More importantly, for Kristeva the effects of abjection lead to the constitution of one's own culture: »The abject is the border, not me, not that...not nothing either. A something that cannot be recognized as thing [...] There, abject and abjection are my safeguards, the primers of my culture« (ibid.: 2).

The political abject in communist countries was certainly the primer of one's own culture – for those feeling discomfort in relation to the political culture the only alternative was not to mix these two elements since the mixture of politics and culture would necessarily have resulted in the political *abject*.

Figure 7.2: A sculpture of the government project
Skopje 2014

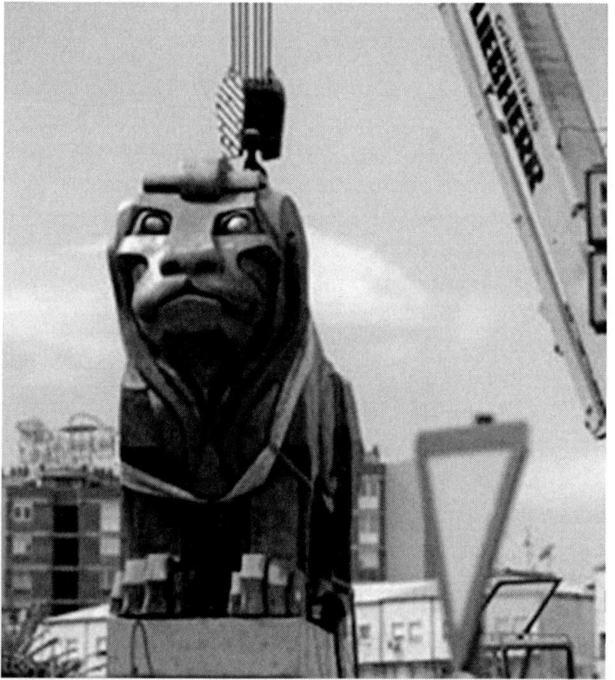

Photo: Sašo Stanojkovik

The local art and institutional critique of culture was never *big* on the analysis of pop culture and media representation, with only a few art critics and theorists even engaging with the omnipresent problems of representation in advertising, print and electronic media, etc. Texts addressing the artistic legacy in Macedonia from a visual culture perspective have been published, but they have not dealt with the uncritical use of the visual field due to the fact that art historians have been primarily concerned with high art and have been completely uninterested in pop culture and other *low culture* phenomena, with only a few exceptions.[4]

One particularly relevant example in this context is the critical response from the blogging community to the building of an Orthodox cross in 2001. To this can be added, after a lag of several years (2006), several debates such as the one around the breach of copyright by the art and culture magazine *Margina* (2003) and, more recently, the debate on abortion (2007) as well as debates on other visual and urban phenomena. Such internet debates show that the visual field is not only affected by taste or pure aesthetics and that it has a wider societal impact, especially when we take into account the number of comments submitted to each of the main posts.

Apart from a short overview of these debates, I would also like to offer an analysis of the possible reasons for bloggers' recurrent concerns about the emerging visual shifts in public spaces and the media. I would also like to sketch out the possible impact of the numerous posts on the emergence of a more critical use of images in the institutional visual culture and the possibility of creating a kind of agonistic visual *public sphere* (Mouffe 2000: 80–112). Chantal Mouffe has written about the impossibility of reaching a rational consensus within the public sphere and argues that this is exactly what deliberative democracy fails to recognize (ibid.: 104). Some bloggers in Macedonia have become so popular of late due to their witty commentary and expressions of dissent that they have started pursuing careers in journalism, politics, literature, art, etc.

VISUAL CULTURE IN PUBLIC SPACE, THE PUBLIC SPHERE AND THE BLOGOSPHERE

The Macedonian government's practice of investing in the construction of huge public sculptures, monuments, religious landmarks, etc. without any public debate has had a significant impact on the blogosphere. A particularly relevant example is the protest conducted via blog against the construction of a 66-metre-high metal cross on Vodno hill in Skopje during the interethnic conflicts of 2001/2002. The cross, which is electrically illuminated and can be seen from as far away as 20 kilometres, provoked many young bloggers into discussing topics such as the power of visual signs and symbols,

---

4   Dr Dona Kolar-Panov was one of the first theorists in Macedonia to employ the arguments of visual culture and critical theory in her analysis of the influence of Hispanic TV soap operas on local audiences, see: Kolar-Panov 1997: 46–59. Such themes have been mentioned only sporadically in daily newspapers columns published by prominent professors (e.g. Venko Andonovski and Elizabeta Šeleva) and only from an isolated expert position.

and the abuse of religious beliefs against a background of political advertising, inter-religious conflicts, etc.[5]

The posts and comments were mainly divided into two conflicting and completely opposing camps: pro and contra the cross. The camp that defended the cross referred to Christian and Biblical sources and mainly leaned towards religious arguments.[6] Comparisons with examples from Hollywood films (a particularly radical example involved a highly superficial comparison with the ›burning cross‹ of the Ku Klux Clan) and political arguments were used to oppose the building of the cross. However, on both sides the arguments ended up sounding very much like critiques addressed to the opposite blogging camp even though the debate started as a critique of cultural policy and political decision-makers. The bloggers often entered into discussions and arguments that ultimately began to sound like the hate speech that had initiated the whole debate in the first place.

A debate very similar to the one around the Vodno cross and involving numerous attacks on the country's religious revival and the power of neo-Christians is currently taking place on the construction of a church on Skopje's main square. The populist move by the ruling conservative party VMRO, presumably to ensure its re-election, inevitably sparked another blogging war among Albanian minority and led to reactionary requests to build a mosque on the very same square. At least now there is a petition that can be signed on Anti Blog that could serve as a more objective instrument for showing the extent of agreement or disagreement among the local population regarding governmental decisions to use public space for building religious or other buildings without ensuring a consensus among the inhabitants and users of this space. Such important debates in the blogosphere confirm that an agonistic democracy can emerge in unexpected media and spaces and is not restricted to discussions within political elites.

---

5   Antiblog, »10 pricini da se otstrafi krstot na Vodno«, 10 December 2006, http://antipunkt.blogspot.com/2006/12/10.html [accessed 11 April 2008]; Vuna »Raspnati pod krstot«, 15 April 2006, http://vuna.blog.com.mk/node/16265 [accessed 10 April 2008]; Iacovibus, »Krstot i Ajfelovata kula«, 10 December 2006, http://iacovibus.blogspot.com/2006/12/blog-post.html [accessed 14 April 2008]; Istorija, »Za krstot na Vodno«, 1 March 2006, http://istoricar.blogspot.com/2006/ 03/blog-post.html [accessed 11 April 2008]; Zombifikacija, »Gjavolska« rabota«, 30 March 2006, http://jasnesumjas.blogspot.com/2006/03/blog-post_1143681627 31773175.html [accessed 11 April 2008].

6   Tribun. »Kontraakcija: Mileniumski krst – Da se dovrsi! Da se zastiti!«, 10 December 2006, http://tribun.blog.com.mk/node/58330 [accessed 12 April 2008].

Pro-Life Debate and Other Issues

One of the hottest issues presented within the blogosphere was the debate sparked around the pro-life billboard campaign in Skopje, which was organized in December 2007.[7] The images of advanced foetuses covered in blood suggesting that abortion is equal to murder were blown up and distributed around the entire city and represented the first such public and aggressive campaign against women's right to choose abortion, which currently remains a legal right for all Macedonian women. The most pertinent comments presented during this debate drew attention to the remarkable fact that the media had not announced who was responsible for putting up the billboards or providing financial and political support for this campaign.[8]

Surprisingly, this new wave of conservatism, which some activists suspected was the work of the Orthodox Church, also caused an unexpected debate between male and female bloggers that was laced with sexist comments. Of course, in general the sex of bloggers is usually unknown and can be faked, but in this case the bloggers did not even try to hide their sex and their hatred of the opposite gender. Although blogs, posts and comments by feminists and women in general are quite common in the Macedonian blogosphere, even quite sophisticated and contemporary debates tend to be peppered with sexist comments.

The complex implications of the *First Architectural Insurgence* and the role of social media in Macedonia in general could be analyzed in terms of Giorgio Agamben's concept of *belonging* and Ernesto Laclau's concept of the *particularity* of belonging (Agamben 1993; Laclau 2000: 139–145). Both Agamben and Laclau express reservations about the particularity of belonging but their arguments are very different. While Agamben regards belonging as complete and unconditional, stating that *whatever singularities* stand for a kind of universal *belonging of a belonging* or *the belonging itself*, in Laclau's view although universality is incommensurable with any particularity, it cannot be completely thought apart from the particular (Laclau 2000: 142).

In my view it is important that we examine the oscillations between universality, collective identities and particularity that characterized the Skopje student protests. I would argue that social media had an extremely sensitive and manifold role in the course of events because they could not be controlled by any one of the groups involved in the conflict and were available to all sides whatever their aims and therefore enhanced the oscillatory nature of identity. What urgently needs to be discussed in this context is the need to fight for legitimate possibilities of negotiation of our own position in society

---

7   Femgerila, »Novi plakati niz Skopje«, 20 December 2007, http://femgerila.blog.
    com.mk/node/124270 [accessed 10 April 2008].

8   Zombifikacija, »Debata za abortusot«, 1 February 2008, http://jasnesumjas.
    blogspot.com/2008/01/blog-post_6545.html [accessed 11 April 2008].

between these two radical oppositions, between the universal *whatever sin-gularities* and the *particularity of belonging* that ultimately result in an end-less process of *oscillation* within visual culture.

The remarks in the report on the fulfilment of the eight benchmarks that accompanied the EC recommendation for Macedonian accession to the EU included harsh criticism of the lack of freedom of speech in the country's media.[9] One of the most frequent critical remarks concerned the accuracy of the information conveyed the monopolisation and politicisation of main-stream media. This is hardly surprising considering the strange attacks on students' rights to protest contained in some of the electronic media reports on the events of 28 March 2009, which mainly came from TV stations close to the government and the ruling party VMRO, which supports the building of the church.[10] A completely different position was taken in media outlets unconnected with the government or linked to the oppositional party SDSM (Social Democratic Union of Macedonia), which acknowledged the absurd-ity of the brutal attack on the unarmed student protesters.[11]

While hardly significant in terms of quantity (barely 150 protesters gath-ered for the first protest) these events certainly refined public discourse and brought a new quality to the social life of Skopje in the sense of an aware-ness of the power of the visibility of counter-communities. Particularly rele-vant here are the Facebook groups Plostad sloboda (Square Freedom), Arhi-brigade (Architectural Brigade) and the student choir Raspeani Skopjani (Singing Skopjeans), which brought together many bloggers who communi-cated with one another in virtual space even before the *insurgence* that saw their communication enter the real public space.[12] It is therefore strange that the EC report made no mention of social media.

What was ignored by the media reports that mostly blamed students for creating violence instead of praising them for having the courage to stand up for their convictions was precisely their expression of the potential of be-coming-together and belonging without claiming to belong to any political

---

9   The report delivered to the Macedonian government on 15 October 2009.

10   Sitel news, »Students manipulate protest«, 28 March 2009, Sitel news, http://www.youtube.com/watch?v=3ArDn9_WUNk and Kanal 5 news, »Group of stu-dents provoked violence directed by SDSM«, 28 September 2009, http://www.youtube.com/watch?v=qEdfZb6iGSE&feature=related

11   A1 News, »Terror over democracy«, 29 March 2009, http://www.a1.com.mk/vesti/video.asp?Video=09/tepanje-28-03.wmv&VestID=106431

12   As of Saturday 11 April 2009 the Facebook group had 385 members, 1,371 con-firmed guests, 1,416 who might attend, 2,749 not confirmed, 1,708 confirmed not attending. See: Facebook group: Plostad sloboda, http://www.facebook.com/event.php?eid=82168370468# The event was recorded and posted on: http://www.facebook.com/event.php?eid=82168370468#/video/video.php?v=1649878 35337&oid=89017711971. For the activities of the group Arhi-brigade see: http://www.facebook.com/#!/group.php?gid=61204922527&v=photos

or national group that impinged on the State or the media that support its opponents. Even more confusing was the fact that this group did not register as a non-governmental association of citizens but only as a Facebook group. There was never any possibility for any negotiations or serious discussions between the government and the students because they communicated only through media. Negotiation is necessary when one party requires the other party's agreement to achieve its aims. Negotiations differ from mere coercion in that negotiating parties have the theoretical possibility to veto or to withdraw from negotiations. But in this case the State recognizes the negotiators' identity.

Figure 7.3: Original antique sculptures from the first and second centuries A.D. in front of the government buildings of the Republic of Macedonia

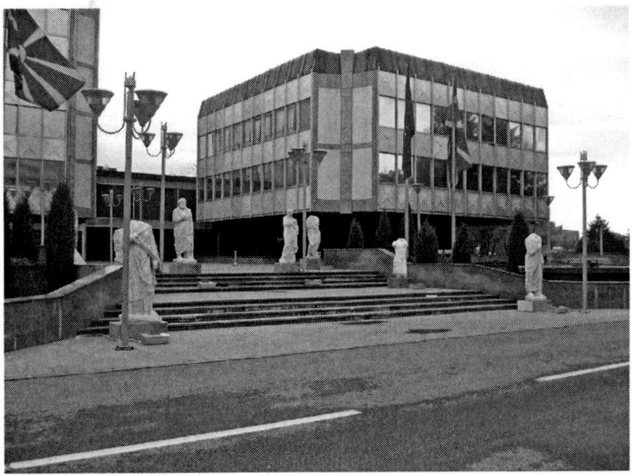

Photo: Sašo Stanojkovik

What the State cannot tolerate in any way, however, is that the singularities form a community without affirming an identity, that humans co-belong without any representable condition of belonging (even in the form of a simple presupposition) (Agamben 1993: 86).

Thus it seems that identity is a crucial anchor of recognition, belonging and the negotiation of one's own identity; belonging to the same, rather than difference, is actually invited and welcomed, or in Agamben's words: »Whatever singularity, which wants to appropriate belonging itself, its own being-in-language, and thus rejects all identity and every condition of belonging, is the principal enemy of the State.« (ibid.: 87). The contemporary globalized condition inevitably pushes towards a hierarchical system of belonging in which belonging to a certain community, region, group or association on the basis of particular properties or attributes becomes the basic requirement on which the negotiation of one's own identity is founded.

However, there is nothing to negotiate in belonging as defined by Agamben: it is complete and unconditional, »being-such«, or more precisely »the belonging itself« (ibid.: 11).[13]

While the concept of human rights developed during the French Revolution was based on implicit assumptions about the homogeneity of the society at that time, today we have no homogenous society in this sense. Such universal notions devoid of particularities have already been questioned by both Laclau and Agamben. Today a multitude of groups with claims against oppressive regimes exist in different relationships to each other, sometimes even opposing each other. Moreover, it is the shared negativity, the collective opposition of emancipatory subjects that unites them against the dominant regime. According to Laclau the naming of emancipatory subjects or groups is not something that precedes the emancipatory struggle (Laclau 2005: x). When various political agents come together to articulate the same demands against an oppressive regime the new political unity—the *people*—emerges as something that is discursively constructed concurrently with this process of emancipatory struggle and its *naming*.

We are currently faced with an urgent need to fight for legitimate possibilities of negotiating our own position in society between these two radical oppositions, between the universal *whatever singularities* and the *particularity of belonging* that ultimately result in an endless process of oscillation. Agamben writes that »the passage from potentiality to act, from common form to singularity, is not an event accomplished once and for all, but an infinite series of modal oscillations« (Agamben 1993: 19). The coming community is therefore founded on the imperceptible oscillations of whatever being that, while attracted to the inwards movement towards the known and familiar, is still curious about the unknown. The deterritorialized subjects seem to long for a position in which a continuous process of negotiating various belongings would give way even to a potentiality *not-to-belong*. Here I refer to the contingency and potentiality of *not-to-belong*, following the Bartlebean formula *I-prefer-not-to*, and thus I am trying to call into question the supremacy of the will to belong over the potentiality *not-to-belong*.[14] In a similar fashion Gianni Vattimo suggests that »[t]o live in this

---

13 It is worth noting here that for Agamben the most distinctive characteristic of the Tiananmen Square events (14 April to 4 June 1989) was the relative absence of determinate contents in the students' demands (except the demand to mourn Hu Yaobang, an official who fought for reforms against corruption that died on 15 April). That is exactly what any state cannot tolerate: that the »singularities form a community without affirming an identity«, that their co-belonging is not determined by any condition of representation be it national, political, gender or another identity (Agamben 1993: 85–87).

14 I use the negative concept *potential not to* here within the framework of the philosophical notion of aporia between potentiality and actuality, one already familiar to ancient and medieval philosophy (see Agamben 1999: 243–271).

pluralistic world means to experience freedom as a continual oscillation between belonging and disorientation« (Vattimo 1992: 10).

FINAL OSCILLATIONS

To conclude, the main problems of negotiating the imposed visual culture within the Macedonian public, media and blogosphere still remains. Social networking and blogging are only available to a very limited user group consisting of members of the young generation, and computer literate and intellectually advanced individuals who do not have the influence wielded by politicians and policy makers. This is not to say that social networks and media cannot become an effective element in the process of democratic decision-making. Some of the blogs involved have already started being published in newspapers and magazines, initially without necessarily gaining the permission of bloggers but more recently by official invitation and even with remuneration.

Nevertheless, bloggers' voices are still not being taken seriously when the government announces open competitions to award commissions for public monuments or major buildings such as churches and museums. If we consider that the deliberative conception of democracy implies that decisions should be collective and should emerge from »arrangements of binding collective choices that establish conditions of free public reasoning among equals who are governed by the decisions« (Cohen, quoted in Mouffe 2000: 87), it is obvious that in Macedonia bloggers' protesting voices are still not being treated as equals in decision-making processes but remain isolated and independent.

However, if instead of deliberative democracy one adopts a perspective such as agonistic pluralism, which »reveals the impossibility of establishing a consensus without exclusion« and »warns us against the illusion that a fully achieved democracy could ever be instantiated,« (Mouffe 2000: 104) then it is obvious that in Macedonia the internet has opened up the first public space of dissent and democratic contestation, a space that is vital to an agonistic pluralistic democracy and a participatory visual culture. All this provides a further argument for the urgent need for an interdisciplinary approach towards the entanglement of visual culture studies, urban studies and other academic disciplines relating to social communications (an approach that could offer methodological support to anyone interested in pursuing an academic career in these fields).

Obviously some of the local debates have already introduced intuitive but relevant arguments in favour of such urgency, perhaps even without the awareness that such arguments coincide with visual culture theories of representation. They point out that public spaces ultimately become unevenly available to different groups or individual citizens and that ever more hierarchies are created. Art in the public space is perceived as problematic and questionable and even though it is a part of visual culture it often functions under different rules.

Interestingly enough—and this is the main conclusion of this essay—besides all other urgent and turbulent political questions such as that of national identity, inter-ethnic conflicts, and the conflict with Greece over the use of name Macedonia, issues relating to visual culture and the use of public space have become relevant points of dissent between different communities. In spite of the lack of theoretically informed criticism, hundreds of posts and comments by non-experts have had concrete impacts due to the large numbers of people involved in areas that would otherwise have been ignored.

I have tried to show here how new social media and social networks have drawn attention to the power of social media and offered new arguments regarding the negotiation identities on a larger scale in the ongoing debate. On the other hand, I have also presented examples of how to a certain extent this role of social media has fuelled negative reactions by the public and even helped the government find *arguments* for prosecuting peaceful protestors.[15] However, I want to argue that although the phenomena of blogging and internet use are also available to politicians and the police, they still offer a means for the public to contest official authority and the potential to question representational and ruling powers. The bloggers in Macedonia took over the available virtual space and became the first committed visual critics to turn the internet into a continuously open and accessible space for visual culture debates. One could easily argue that these virtual public media and social networks offer the means and space for a more critical public voice and could thus become unofficial control mechanisms that monitor what enters our public visual field and how such visual phenomena influence the societal, political and cultural realm.

BIBLIOGRAPHY

Agamben, Giorgio (1993): *The Coming Community,* trans. by Michael Hardt, Minneapolis, MN: University of Minnesota Press.

——— (1999): *Potentialities,* Werner Hamacher and David E. Wellbery (ed. and trans.), introduction by Daniel Heller-Roazen. Stanford, CA: Stanford University Press.

Cohen, Joshua (1988): »Democracy and Liberty«. In: Jon Elster (ed.), *Deliberative Democracy*, Cambridge, MA: Cambridge University Press.

Foucault, Michel (1986): »Of Other Spaces«. *Diacritics* 16, spring 1986, p. 22–27.

---

15 A1 News, http://www.a1.com.mk/vesti/video.asp?Video=09/predrag-16-10.wmv &VestID=115059

Kolar-Panov, Dona (1997): »Ednostavni zadovolstva – Kasandra i politikata na vkus«. *Kulturen zivot*, 4 December 1997, p. 46–59.

Kristeva, Julia (1982): *Powers of Horror – An Essay on Abjection*. New York: Columbia University Press.

Laclau, Ernesto (2000): »Power and Social Communication«. *Ethical Perspectives* 7(2–3), p. 139–145.

——— (2005): *On Populist Reason*, London and New York: Verso.

Mitchell, W.J.T. (1986): *Iconology: Image, Text, and Ideology*, Chicago, IL: University of Chicago Press.

——— (1995): »Interdisciplinarity and Visual Culture«. *Art Bulletin 77*, December 1995, p. 540–41.

Mouffe, Chantal (2000): *The Democratic Paradox,* New York: Verso.

Vattimo, Gianni (1992): *The Transparent Society,* trans. David Webb, Baltimore, MD: Johns Hopkins University Press.

Geographies of Circulation

Motor City Illusions, Driven Over the Sea

Dan S. Wang

On a dewy May morning of 1876, the United States of America's centennial year, General George Armstrong Custer led the Seventh Cavalry out of a garrison in the Dakota Territory for what would be his last time. According to those who were there, as the column marched out of the river valley the sun broke through the mists, creating a mirage that suspended the column between sky and earth: Custer and the Seventh Cavalry appeared to depart »from the Dakota prairie and into the timeless mists of the heavens« (Lehman 2010: 79). This apparent levitation and celestial send-off was driven not only by the interaction of light and moisture, but by the pressures of a settler nation hungry for the hunting lands of the indigenous Lakota, Cheyenne, and Arapaho peoples. In setting out from Fort Abraham Lincoln that morning, the Seventh Cavalry's sole mission was to find and compel, by force if necessary, the remaining bands of nomadic and hostile Indians to accept reservation life.

Custer's march into the mists was carried out in the service of the deeper illusion, that of manifest destiny itself. The processes of disfigurement, including everything from the shameful and deceitful efforts at ›civilizing the savages‹ to Custer's self-aggrandizment and delusional battle tactics, only proceeded as practical inevitabilities. The point of relating this story is to suggest that the contradictions of that time persist as the deeper illusions of *our* time and of the world—now gone utterly and unavoidably global—that *we* have grown up in. Partly told through an explication of method, the basic inquiry of this essay concerns the seeing of a superstructure woven from threads of connection between two places across time and space, from the theater of manifest destiny to the politics of unemployment and foreign reserves.

I work periodically with a group of artists, activists, and writers who when we need a group identity call ourselves Compass. Over years of acquaintance and collaboration we found that we share concerns having to do with placemaking and belonging to place. The mutual realization came out of the fact that we all live in a part of the United States known generically as

Figure 8.1: Eight Immortals in Penglai, 2010

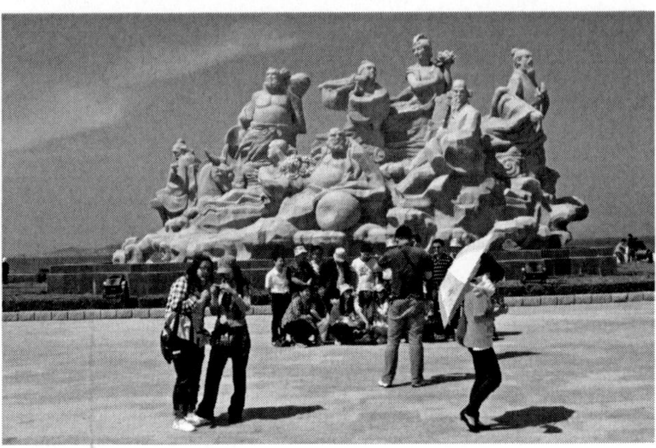

Photo: author

the Midwest, or more particularly the Upper Midwest, or the Great Lakes region, or the Manufacturing Belt, or the Rust Belt, or, most recently, the Water Belt. The multiple inexact ways of naming this multi-state region, in a radius extending about a full day's automobile drive from Chicago, speaks to the different ways of framing the experience of being in, working in, living in, travelling through, and belonging to this part of the world—and maybe any part of the world. Dissatisfied with the conventional language, through extended conversations we began to work out some key terms for understanding this place, for understanding where we are, and how we live in it. I will introduce three of these terms and use them to frame my research.

The first term is *midwest radical culture corridor*. *Midwest*, despite bearing the residual imperialist voicings of manifest destiny as an orientation in relation to the North American continent, is from where we start. We are in the middle of the continental landmass, part of neither coast, nor the mountain west, the boreal forest north, the desert southwest, the hilly mid-south, nor the red-clay and swampy deep south. We live in lands in which a great many migrations intersect, economic trends leave crossed traces, the ends of the political spectrum meet, and extremes get moderated. *Radical*, because of our politics, the histories we find in our region, and the present day creative projects we see around us that open up different possible futures. *Culture*, because it is trump. All of the factors informing human existence, our systems of governance and agriculture, even economics and now climate, are matters of culture. *Corridor* because we experience a particular place always in relation to another particular place, moving between places, travelling passageways between the two, physically, economically, historically, mentally. And because people, ideas, capital, and materials are always moving point to point, with all points along the way presenting questions of relevance.

To sum up the term as four words put together, let me quote from our website:

»Driven by the pressures of corporate competition, Midwestern capital elites envision a network of highspeed trains linking the scattered cities of flyover land into a dense urban grid. Oblivious to territories, histories, and peoples, you would whisk your way from centre to centre like a roulette ball spinning aimlessly through the global casino. What gets lost in the dreams of power are the connections between the city and the country, the earth and the sky, the past and the future.«

The *midwest radical culture corridor*, or mrcc for short, as a place, an idea and a possibility, is a call for longer, slower, deeper connections between the territories where we live. It is a cartography of shared experience, built up by those who nourish lasting ties between critical groups, political projects, radical communities and experiments in alternative existence.[1]

The corridor I highlight here, literally conceived and critically considered, connects post-industrial Detroit with the seaside town of Penglai, China. The great distance between these two places immediately brings to the fore the second term, *ethics of scale*. How we know, or think we know, where we live and work, depends on the scale of space and measurement we are talking about. Ethics enters the picture when we realize that the inequalities and control regimes enforced by power become manifest at and across all levels of human existence: molecular, personal, city, regional, national, and continental. Conceived in this way, we can well imagine the corridors of the Midwest that connect points from within our own bodies, to the fields of corn surrounding our subdivisions and university towns, to the electronic bets coming in to the Chicago Board of Trade from around the world—all vectors at all scales seamlessly intersecting. Then the questions are, what are the particulars of the connections, what historical-cultural conditions do they reveal, and where do they leave us politically, as citizens of the globe?

Penglai City in Shandong province, on the southern shore of the Bohai Sea, a day's ferry ride from the Korean peninsula, is described in cheerful promotional material as a place of old fairytales. The stories are Taoist in origin and have to do with the quasi-historical journey of the Eight Immortals (*ba xian*) in their quest for immortality over the seas, a story long represented as a thematic trope in *guohua* painting, poetry, and literature. As it happens, Penglai is also renowned for its naturally-occuring sea-borne mirages that appear every few years as a vaporous, stunningly reflective image

---

1   Text available on www.midwestradicalculturecorridor.net The texts on the website, including that quoted, are written collaboratively by the principals of Compass. They are Claire Pentecost, Ryan Griffis, Bonnie Fortune, Sarah Kanouse, Heath Schultz, Matthias Regan, Rozalinda Borcila, Brian Holmes, Nicholas Brown, Sarah Lewison, Sarah Ross, Brett Bloom, Amy Partridge, Mike Wolf, and Dan S. Wang.

over the waters. As with Custer on his way to battle, the mirrors of nature tend to create legend out of history. Nowadays this folkloric history is delivered through package tours that bring tourists in for one night between other stops, day after day. As a site of research, at once far-flung but shaped by the politics of the intimate, placing Penglai in the context of Compass's inquiry into the ethics of scale reveals the corridors that connect. At the level of the intimate, I only learned about Penglai because I went to visit relatives in a nearby ancestral village. In other words, for me the discovery of Penglai arrived along the pathways of transnational kinship networks, which, in an

Figure 8.2: Advertisement from The China Sphere, *1927*

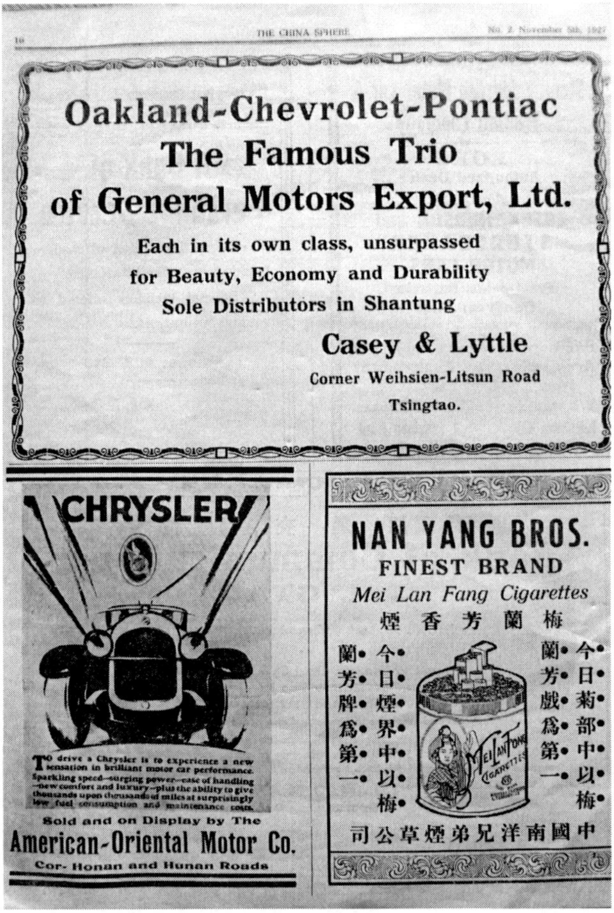

THE CHINA SPHERE   No. 2, November 5th, 1927

**Oakland-Chevrolet-Pontiac
The Famous Trio
of General Motors Export, Ltd.**

Each in its own class, unsurpassed
for Beauty, Economy and Durability
Sole Distributors in Shantung

Casey & Lyttle

Corner Weihsien-Litsun Road
Tsingtao.

CHRYSLER

To drive a Chrysler is to experience a new sensation in brilliant motor car performance. Sparkling speed—surging power—ease of handling —new comfort and luxury—plus the ability to give thousands upon thousands of miles at surprisingly low fuel consumption and maintenance costs.

Sold and on Display by The
American-Oriental Motor Co.
Cor. Honan and Hunan Roads

NAN YANG BROS.
FINEST BRAND
Mei Lan Fang Cigarettes

梅蘭芳香煙

今日菊部中以梅蘭芳戲為第一

今日煙界中以梅蘭芳牌為第一

中國南洋兄弟煙草公司

Source: author's archive

age of universal diaspora, are themselves produced by economic conditions and political events. From the personally political, threads attach to our Midwest, through time and space.

Like people from other modernizing economies before them, people from a segment of Chinese society are learning to consume experiences through tourism as leisure (MacCannell 1976: 34–35). As such, it is one of the most visible of performed behaviours by the emerging consuming class of China. The administrators and business people of Penglai are capitalizing on this new disposable income by inflating the historical associations of their town, to the tune of it undergoing something of a minor economic boom. How the developers of Penglai and the tourists themselves choose to represent a lifestyle that matches their understanding of a modernized people in a modernized nation is the point at which some critical evaluation seems necessary. The at-once familiar and novel observed ways of the tourists visiting Penglai harkens to the mimicry of the ›savages‹ noted by Michael Taussig:

»Pulling you this way and that, mimesis plays this trick of dancing between the very same and the very different ... Creating stability from this instability is no small task, yet all identity formation is engaged in this habitually bracing activity in which the issue is not so much staying the same but maintaining sameness through alterity« (Taussig 1993: 129).

Certainly there is a layered mimesis in the universal aiming of cameras or the purchasing of cheap souveniers, and an alterity in the behaviours transposed from the pre-boom years. But I believe the sameness of grand significance—and the difference—is most clearly visible not at the Penglai Pavilion, the historic seaside fort-turned-pleasure garden that the tourists visit, but rather just outside Penglai.

The Shanghai General Motors Dongyue factory sits along the coast, about 25 kilometres outside of Penglai. According to its own promotional information, the 500,000-square-metre plant is set to produce more than 400,000 vehicles a year. That the creation of the consuming classes is partly enabled by an automobile-based manufacturing economy, in this case by the same corporation, in its Chinese joint venture incarnation, that stamped such a heavy mark on Detroit, exposes the conundrum and the uncanniness of mimesis as no observed personal behaviour could.

The alterity comes in a little further down the same road with the Foxconn facility. Part of a massive empire that assembles iPhones, iPods, iPads, Kindles, Motorola cellphones, components for Dell and Hewlett Packard, Playstations and xBoxes, just to name a few of the best known products coming out of their factories, Foxconn's Yantai plant employs some 80,000 workers. In the spring of 2010, around when I first visited Penglai, Foxconn was in the throes of a full blown crisis, brought about by a rash of suicides by young workers in their main facility in southern China. The discontent and high profile incidents forced the appearance-sensitive company to publicly trumpet an across-the-board 30 per cent increase in wages along with big morale-boosting programmes. This happened at the same time that work stoppages forced carmaker Honda to increase pay in their Chinese factories. So, while there were no mirages reported in Penglai in 2010, the first half of that year seemed to be a key moment in the continuing dissipation of a neoliberal mirage, in this case among the young industrial workforce in China. With a business model that relies on military-like controls over vast numbers of workers on sprawling private campuses, beyond anything experienced in the US now or ever, I see the economy of China as indeed ›maintaining sameness through alterity‹. That is, a sameness of consumer behaviours and habitus maintained through a major difference in scaled economics—in a word, bigger, but not only in geographical distance, but in volume, in the length and complexity of supply chains, and in vastly accelerated production schedules.

There around Penglai, where the timeless Taoist quest for immortality now only exists as a tourist product, the greatest illusion of our time—i.e. the mirage of neoliberalism in the form of large-scale neo-Fordist industrial capitalism—takes solid form as the most winning American export, embraced without reservations. If this recent export has proved to be a little *too* successful for Detroit and the United States, it is not because Americans had not been trying earlier. From at least the 1920s, even while China's domestic situation was a mess of uncertainty, Detroit looked for inroads to new Asian markets. And the way to selling a vision to the Chinese was paved by the many zealous Christian missionaries even decades before that. From that past, another thread that binds: Henry Luce, the American cold warrior media tycoon of the twentieth century, was born and raised into his teenage years in Penglai. It was he who coined the term ›the American Century‹, a concept that in its vision of globally projected American power conveniently continued where manifest destiny left off. Henry Luce carried with him for the whole of his life an understanding of China and America's relationship to it that could only come from the contradictory idealism of missionary life in Shandong province, in which the Americans served and proselytized, but also employed servants for every small want and segregated themselves socially. Not understanding the Chinese Revolution, Luce blamed the Truman Democrats for ›losing China‹ instead of subjecting his fantasies about that country and its people—which at least one scholar has described as a ›fairytale‹—to the realities of China's situation (Hunt 1999: 326).

Luce had no such illusions regarding Detroit. In an extended *Life* magazine feature titled »Detroit Is Dynamite« published in August of 1942, only about a year after Luce's famous ›American Century‹ editorial, the magazine described a city on the verge of a social breakdown, with complicated ethnic divisions, extreme housing shortages, and, above all, workers and bosses at each other's throats. The magazine all but declared industry's inability to properly discipline labour of putting the American war effort at risk:

Figure 8.3: US Social Forum Work Brigade, Detroit, 2010

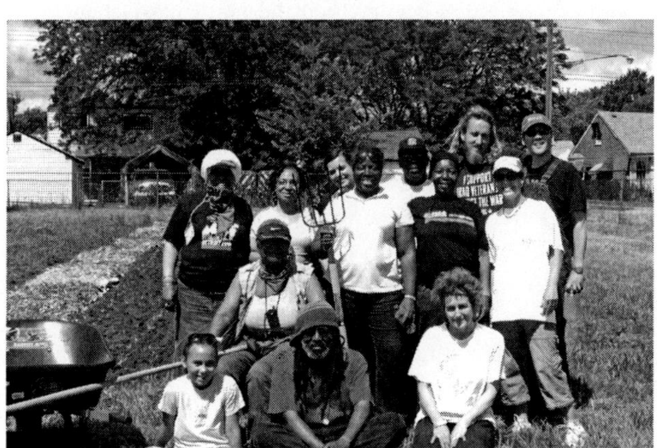

Photo: author

»Wildcat strikes and sitdowns, material shortages and poor planning at the top have cut into Detroit's production of war weapons. Detroit's workers, led by the lusty U.A.W., seem to hate and suspect their bosses more than ever. Detroit's manufacturers, who are the world's best producers, have made a failure of their labour relations [...] it is time for the rest of the country to sit up and take notice. For Detroit can either blow up Hitler or blow up the US« (Uncredited 1942: 15).

If conservatives such as Luce saw Detroit's situation clearly, Detroit's deep roster of leftists, too, saw through the illusions earlier than the rest. To cite only a few examples, even as many on the left today continue to clamour for jobs as the end point of a progressive economics, forty-eight years ago Detroit autoworker Jimmy Boggs was saying, due to the logics of automated efficiency and the increasing redundancy of workers, that »a job ain't the answer« (Boggs 1963: 33–41). Fredy Perlman, a Detroit radical who participated in the May-June strikes of Paris, saw the direct connection between the Situationist critiques and his home environment. Together with others at Detroit's Black & Red press, he produced the first, and for several decades the only, English translation of Debord's *Society of the Spectacle*. True to its radical vision and life as an underground publication, the volume was and remains copyright-free. The Detroit Geographical Expedition and Institute, a collaboration between radical geographer William Bunge and a student from the inner-city named Gwendolyn Warren, mapped factual trends and phenomena like money transfers, rat-bitten babies, and black children hit by automobiles. The DGEI mixed cartography, radical pedagogy, visual media, and activist research in an intense combination thirty-five years before the critical art trends of the 2000s.[2]

---

2   For an excellent introduction to the work of William Bunge and the DGEI, see http://indiemaps.com/blog/2010/03/wild-bill-bunge/

Given this history of visionary radicalism come to life in America's grittiest city (which goes much deeper than the elements just mentioned), Detroit has been an obvious destination for our explorations along all the possible midwest radical culture corridors. All the more so considering the conditions in the present day. Though Chicago gets tagged as the pulsating global city of the Great Lakes, in the *mrcc* Detroit is more appropriate as the regional capital. Scores of cities around the Rust Belt look, feel, and have followed similar patterns of development, as smaller versions of Detroit. What one finds in Detroit these days is not merely the romance of ruins, but what I like to call ›What comes after the working classes flex their muscle.‹ That is to say, when capital is driven out of town, when an illusion is driven over the sea, we are left with what we have in Detroit: apart from the urban decay and despair, bright efforts at self-sufficiency, an emerging urban land ethic, and models of autonomous self-administration—made all the more real for it happening in the shadows of capital's abandoned investments, landscapes of both architectural and social devastation. Over 900 farming and gardening projects in the city, international inflows of artists and musicians, and in the summer of 2010, the second US Social Forum—that is today's Detroit, in which the abiding view of residents of all proposed top-down economic initiatives is disbelief and suspicion, that is to say, realism. Our Detroit friend of Compass and comrade Grace Lee Boggs, ninety-five years old, a principal of the Johnson-Forest tendency, child of Chinese immigrants who escaped the brutal upheavals of late Qing China, Asian American activist heroine, ally of African-American struggle, and six-decade resident of Detroit, brings the vision up to date when she speaks of projects in that city as the making of the ›Chiapas of North America‹. No illusions, just a prescription of dirt, love, hard work, and each other.

The radical economist Li Minqi argues that China and India, from the perspective of a world-systems analysis, are the strategic reserves in the global system of endless accumulation. Due to the shrinking ecological space for wastes and other finite resources, that a system founded on endless accumulation can continue with the rise of China and India is highly questionable, if not impossible (Li 2008: 131–133). In this end of days scenario, in which the new bourgeoisie of China will inevitably play a major role, what comes next can only be that pairing exotically misattributed to classical Chinese wisdom: crisis = danger + opportunity.[3] If this systemic bifurcation opens up a contemporary search for immortality, the most promising may be in the work happening in and around the Midwest, based on the lessons of the native prairie ecology. The scientists at the Land Institute in eastern Kansas are working to breed drought resistant, petro-chemical independent perennial grains. All around the region there are prairie restoration projects that conserve soils and provide habitat for threatened bird and in-

---

3   Victor H. Mair debunks this widespread misreading of symbolism in Chinese
    writing. http://pinyin.info/chinese/crisis.html

sect species. Whether these efforts prove to be as phantasmagoric as the Taoist search for the Peaches of Immortality may depend on whether and when native ecosystems get outstripped by climate change, humanity's ultimate test in the struggle of illusion versus reality.

Figure 8.4: Corridors to Clarity, 2010

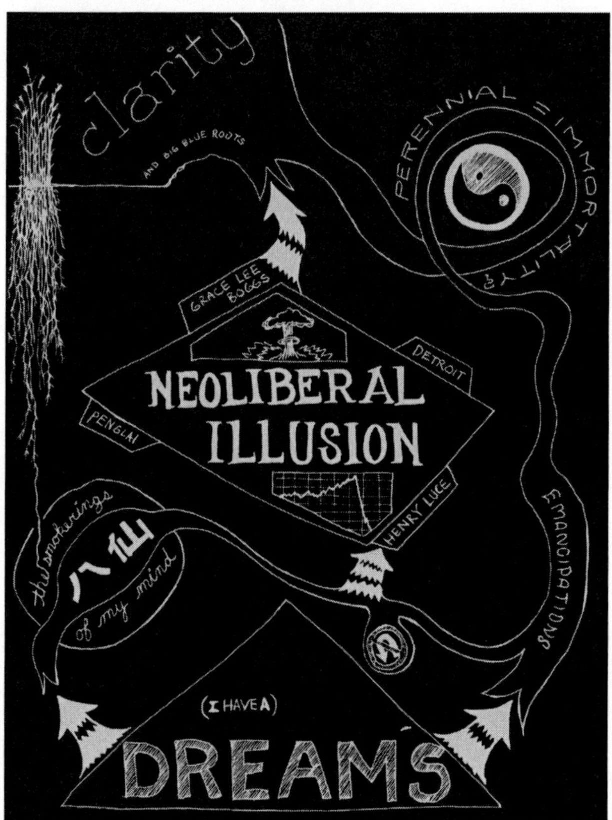

Drawing: author

Here, I finish by introducing the third and latest term from our working lexicon: *petroleum space-time continuum.* From our region's airports and highways to the fields of corn between them and the seams of coal below those, the Midwest of my life up until now has been lived in the petroleum space-time continuum. My speed of mobility is enabled, the light of my days gets extended, my media is prepared and delivered, and my food is raised and transported—almost all of these things—by an economy of fossil fuels. My experience of time and space, one that brings into connection in more ways than ever points once far apart, such as Detroit and Penglai, or, for that matter, my brain cells and yours, is the time and space of the petroleum space-time continuum. Where this continuum ends, is not necessarily where history ends, but just maybe where the perennial grains and the immortality begin.

BIBLIOGRAPHY

Boggs, James (1963): *An American Revolution*, New York: Monthly Review Press.

Hunt, Michael H. (1999): »East Asia in Henry Luce's ›American Century‹«. *Diplomatic History* 23(2), p. 326.

Lehman, Tim (2010): *Bloodshed at Little Bighorn*, Baltimore, MD: Johns Hopkins University Press.

Li, Minqi (2008): *The Rise of China and the Demise of the Capitalist World Economy*, New York: Monthly Review Press.

MacCannell, Dean (1976): *The Tourist*, Berkeley, CA: University of California Press.

Taussig, Michael (1993): *Mimesis and Alterity*, London and New York: Routledge.

Uncredited (1942): »Detroit Is Dynamite«. *Life* 13(7), p. 15–23.

Making Do

PETER MÖRTENBÖCK AND HELGE MOOSHAMMER

URBAN DIALOGUES

The Venice Architecture Biennale, with its plethora of national pavilions dotted around the Giardini and the city of Venice, is often claimed to function as a global showcase that brings together advances in the design of the built environment and critical debate. This claim can be substantiated with reference to numerous examples from past biennales, from the first exhibitions curated by Vittorio Gregotti in the 1970s to the more recent engagements with what Aaron Betsky in 2008 termed ›building-free architecture‹ as a way of dealing with important societal issues. The very setting of the Venice Architecture Biennale, with its changing themes, individual curatorial interpretations and delightful scattering of shows in lush gardens and a city steeped in history, seems to evoke a sort of walk-in dialogue between the city of Venice, the directors, the curators and the global audience. But what kind of dialogue can be achieved by staging or provoking responses to a finished object?

Or are there other ways to engage in dialogical situations in the urban realm, to extend—in Deleuzian terms—the co-existence of polyphonic, multi-vocal compounds (Deleuze/Guattari 1991: 178)? In Mikhail Bakhtin's concept of *dialogism* words constitute subjectivity by generating a social space that is fundamentally interpersonal and thus facilitates a constant appropriation and transformation of the voice of the other (Bakhtin 1984). What emerges in such dialogues is not merely a reproduction of self-contained worlds but a complex map of intensities whose distribution, rather than according with a predetermined logic, develops out of reciprocal points of contact: singular encounters, movements, gestures and spontaneously co-ordinated actions. None of the links appearing between the encounters is required to be part of an overarching plan, part of the grammar of a common project. Dialogues evolve in the acts of speaking and hearing, in processes of interruption and sedimentation and not in the planning of a common outcome.

Figure 9.1: Re:Orient – Migrating Architectures,
Hungarian Pavilion, 10th International Architecture
Biennale Venice, 2006

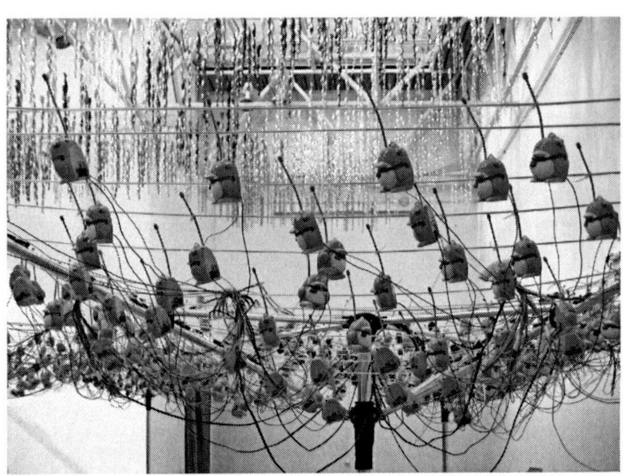

Photo: authors

Approaching the Hungarian pavilion at the Venice Architecture Biennale in 2006, visitors were treated to a cacophony of sounds—a twittering and hissing, chirping and clucking, all seeping out from what looked like a brightly coloured ›Garden of Eden‹ tucked away in the courtyard of the pavilion. As one drew closer, however, it became apparent that these sounds were not being produced by birds or other happy creatures and that the garden was not composed of trees and plants but of strange, artificial structures that looked like a landscape of rotary clotheslines that were loaded and interconnected with thousands of little Chinese toys the mechanics of which were producing this ragtag soundscape. The installation by Usman Haque and Adam Szaboles Somlai-Fischer took its inspiration from the spread of Chinese markets into the everyday life of even the smallest villages in Hungary. What, the work seemed to ask, would happen if the Chinese mass production of disposable commodities did not just flood these spaces with cheap toys and textiles but also provided an excess of cheap, basic building material that could be shipped around the globe from China? What would become of the European cityscape and its aura of longevity and cultural rootedness if it were transformed into a commodity of global capitalism? What impact would this have not only on the physiognomy of the built environment but also on cultural identifications geared towards a concurrence of the notion of place and vernacular ways of making oneself at home.

These items do not just flood the European market by themselves. They are transported, handled and distributed by an army of nomadic Far Eastern workers. A particular accumulation of this presence and a reference point for Haque and Somlai-Fischer's project is the Four Tigers Market in Budapest's Jósefváros district, a mile-long stretch of containers stacked on the sidings of a disused freight terminal. The Four Tigers Market is a major node of the Far Eastern migrant economy. It is *the* place in Budapest to buy smuggled cigarettes and bootleg versions of brand-name goods; imitation Adidas tracksuits, fake fragrances, fashionable sunglasses, car accessories and counterfeit CDs can all be purchased quickly here. Built around simple forms of economic exchange with an anonymous externality, the market offers visible traces of the immigrants' presence in Budapest as does the associated network of transient commercial establishments that fill the abandoned spaces of the city. But although the makeshift structures of the market—metal containers, tent-like constructions, cardboard stalls and other improvised sales areas—are the most obvious manifestations of the urban activities of Far Eastern immigrants in Budapest, they appear to have escaped the regulatory mechanisms of the state (Nemes 2006). The market has its own regulatory forces that thrive on a climate of murky deals, shadowy figures, dubious contacts, liabilities, debts and unregulated control. It is part of a globally dispersed network of informal marketplaces, whose European nodes manage to create transient eruptions in the ideational matrix of how the economy is supposed to link up with an idealized vision of civic society. From Jósefváros' Four Tigers Market and the ›Seventh Kilometre‹ container market near Odessa to the infamous Arizona Market near Brčko in Bosnia and Herzegovina, these major European hubs contain streams of human activity centred around ›spontaneous‹ economies, informal trade and dreams of a better life.

Figure 9.2: Four Tigers Market, Budapest, 2008

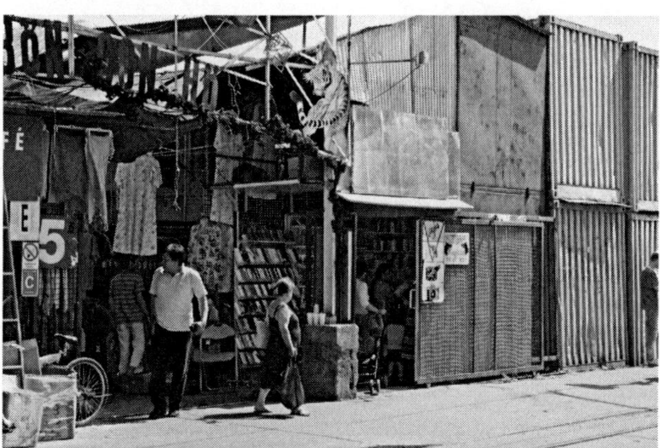

Photo: authors

The mobilization of Far Eastern cultures and the opportunities they find in European cities do not just combine to constitute the local presence of migrant subjectivities within a uniform global labour regime. Interacting with flexible technologies of governance and citizenship that push migrant workers into illegality while benefiting from the availability of cheap labour, they produce conditions that change the rationalities of urban space and provide the grounds for an unexpected and unsolicited place-making in its most elementary form. Driven by new imperatives of social mobility and the expansion of transnational spaces brought about by the unequal movements of tourism, migration and flight, marketplaces have come into being that have created novel and extreme physical configurations from local opportunities. These spatial structures are intermediate zones that are being seized by diverse interest groups, irrespective of whether they are local or global, formal or informal, or have access to a great deal or very little capital. Their unstable positioning is allied to the ambivalent logics of mobility and circulation and to a range of unsolicited processes within the streams of global geopolitics.

Place-making practices are thus deeply intertwined with the organization of the world economy. In his book *Networking the World*, Armand Mattelart locates the struggle over territorial resources within a restructured organization of economic space in which the orientation of the world economy towards network organization is characterized by two distinct processes: the relocation of economic activities towards regions with low labour costs combined with liberal environmental regulations, and a highly flexible agglomeration of capital investments in ›innovative‹ world regions. The dynamics of this development are threatening to create a two-speed social geography made up of a network of megalopoli and deteriorating areas in between global nodal points (Mattelard 2000: 98–99).

Commons Markets

»What is common to the greatest number has the least care bestowed upon it. Everyone thinks chiefly of its own, hardly at all of the common interest.«[1] In the introduction to her seminal 1990 book *Governing the Commons* Elinor Ostrom quotes Aristotle to underline how the so-called ›tragedy of the commons‹ has come to dominate Western thinking about the individual use of common-pool resources. For centuries the all-pervasive conclusion has been that »where a number of users have access to a common-pool resource, the total of resource units withdrawn from the resource will«—inevitably it appears—»be greater than the optimal economic level of withdrawal« (Ostrom 1990: 3). As Ostrom points out, the two most commonly recommended solutions to this problem are based on an intervention by an external agent that either puts the management of a common-pool resource into the hands of private enterprise or a centrally organized state authority. The latter solution is based on the reasoning that if »private interests cannot be expected to

---

1   Aristotle, *Politics*, Book II, ch. 3; quoted in Elinor Ostrom, *Governing the Commons* (Ostrom 1990: 2).

protect the public domain then external regulation by public agencies, governments, or international authorities is needed«[2].

This view has become particularly prevalent and all-encompassing when it comes to the utilization of space as a key resource of ›society‹ itself—to issues of how to co-exist in space and how to interact spatially as a society. The presence of a monitoring and controlling authority, it is widely perceived, is crucial to ensure a, if not fair then at least safe, way of co-existing. The aim of planning with regard to common resources such as air or light is thus predominantly directed toward maintaining order vis-à-vis an otherwise chaotic and anarchic urban conduct. Hence, every spatial activity that falls outside the reach of the planning authority and evades its planning regulations, such as informal spatial arrangements, is considered to be a failure of planning, of its institutional mandate to ensure a safeguarded usage of space. In most cases these activities are regarded as signs of unsustainable and unsocial exploitation, both of the people existing in that space and the resource of space itself.

However, as Ostrom has also pointed out, one of the main difficulties for any centrally controlled agency of resource management lies in the sheer impossibility of always having all relevant information at hand to substantiate its regulations and decisions in a way that is appropriate to the actual demands and situations on the ground. Particularly in a globalized world, where it is not only the case that local situations are becoming ever more implicated in global developments but where macro-constellations themselves are subject to rapid change, the sufficient development and successful application of up-to-date and appropriately adapted regulations seems to be becoming an insurmountable challenge.

In the light of this problematic, the last decades have increasingly seen hope placed in models of self-organization, and there is growing interest in both scholarly and artistic circles in investigating and exploring what settings might foster the capabilities of individuals to organize collective action for the general good. One notable work in this regard is Minze Tummescheit's documentary on *Jarmark Europa* (Europe Fair), a sprawling site for unregulated small trade that operated for some twenty years in and around Dziesięciolecia Stadium in Warsaw. Initially used as a major sports complex for mass events, the grounds of the stadium were transformed into a market filled with thousands of makeshift stalls that effectively connected the Polish capital with cities in the former Soviet Union, China and Vietnam (Bendyk 2006: 332–335). Tummescheit's film portrays the lives of several suitcase traders or *chelnoki* (meaning ›shuttles‹), as the traders from the former Soviet Union in this bazaar-like marketplace were known, and highlights the self-organized structures that made this market economy a social space for its participants. It features, amongst other things, a bazaar library

---

2   D.W. Ehrenfield 1972, *Conserving Life on Earth*, 322; quoted in Elinor Ostrom, *Governing the Commons* (Ostrom 1990: 9).

run by one of the women traders that served the thousands of Russian-speaking *chelnoki* and created a focal point for cultural exchange. Another example of such investigations can be found in Ursula Biemann's ›video geographies‹: works that lay bare highly complex topological relations by exploring the tactics and disguises used by smugglers in the Spanish-Moroccan border region, by documenting the geo-strategic rivalries and representational politics around the trans-Caucasian oil pipelines, and by tracing the nomadic economies of sub-Saharan migration.[3]

These studies investigate geophysical conflicts not from a top-down view but from the perspective of creating social environments, foregrounding the spontaneity of social interaction and the ways in which it fashions a complex network of detours, back doors, ›underground relays‹, hiding places, tunnels and tricks that make up everyday life on the fringes. What emerges through such examinations is a horizontal and relational aspect of global economic, political and cultural processes, one that complicates the clear distinction between formality and informality, legality and illegality, inside and outside when it comes to dealing with material and symbolic goods. It also becomes clear that what are currently often referred to as ›peripheries‹ in fact constitute a highly mobile situation that permeates the disintegration of the old binary system of centre and periphery. Territorial distributions emerging from such mobilizations are both conditioned by a transformation of political economies through the opitimizing technologies of neoliberalism as well as by an intuitive eco-logical praxis (Cooley 2008: 269)—diverse and contingent human activities, empirical attunements to local cultural sensibilities, trespassings and bottom-up explorations of possibilities and resolutions, all grounded in the ecologies of everyday life.

While most conceptualizations of an alternative response to the ›tragedy of the commons‹ promote the capacity for self-organization as one of the key ingredients to its success, almost all of them also point to the necessity of certain impulses or creative constellations in order for forms of such biopolitical reasoning to become effective. The architect and artist Azra Akšamija has proposed such a creative incentive for the Arizona Market in Bosnia, one of the largest of the informal marketplaces that have recently sprung up in south-eastern Europe, in order to intensify some of the creative potential of what she sees as urbanization from below. Stating that »a formal system cannot function without its informal counterpart, and vice-versa«, she advocates »urban planning [...] as a rhizomatic interweaving of actions and programmes that come from both, the formal and the informal systems.«[4] Redefining the role of the architect as a sensor, a provocateur, and a guide through urban processes which do not result in a final order but are

---

3   See Ursula Biemann 2008, *Mission Reports. Artistic Practice in the Field: Video Works 1998–2008.*

4   Azra Akšamija, »Arizona Road«, http://www.mit.edu/~azra/Arizona.htm [accessed 1 March 2011].

left open-ended, she conceives of architectural intervention as accompanying and inspiring the ever-evolving process of sustainable urban development.

Questioning the efficiency of the master plan developed by the government that is threatening the further existence of the market people, she proposes so-called *Provocateur Poles*, infrastructural elements providing access to electricity, water, sewage systems, television and advertising. Here, the work/practice of the architect is understood as a method of informal provocation. It uses existing conditions to create new ones, which the next generation of users can continue, abandon or modify—a dialogical cycle that continuously reshapes urban conditions and communication processes.[5] In advocating self-organization that uses existing conditions to create new ones, her method of informal provocation suggests an alternative to the ›normalization‹ of the market through privatization induced by an interaction of political, economic and military claims.

The strip of land occupied by the Arizona Market is a part of the war zone that was fiercely fought over by Serbian, Croatian and Bosnian Muslim units because of its strategic position after Bosnia-Herzegovina had left the federal state of Yugoslavia in 1991. In the Dayton Peace Accords of November 1995, the disputed territory around the town of Brčko was placed under the direct supervision of a special supervisor from the Office of the High Representative (OHR) of the international community of states in Bosnia and Herzegovina. After the checkpoint set up at the interface between the three ethnic groupings had evolved into an informal meeting place where cigarettes and cattle were traded and coffee was served at the roadside, the local commander allegedly decided to encourage initial encounters between members of the different ethnic communities by proclaiming a ›free-trade zone‹, which was designed to consolidate peace.

In the years that followed, the convergence of economic activities at the site and the self-organization of this grey trade area were hailed as a model for promoting the sustained development of communications and community structures between former wartime enemies. Supplementing the simple market facilities and mobile sales outlets, the first buildings were soon constructed, presaging the emergence of a self-organized urbanisation process on the site. However, hopes that the Arizona Market might become a model for self-organized place-making were dashed when a kind of market arose whose existence and development were far more extensively tied to the presence of the international peace-keeping force than initially expected. Ever more bars and motels operating in the various huts and buildings started to accommodate a form of trade that made it increasingly difficult to sell the success story of peace based on establishing a free market economy. For at the Arizona Market, the real money was made through prostitution

---

5   Ibid.

and trafficking in human beings: women and girls being brought in from Eastern Europe.[6]

The most striking aspect of the ensuing attempts to regain control over the Arizona Market—which ultimately culminated in the ceremonial opening of a new shopping centre in 2004—was the way the international community, which exercised politico-territorial control, and an international investor co-operated in privatizing public space. In February 2001, the International Supervisor of Brčko District ordered the closure of the existing market. In December that year, ItalProject, an Italian-Bosnian-Serbian consortium, won a tender to establish and operate a new market. The consortium signed a twenty-year leasing agreement with the district administration that granted it the right to retain 100 per cent of the rental income for a period of seventeen years in return for developing the infrastructure. The project envisaged the development of a complexly structured trade base for the entire south European area that would include multiplex cinemas, hotels, casinos and a conference centre. Resistance by landowners and traders to this total takeover was met with compulsory dispossessions. This response was justified with the argument that it was in the public interest to ensure that the district administration of Brčko complied with the agreements concluded with Italproject. Demonstrations and road blockades staged to oppose the demolition of the old site were cleared by the police. As most of the landowners affected were Croatians who sought the support of nationalist groups to assert their cause, the maxim of achieving reconciliation by taking economic measures came dangerously close to fomenting an ethnic conflict as a result of what was seen as an arbitrary allocation of economic options.

In only ten years, the Arizona Market has been transformed from a space of bare survival into a centre of ubiquitous consumption. What was once a mere border guard post has now become a post-metropolitan territory. The convoluted flows of international money and goods at the Arizona Market may have now entered a new phase, yet the form of capitalism that prevails there is no less ›rampant‹ than it used to be. Its aggressiveness resides in an all-pervading motivation to gain some form of control—ranging from the need to survive at one end of the scale to international relations at the other—by seizing anything that is not yet subject to controls. All these different levels of exchange have created the countless trading situations that one finds at the Arizona Market, which promise everyone an opportunity to exploit the market to their own ends. What appears to be a random remaking of territorial, economic and cultural claims eventually comes to constitute a continuous displacement of boundaries that results from local interpretations, arrangements and deals. There is no specific logic shared by all participants but only a contingent operating mechanism—an economic fabric

---

6   The UNHCHR attributes the crisis to, among other things, the presence of over 30,000 peacekeepers in BiH. Bosnia was not so much a transit country as a destination for women victims of trafficking. See Rees 1999.

geared to situational opportunities, instead of being subject to established protocols of trade.

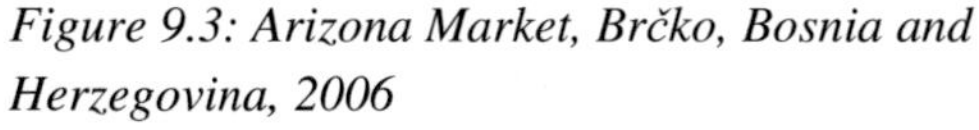

Figure 9.3: Arizona Market, Brčko, Bosnia and Herzegovina, 2006

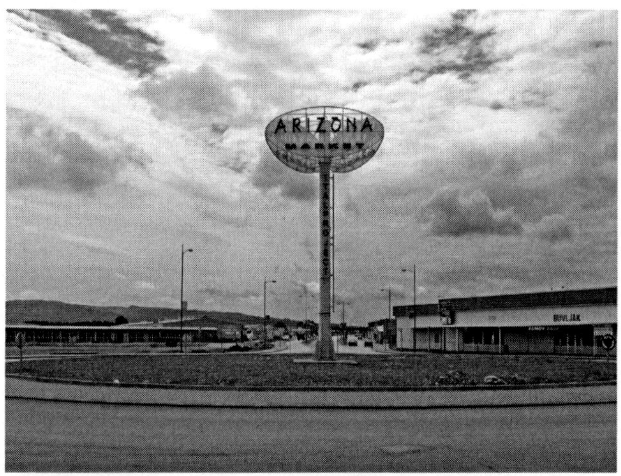

Photo: authors

EXTENDED CITIES

This brief history of the transformations that the Arizona Market has undergone during its short existence of ten to fifteen years may not necessarily be particularly supportive of an alternative model of self-organization and self-regulation, but it highlights the problematic aspects of the two dominant models of common resource management, one being privatization and the other being control by a centrally organized agent. It clearly indicates how, in most cases, both trajectories are intrinsically intertwined and that a state body—a supposedly independent agent—might itself be pursuing some rather ›private‹ interests such as cashing in on tax revenue, developing its own enterprises or endeavouring to accumulate the resource of control. Furthermore, it reflects the dual challenge we face when thinking and creating something we might understand as representing a global public sphere: firstly, the dispersion and fragmentation of the public realm in what Stephen Collier and Andrew Lakoff have defined as ›regimes of living‹ (Collier/ Lakoff 2005), i.e. the production of unstable subject formations through ongoing segregations, both spatially and culturally, and, secondly, the formation of globally interacting networks whose sense of a ›public sphere‹ is not invested with the old logic of publicness.

Yet our point here is not just simply to illustrate the failures of informal systems or official planning protocols, but also to use the unfolding drama of their applications as a basis for speculating about the spaces of informal markets as a kind of breeding ground for contemporary biopolitical reason, where collective actions can succeed in community-making that transgresses the boundaries set by either of the two concepts, be it the nation state and its sanctioning principle of citizenship or the privileging of private ownership and materialized entitlements. Rather than seeing informal markets as a victim of the failures of centralized governance we can understand the developments at the Arizona Market and many sprawling agglomerations of this kind as indicative of a new kind of urban system that has arisen from the multi-directional movements of transnational urban deregulations and re-alignments—the ›extended city‹ as a cluster of networked sites produced by political upheaval, migratory movements, regulatory bodies, laws, technologies, and other translocal forces that are acted out locally. This new urban form points toward a shift from a ›citizenship of borders and confines‹ (Balibar 2004: 6) to diverse forms of ›latitudinal citizenship‹ (Ong 2006: 123–125) associated with the exertion of lateral influence across social and political domains. It signals a complex entanglement of neoliberal technologies of government with forms of self-organization. In this environment, informal markets behave as performative frames that build increasingly complex webs of relationships linked to a redefinition of the urban system not purely as an effect of accelerated globalization but as a set of situated cultural practices and interactions between particular emergent assemblages.

In light of these mechanisms, it seems that an intensifying network of nodalized informality emerges where different cultures coincide locally and yield volatile, contradictory and contested space-time ecosystems. Informal markets incubate this ›globalization from below‹ fuelled by a deterritorialization of cultures. Their dialogical gestures constitute a common space beyond the mere agglomeration and exchange of fixed entities. Looking at the self-spun regimes of these ecologies, not with regard to what they are or what role they are supposed to fulfil but by asking what they make possible beyond themselves, allows us to reframe the present contestation of rationalities around rights and entitlements, participation and control. It opens up a space to think about markets in relation to processes of self-constitution and technologies of globalized political economies, such as the oblique worlds experienced and facilitated by black marketeers or the creation of distinctive ›ecosystems‹ through alignments of particular networks, labour conditions, citizenship arrangements and venture capital. Making their place within the porous nature of the extended and flexibilized city, the transnational subjects of the sprawling container markets maintain their quest for ›other markets‹ by intruding on and remaking the regimes of global exchange.

In order to imagine the possibilities, practicalities and difficulties of an emerging global public sphere requires us to take a closer look at the cultures of making do not merely as a contamination of institutional high culture but as a source of the actual fabric of its piecemeal morphological transformation. Indeed, the subtle infiltration of spatial hegemonies, as imagined by the designers and curators of the Hungarian pavilion at the Venice Architecture Biennale of 2006, is already underway, as indicated by the fact that the chirping and clucking washing lines of the Hungarian installation that year found their way back into the main pavilion of the 2008 ›Out There—Architecture Beyond Building‹ exhibition. Recycled, mended and dolled up for a second run, they came to demonstrate what makes us feel at home in the world.[7]

BIBLIOGRAPHY

Akšamija, Azra: »Arizona Road«, http://www.mit.edu/~azra/Arizona.htm [accessed 1 March 2011].

Bakhtin, Mikhail M. (1984): *Problems of Dostoevsky's Poetics*, edited and translated by Caryl Emerson, Minneapolis, MN: University of Minnesota Press.

Balibar, Étienne (2004): *We, the People of Europe? Reflections on Transnational Citizenship*, Princeton, NJ: Princeton University Press.

Bendyk, Edwin (2006): »Warsaw – Citizens against the City«. In: Katrin Klingan and Ines Kappert (eds.), *Leap into the City: Chişinău, Sofia, Pristina, Sarajevo, Warsaw, Zagreb, Ljubljana (Cultural Positions, Political Conditions. Seven Scenes from Europe)*. Cologne: DuMont, p. 326–341.

Biemann, Ursula (2008): *Mission Reports. Artistic Practice in the Field: Video Works 1998–2008*, Bristol: Arnolfini.

Collier, Stephen/Lakoff, Andrew (2005): »On Regimes of Living«. In: Stephen Collier and Aihwa Ong (eds.), *Global Assemblages: Technology, Politics and Ethics as Anthropological Problems*, Oxford: Blackwell.

Cooley, Heidi Rae (2008): »Ecologies of Practice«. *Journal of Visual Culture* 7(3), p. 267–276.

Deleuze, Gilles/Guattari, Félix (1991) *Qu'est-ce que la philosophie*, Paris: Les éditions de Minuit.

Mattelard, Armand (2000): *Networking the World, 1794–2000*, Minneapolis, MN: University of Minnesota Press.

Nemes, Attila (ed.) (2006): *Re:Orient – Migrating Architectures*, Műcsarnok/Kunsthalle Budapest.

Ong, Aihwa (2006): *Neoliberalism as Exception: Mutations in Citizenship and Sovereignty*, Durham, NC: Duke University Press.

---

7   See: http://www.labiennale.org/en/architecture/history/11.html [accessed 1 April 2011]

Ostrom, Elinor (1990): *Governing the Commons. The Evolution of Institutions for Collective Action*, Cambridge, MA: Cambridge University Press.

Rees, Madeleine (UNHCR Sarajevo) (1999): »Markets, Migration and Forced Prostitution«. *Humanitarian Exchange Magazine* 14, June 1999.

Uglyville

A Contention of Anti-Romaism in Europe[1]

EDUARD FREUDMANN AND IVANA MARJANOVIĆ

The term ›Universiade‹ is composed of ›University‹ and ›Olympiad‹. It designates a biennial multi-sport event, the second largest in the world, besides the Olympic Games. The 25th Universiade took place in Belgrade, in July 2009. At the same time, Serbia held the presidency of the Decade of Roma Inclusion, an international initiative which aims at improving the socioeconomic status and social inclusion of Roma. The Decade of Roma Inclusion consists of European integration organizations, global financial players, NGOs and national governments.

At the temporal conjunction of Decade and Universiade, certain phenomena come to the fore, which define reality in Serbia and Europe and can be understood as a paradigmatic example of the discrimination that Roma face today—discrimination that has to be defined as structural and institutionalized as it traverses the social fabric and its institutions so deeply and systematically.

Before we can reflect on these events, we have to make ourselves aware that we cannot refer to human rights that are regulated by international conventions or national constitutions, because there is no such thing as universal human rights, guaranteed by the present world order. There is only the power of capital, and related to it, the power of sovereignty that determines who does and who does not have the right to be human and therefore have human rights or not.

---

1 This essay is the script of the film with the same title based on the text »Contention of Anti-Romaism as a Part of the Process of the Decoloniality of Europe« by Ivana Marjanović, published in: *Reartikulacija* 7, http://www.reartikulacija.org/?p=647. For the need of the film, which was produced in 2010, the text was extended, edited and adapted by Eduard Freudmann and Ivana Marjanović.

Figure 10.1: Uglyville. A Contention of Anti-Romaism in Europe *(dir. Eduard Freudmann and Ivana Marjanović),* 2010

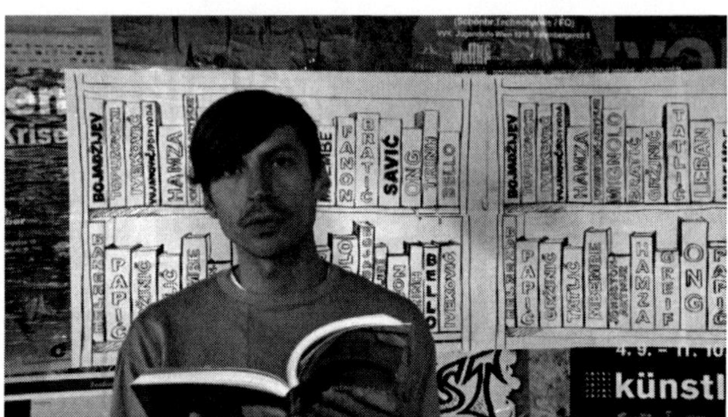

Film still

Sport is one of the key elements of national cohesion and national pride in Serbia. Athletes are considered to be international ambassadors of Serbian superiority. Roma, on the other hand, are constructed as a threat to the Serbian national body, and the visibility of their discriminated position endangers the international image of the nation.

From July 2008 to July 2009, Serbia held the Roma Decade's presidency. For that year, one would expect Serbia to make serious efforts towards improving the discriminated position of Roma and decreasing the effects of a policy of anti-Romaism that has lasted for centuries in the region. The opposite was the case. What we witnessed was the total disregard of the Decade's objectives and even an intensification of discrimination by Belgrade authorities, citizens and media. At the same time, all public attention was drawn to the international sports event Universiade.

Because of the lack of infrastructure for accommodating the eight thousand international athletes and officials of the Universiade, the city of Belgrade made a deal with a private investor, the multinational consortium Blok 67 Associates. The consortium consists of two companies. The first is Delta Real Estate which is owned by Miroslav Mišković, Serbia's biggest tycoon, who owes his wealth to his closeness to the former regime of Slobodan Milošević and its war politics. The second is the Hypo Alpe-Adria-Bank, one of the numerous Austrian banks exploiting Eastern European markets. The city provided public land on which the private investors erected a building ensemble called Belville, which is French for ›beautiful city‹. The buildings were used to accommodate the international guests during the Universiade and its flats, shops and offices were ready to be purchased from the consortium after the end of the event. Belville was strategically located next to the largest shopping mall in the Balkans, Delta City, which is also owned by Miroslav Mišković. This proximity brought in extra profit as the international guests of the Universiade mostly spent their leisure time shopping there.

Having lived in Europe for centuries, Roma must be considered as a constitutive part of it. They settled long before the concept of nations was constructed, thus we could ask on which basis they are regarded as something exterior, which must be ›included‹. Therefore, the concept of inclusion, pushed by the Decade of Roma Inclusion, seems paradoxical. But if we take a look at how power functions and to which extent coloniality (Quijano 2007) is embedded in capitalism, we realize that it is not a paradox at all.

Figure 10.2: Uglyville. A Contention of Anti-Romaism in Europe *(dir. Eduard Freudmann and Ivana Marjanović),* *2010*

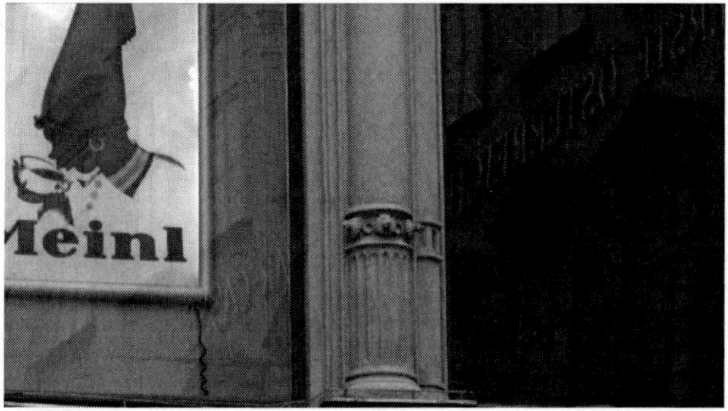

Film still

Hundreds of thousands of Belgrade citizens reside in so-called ›informal settlements‹, settlements that are not part of the regulated framework of the government. It is said that they cover 43 per cent of Belgrade's residential area. Although their legal status is equal, there is a tremendous qualitative difference between informal settlements inhabited by non-Roma and most of informal settlements inhabited by Roma: the Roma settlements are in constant danger of being demolished and have no chance of becoming formalized. These facts, and the poverty level of the inhabitants, turn most informal Roma settlements into slums.

Whenever a slum is about to be demolished, the authorities as well as the media, conceal the history of racism and discrimination. They do not ask why Roma are forced to live in miserable conditions and why the segregation within the social fabric is so extreme. They do not mention how deeply the reasoning of the so-called ›majority population‹ is rooted in racism and how this racism makes it impossible for most Roma to access regular education, have a legal job, social insurance or proper housing. They do not pose the question of why the average Roma are seven times poorer than the average non-Roma citizens and their life expectancy is half as high, why Roma are forced to dig in garbage bins in order to survive and are dying of diseases that are regarded as eradicated in Europe. They do not mention that Roma in Serbia live in perpetual fear of being exposed to attacks by fascist groups or police violence, that they get beaten to death and their houses are set on fire nor do they mention that Roma are illegalized by being deprived of basic legal documents and are thereby completely invisibilized when it comes to citizenship and civil rights.

Examining contemporary racism in Europe, Manuela Bojadžijev explains:

»Like anti-Semitism, neo-racism is an ideological practice, in which its specific object is constituted and constructed. This presumption implies a crucial challenge: something that does not exist, such as race, is coming into being through different forms of praxis by individuals, groups, institutions, or states and therefore a reality, a social relation and a policy. The fiction of race is produced by a vast number of narrations: gestures, rituals, images, texts. [...] Ethnicity and race—to take up a metaphor of Adorno—is a rumour, once it is the rumour about the Jews, the other time the rumour about the migrant or the refugee« (Bojadžijev 2006).

To understand the events around the Roma Decade and Universiade, we must return to the core of capitalist exploitation, because its mechanisms still define human relations. The core of capitalist exploitation is the colonial history of Europe and slavery that was conducted for the sake of capitalist progress and the development of Western Europeans.

For centuries, the colonial history has been and is normalized by European knowledge production, such as school and university books, encyclopedias, artworks, etc. Colonialism is thus trivialized, and thereby justified, as the modernization of so called backward areas, spice trade, geographical discoveries or Christianization missions, and not named as cruel exploitation, mass murder, enslavement and expropriation in the name of European progress and modernity.

The history of the construction of the Delta City shopping mall and the athlete's village Belville began with destruction. Both complexes of buildings were erected onto the ruins of Roma settlements, which had to be erased, before starting the construction. First, the inhabitants were expelled from their homes, prior to the construction of the shopping mall. Several of them settled a few hundred metres away. Then, two years later, prior to the construction of Belville, they were expelled from that location as well. Both expulsions did not cause any public attention nor did anyone protest. Finally, in order to accomplish the total cleansing of the territory around Belville, before the beginning of the Universiade, the authorities decided to erase the last remaining parts of the Roma settlement in spring 2009.

Roma in Serbia are caught in a net of state politics that is spun by the interests of capital and should be termed ›necropolitics‹ (Mbembe 2003). Its authorities and businessmen acquired their governing knowledge in the

1990s within Milošević's ›turbo-fascism‹ (Papić 2002). The remnants of the ideology that ethnic cleansing and genocide was immanent still determine the present Serbian politics and its propagators are still represented in the Serbian parliament and government. We have to bear this continuity in mind when we contemplate the conjunction of two governmental initiatives prior to the Universiade. One was a public campaign launched by the Ministry for Environment and Spatial Planning. It depicted a popular Serbian sportsman, the notorious nationalist Novak Djoković, swinging a broom like his tennis racket and calling his fellow countrymen out to »Let's Clean Serbia!« The other governmental initiative is the necropolitical spatial plan to erase the Roma settlement next to Belville.

While the government plastered Belgrade with the campaign's giant billboards, media and politicians prepared the field for the eviction of the settlement by addressing the broad anti-Romaist consensus in Serbia through typical racist propaganda.

Figure 10.3: Uglyville. A Contention of Anti-Romaism in Europe *(dir. Eduard Freudmann and Ivana Marjanović),* *2010*

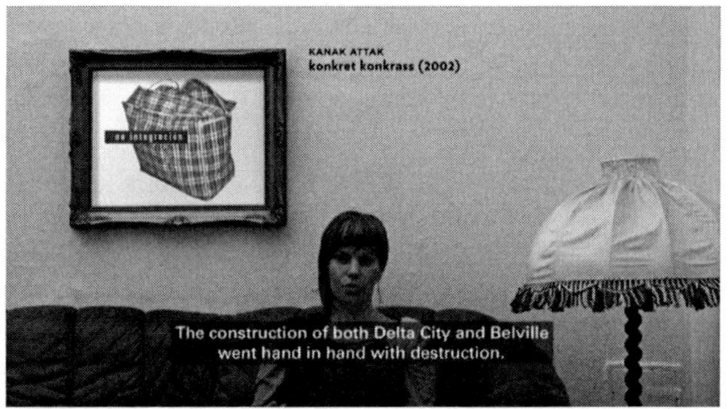

Film still

The media focused on constructing the contrasting image of a kind of ›Uglyville‹ that allegedly popped up overnight and was growing out of control. It was reported that the organizer of Universiade, the International University Sports Federation, insisted on the removal of the eyesore before the beginning of the event. One thing was made perfectly clear: Roma will not be allowed to pollute the beautiful image of Belgrade and Belville that was supposed to be sent to the world.

Colonial history determines the present. Normalized, it is perpetually maintained in the First capitalist world and outside of it, through migration politics, globalization, debt slavery, ongoing confiscation of natural resources and contemporary wars and invasions.

The colonial matrix of power and racism, as its main technology, is not only functional outside of Europe but also within it. It subjugates all those who do not fit into the category of so-called ›white Christians‹, the ones who are constructed as the most worthy.

After the public opinion had been prepared, the operation could start. One early morning in April, several bulldozers guarded by the police began the eviction of the inhabitants of the settlement and destroyed around 40 houses. The demolition came like a bolt out of the blue for the inhabitants. Most of them were even prevented from rescuing their personal belongings from their homes before they were destroyed.

Being constructed as people of colour, and assumed to be pagans, Roma were targeted by the colonial matrix of power from the time of European modernity and enlightenment on. For centuries, kingdoms, holy empires, totalitarian regimes and democracies of Europe issued great many decrees and laws to torture, banish, enslave, expel and exterminate them. Examples are numerous from the sixteenth century on, from England, Romania and Nazi Germany to contemporary Europe. Roma were slaves of Christian monasteries and other feudal rulers; they were banished from many countries; they were marked with branding irons; they were forbidden to use their language or marry among each other; children were abducted from their parents to be brought up in Catholic families in the Habsburg Empire; they were massively exterminated by the Nazis throughout Europe; Roma women were coercively sterilized until the 1980s in Czechoslovakia, Hungary, Sweden, Norway, with recent cases having been made public in the Czech Republic. In collaboration with EU candidates, as part of their application process, Germany has been expelling Roma and deporting them to their countries of origin. In Italy, the state of exception was proclaimed in order to fingerprint entire Roma communities, including minors (Jeremić/Rädle 2009; »Rights Groups Demand European Commission Clarify Its Position on Fingerprinting Roma in Italy« 2008). Roma have recently been exposed to pogroms, murder and expulsion all over Europe: in Austria, the Czech Republic, Finland, Germany, Hungary, Ireland, Italy, Serbia, Slovenia and Slovakia, as well as in other countries (Petrova 2004; »UN Presses Czech Republic on Coercive Sterilization of Romani Women« 2006; Rakić-Vodinelić/Gajin 2009; Ostojić 2006; »Snapshots from around Europe. Report reveals that Romani women were sterilized against their will in Sweden« 1997).

As a reaction to the demolition of the settlement, something exceptional happened: A series of public protests were organized in the streets of Belgrade. They were initiated by the inhabitants and joined by Roma representatives, NGOs, activists, students, independent cultural workers, artists and other citizens in solidarity.

One has to have in mind that Roma living in slums are extremely deceived, blackmailed, silenced and frightened by authorities, and thus hardly ever formulate their demands publicly. Being at the very bottom of society, what is just something for others, is everything for them. They have the most to lose and—as personal and historical experience has taught them—the least to win. The protests against the demolition have shown that this is not the ultimate rule. They mark one of the important moments, when Roma resisted and gained something.

The protests attracted the attention of international humanitarian organizations and put public pressure on the city's decision-makers to an extent that they had to momentarily interrupt what they had started: the total erasure of the settlement. Nevertheless, the mayor insisted on the demolition of the settlement, because he said it would endanger the growth of Belgrade. As a concession to the protests, the city authorities offered what they called a ›temporary alternative accommodation‹ to some of the now homeless Roma by installing a few modified freight containers in a village near Belgrade. The village is well-known, because a Roma teenager was killed there two years ago. As soon as the news spread, the villagers started to protest against their potential new neighbours; a reaction that is a common practice in Belgrade, whenever it is rumored that Roma should be relocated to a certain neighbourhood. The villagers burnt down one of the containers and announced that they would burn down more of them, including the inhabiting Roma, in case they dare move in.

The mayor expressed his understanding of the behaviour of the villagers and announced that all inhabitants who do not hold a residential registration in Belgrade have to return to their home towns; the city would pay for their one-way tickets. Finally, in order to stop the protests, one of the organizers was arrested. He was accused of having rented houses in the settlement; a ›delinquency‹ that no one had ever heard of before.

The constellation of the Roma Decade consists of proactive and reactive players. The proactive ones are the main powers of contemporary capitalism and those that maintain its status quo: the World Bank, the Council of Europe and its Development Bank, the Organization for Security and Cooperation in Europe, the Open Society Institute and the United Nations Development Programme as well as other UN sub-organizations. These agencies' engagement in globalization processes and in the European colonial project of the past and the present, warn us against being naïve and believing that the Decade is about the elimination of discrimination and poverty of Roma (Bello 2005). It rather gives us information about the functionality of the colonial matrix of power in the context of the European Union and global capitalism.

The events at the conjunction of Roma Decade and Universiade show that it is not discrimination that is unacceptable. On the contrary, it is needed, because it sustains the capitalist system. What is unacceptable is the visibility of discrimination, because it disturbs those who are supposed to believe in the justness of the system and bears the potential to make them realize that Belgrade's slums result from inequality and exploitation and not from difference as the widespread racist stereotype of Roma, who are poor because it ›suits their nature‹, wants to make them believe. The visibility of discrimination decreases the value of the investors' real estate, and it decreases the value that Belgrade gains by organizing the Universiade. It obstructs the pleasant panoramic view and reminds one too much of the Third World rather than of the Western Europe, which is the object of fixation of every Serbian citizen. The visibility of discrimination interferes with the athlete's quality of life and the one of the white Serbian-Orthodox family who bought the appealing flat from a Serbian war profiteer and his Austrian capitalist partners. All in all, it is that very visibility that endangers Belgrade's growth.

Figure 10.4: Uglyville. A Contention of Anti-Romaism in Europe *(dir. Eduard Freudmann and Ivana Marjanović), 2010*

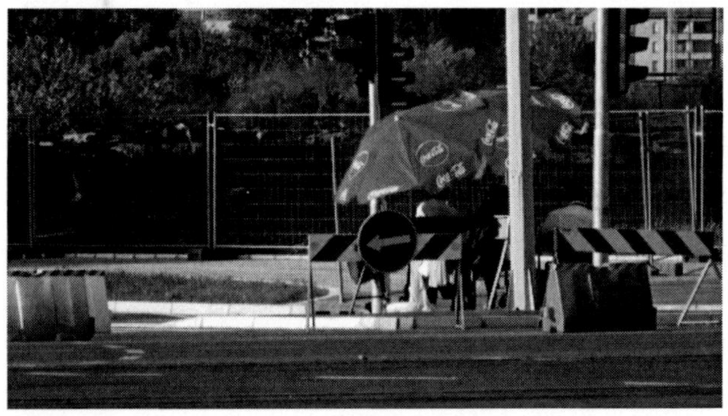

Film still

The reactive players of the Decade are Eastern European countries that either recently joined the EU or are about to join in the near future. One could think that the absence of Western European countries results from the fact that Roma are not discriminated there, and thus no need for such a programme exists. As we know that this is not the case it becomes clear that the Decade is in fact about the inclusion of the new and future EU countries and serves as a tool that enables Europe to ensure Roma's position in the colonial matrix of power. The ideology behind it is a neoliberal capitalist ideology rooted in its colonial past, which uses racism as a tool for exploitation. Its goal is not to bring pluriversality of human relations, but to enforce the inclusion of Roma in the capitalist system of exploitation. Inclusion, thus, does not mean that Roma will have equal rights, but it means that they will be exploited in a more subtle and low-key way as is the case in Western EU countries.

As the Universiade approached, it turned out that the total eradication of the settlement would not be possible due to the protests, so the sovereign power reorganized its strategy. Two weeks before the opening of the Universiade, a metal fence was erected around the settlement, justified by referring to the event's security measures. In order to invisibilize the settlement, a banner was installed onto the fence, which was guarded by security staff and police. The inhabitants were blocked from leaving the settlement and threatened with arrest if they were to be seen in the streets around Belville, particularly if caught searching for secondary materials in trash cans. Therefore, not only was their freedom of movement withdrawn, but they were deprived of their existential basis by being prevented from carrying out regular daily work in the streets of Belgrade. Surprisingly, the Delta City shopping mall was not fenced in for security reasons, commodities were in circulation and profit was accumulated without any barriers.

Giorgio Agamben refers to the camp as the biopolitical paradigm of modernity. He claims:

»To an order without localization (which is the state of exception, in which law is suspended) there now corresponds a localization without order (the camp as permanent space of exception). The political system no longer orders forms of life and juridical rules in a determinate space, but instead contains at its very centre a dislocating localization that exceeds it and into which every form of life and every rule can be virtually taken. The camp as dislocating localization is the hidden matrix of the politics in which we are still living, and it is this structure of the camp that we must learn to recognize in all its metamorphoses into the zones d'attentes of our airports and certain outskirts of our cities« (Agamben 1998).

This situation caused actions by citizens in solidarity, publicly demanding that the fence had to be removed. An international petition and a web campaign were launched, unofficial and official gatherings, workshops and food preparations were organized in the settlement and activities were initiated that aimed to inform the athletes, international delegations and journalists that what was going on behind the so-called ›security fence‹ was not a film set, as the Universiade's organizers wanted to make them believe. A press conference that was organized in the settlement pressured the authorities so they removed the banner and thereby re-visibilized the settlement. The solidarity actions form a crucial element of the process of the decolonization of knowledge that the activists started to undergo, which represents the dismantling of internalized colonialism, as well as detecting one's own position in the colonial matrix of power. Only when their knowledge is decolonized, can subjects delink from the colonial matrix of power.

The living conditions of Roma in slums, their reduced life expectancy, their constant historical and contemporary exposure to violence and death, their illegalization through deprivation of citizenship, the fact that they can be expelled from their homes at any moment, has to be understood in relation to the concept of necropolitics: exposed to the power of death and made invisible when it is about civil rights, while on the other hand, visible when it is about exploitation and the need for the cheapest labour force.

Achille Mbembe argues that the notion of biopower is insufficient in accounting for contemporary forms of subjugation of life to the power of death. Therefore, he introduced the notion of necropolitics and necropower to account for the various ways in which, in our contemporary world, weapons are deployed in the interest of maximum destruction of persons and the creation of death worlds.

»Those are new and unique forms of social existence in which vast populations are subjected to conditions of life conferring upon them the status of the living dead« (Mbembe 2003).

To understand in which continuity the recent concept of inclusion, proposed by the Roma Decade, is embedded, we have to take into consideration that Roma are confronted with two categories of strategies that were conceived for dealing with them as the othered: incorporation and excorporation. Incorporation has to be understood in the literal sense of including an exterior element in an already conceptualized corpus. Excorporation refers to the exclusion of an element that is considered to be interior to that corpus, respectively one that is really or assumedly in the process of incorporation. At first, incorporation and excorporation may appear antagonistic, but in fact they relate to one another in continuity and complementation.

Excorporative strategies have been practiced since the first day Roma have lived in Europe to this very day and range from expulsion to existential extermination. Incorporative strategies can be traced back to the era of enlightenment when forced assimilation was first imposed. However, their emergence cannot be understood as a paradigmatic shift. First of all, both strategies are co-existent, those who rejected incorporation through assimilation were excorporated through expulsion or extermination. Secondly, assimilation itself has to be considered as both, an incorporative as well as an excorporative strategy, because its mechanism of incorporation requires the excorporative act of exterminating all differences of the subjected individual. Finally, as the Nuremberg Laws and Shoah evidenced, assimilation does not protect the subjected individual from existential extermination.

Marina Gržinić proposes to think about necropolitics as the re-politicization of biopolitics and its genealogy. She claims that the concept of necropolitics, primarily envisioned for Africa and the Third World, develops a different biopolitics and is taking place in the First capitalist World more and more.

»With this proposed ›transformation‹ of biopolitics into necropolitics,« she states, »I am NOT asking to de-link biopolitics from necropolitics, but to understand that the maximization of exploitation and expropriation of life, labour, and ›humanity‹ that is put forward here and now by capital asks for the reformulation, or, better to say, re-politicization of biopolitics!« (Gržinić 2009).

Although assimilation is still the most practiced strategy the othered are subjected to, additional incorporative strategies have meanwhile been conceived, such as integration or inclusion. Contrary to assimilation, integration does not require the total abandonment of all differences and accepts a certain extent of heterogeneity of a social group. At the same time, it demands the structural, cultural, social and identitary incorporation of the othered. The strategy of inclusion departs from the assumption that a certain heterogeneity marks normality. It does not denominate the othered as an other, but pretends to include it in a participatory manner. The fact that both, integration as well as inclusion, are found in the pedagogical concepts of the integrative pedagogy and the inclusive pedagogy is symptomatic for the way the othered are perceived by dominant society: As an emotional infantilized object that is not able to speak rationally for itself, but has to be domesticated, civilized and educated by the rational constant of the dominant society.

Describing assimilation through the internalization of coloniality, Jelena Savić explains that in order to be part of society one has to be ›normal‹— meaning, having white skin and being rich. Those who cannot colour their skin have no other choice than

»to become invisible in the mass, to look as white and rich as possible, to be educated, employed [...] not to expose in any way [...] not to declare yourself as Rom or Romni, to insist as little as possible on your difference, [...] not to look as a Rom or Romni, not to speak Romani language in public space, not to walk with a group of greater number of ›evident‹ Roma,« but instead, »to be silent and laugh about jokes of stupid Roma men and venal Roma women, to pretend that you don't see poor Roma in the streets nor the rude treatment of female Roma beggars with babies, to agree on the proposition that everybody can succeed only due to his/her own work, that Roma like to live like that, on the street, and that you have nothing to do with this Roma [...]« (Savić 2009).

Unlike assimilation that exterminates any difference, the strategy of inclusion accepts difference to a certain extent: as long as it can be regulated and controlled to prevent the obstruction and endangerment of the growth of capital. Exoticized Roma music is welcome, because it fertilizes consumerism. Roma women are coercively sterilized, because their children demographically endanger the body of the nation and the capitalist order.

The Decade of Roma Inclusion must be seen in relation to EU security politics: Roma should be prevented from migrating from poorer Eastern European countries to the richer Western European countries. Thus, the participating countries are required to improve the living conditions for Roma, thereby securing that Roma stay where they are. The recent case of 100 Roma migrating from Romania caused immense panic in Germany. After being expelled from a park in Berlin, they were paid money to return to Romania (Fuchs/Marschall 2009)! This panic actually results from the fear that a growing number of Roma could reveal anti-Romaism in Germany, the country in which anti-Romaism had been exercised in its most extreme form. After Porajmos, the genocide of Roma people conducted in the Third Reich, it had been switched to a kind of slumber mode, due to the lack of its target objects. The re-visibilization of Germany's latent anti-Romaism would disprove the Western European cultural-racist conviction of being less racist and thereby more civilized than Eastern Europeans.

In the end, we can conclude that the concept of incorporation and its strategy of inclusion are ideological concepts targeting the production, reproduction and maintenance of hierarchies and relations of domination, because they do not depart from the equality of people, but from their inequality. This means that they take an ideological division that was invented and maintained by capitalism for granted. Based on this, however, a setting where one is part of the corpus ›per se‹ or by ›nature‹, whereas the other having to be incorporated, cannot lead to any promising anti-discriminatory politics. The only way to eliminate discrimination is to eliminate the system that produces it.

Bibliography

Agamben, Giorgio (1998): *Homo Sacer. Sovereign Power and Bare Life*, Stanford, CA: Stanford University Press.

Bojadžijev, Manuela (2006): »Does Contemporary Capitalism Need Racism?«. eipcp.net, http://translate.eipcp.net/strands/02/bojadzijev-strands01en/print

Bello, Walden (2005): *Deglobalization: Ideas for a New World Economy*, revised edition, London and New York: Zed Books.

Fuchs, Claudia/Marschall, Marko (2009): »Bargeld für die Rückkehr nach Rumänien«. *Berliner Zeitung*, http://www.berlinonline.de/berliner-zeitung/archiv/.bin/dump.fcgi/2009/0612/berlin/0031/index.html

Gržinić, Marina (2009): »Subjectivization, Biopolitics and Necropolitics: Where do we stand?«. *Reartikulacija* 6, http://www.reartikulacija.org/RE6/ENG/reartikulacija6_ENG_grz.html

Mbembe, Achille (2003): »Necropolitics«. *Public Culture* 15(1), p. 11–40.

Jeremić, Vladan/Rädle, Rena (2009): »Antiziganism and Class Racism in Europe«. http://www.octogon.hu/in+english+1/antiziganism+and+class+racism+in+europe+by+vladan+jeremic+and+rena+r%C3%A4dle+1.html

Ostojić, Tanja (2009): »The Roma Question 2006«, archive. In: Marina Gržinić and Tanja Ostojić (eds.), *Integration Impossible? The politics of Migration in the Art Work of Tanja Ostojić*, Berlin: argobooks, p. 152.

Papić, Žarana (2002): »Europe after 1989: Ethnic Wars, the Fascization of Social Life and Body Politics in Serbia«. In: Marina Gržinić (ed.), *Filozofski vestnik* (special issue: The Body), Ljubljana: FI ZR SAZU, p. 191–205.

Petrova, Dimitrina (2004): »The Roma: Between a Myth and the Future«. http://www.errc.org/cikk.php?cikk=1844&archiv=1

Rakić-Vodinelić, Vesna/Gajin, Saša (2009): »Kratka istorija pravnog položaja i diskriminacije Roma u nekadašnjoj Jugoslaviji i nekadašnjoj i današnjoj Srbiji« [Short history of legal status and discrimination of

Roma in former Yugoslavia and today's Serbia]. Peščanik, http://www. pescanik.net/content/view/2965/171

»Rights Groups Demand European Commission Clarify Its Position on Fingerprinting Roma in Italy«, 2008, http://www.errc.org/cikk.php?cikk= 2980&archiv=1

Savić, Jelena (2009): »Nenormalni i nemoralni« [Abnormal and unmoral]. http://usernameka.wordpress.com/diskriminacija-roma-kinja-2/ nenormalni-i-nemoralni

»Snapshots from around Europe. Report reveals that Romani women were sterilized against their will in Sweden«, 1997, http://www.errc.org/cikk. php?cikk=1521

»UN Presses Czech Republic on Coercive Sterilization of Romani Women«, 2006, http://www.errc.org/cikk.php?cikk=2626

Quijano, Aníbal (2007): »Coloniality and Modernity/Rationality«. *Cultural Studies* 21(2), p. 168–178.

Fortified Knowledge

From Supranational Governance to Translocal Resistance[1]

LINA DOKUZOVIĆ AND EDUARD FREUDMANN

The international economic crisis has been remedied with the development of a knowledge economy, at the cost of those constituting knowledge production. One of the consequences of the expanse of education has been the geopolitical restructuring of spaces of education, not only as another sphere of life appropriated by capital, but in terms of national narratives on a supranational level, echoing the corporate agendas in and around education. That expansion builds ›areas‹ and ›zones‹, in which a greater marketability and exchange of ›education units‹ can take place on behalf of supranational market agendas.

Contemporary educational structures are a basis for the reproduction of capital, and a laboratory for the creation of branded epistemologies, which are the centre and the starting point of their reproduction both inside and beyond the walls that fortify it. The consequences of this process are manifold and as interlinked as capital and nation, exposing the two as joint partners in the enterprise of the knowledge economy. A shifting foundation ebbs and flows in relation to the needs or crises of the centre.

The consequences of this structure have echoed worldwide, ranging from lack of access to education, to the loss of homes to student debt, to an increase in police forces on university campuses, regulating and preventing discord, worldwide. However, such conditions are not being tolerated and

---

1 This shortened and edited version of the article was presented at the *space RE:solutions conference* organized by the Visual Culture Department at the Vienna University of Technology. The full-length article was originally written for and published in: Volume 3, Dossier 2, »On Europe, Education, Global Capitalism and Ideology«, edited by Marina Gržinić as part of the web dossier »Worlds & Knowledges Otherwise (WKO)«, published at Duke University, July 2010; http://trinity.duke.edu/globalstudies/volume-3-dossier-2-on-europe-education-global-capitalism-and-ideology-2

the antagonism which has erupted, despite and due to the forces of regulation, has expanded as far as the problems being contested. Individuals in Europe have been protesting against the current Bologna Process reforms, in the US against high tuition fees and cutbacks, Indians in Australia against structural racism and abuse, and in the ›developing world‹ against the ever-changing institutions following Structural Adjustment Policies implemented decades ago, to name a few. In the US, protestors have referred to the ›war on our universities‹, in which public funds are invested in financing the war effort and prisons, rather than invested in improving the school system. All the while, education, militias and prisons become increasingly privatized, placing public moneys into private pockets. The common elements in these worldwide issues are part of a complex system, building a knowledge economy, as a purported solution to a failing global capitalist order.

This analysis will, therefore, approach how supranationality substantiates a regulated spatial organization of movement and its restriction, based on a centre, semi-peripheries, peripheries and zones of suspension, accumulating profit from education and using education as a tool for reproducing that very logic. The concept of transnational struggle against supranational structures will thus be questioned in terms of the entanglement of state and capital, proposing alternatives for a struggle against both capitalism and nationalism in their variegated and obfuscated forms.

SPATIAL REGULATION

The ›dependency theory‹[2] claims that a centre and a periphery must exist, in which the periphery provides the resources and cheap labour, to stabilize and support the development and wealth of the centre in a traditional colonial format. The ›World Systems Theory‹ extended that notion into analyzing a globalized context, in order to display a more complex and shifting relationship between the colonizer and colonized, with the semi-periphery playing an increasingly significant role as the balancer of the system and the disguise of the wealth gap between the ›developed‹ and the ›developing‹ in global capitalism.[3] The following analysis of competitive higher education

---

2   The idea originates from the Singer-Prebisch thesis, introduced in 1949. Hans Singer and Raúl Prebisch, in two separate papers, claimed that a centre and a periphery must exist in which the periphery provides the resources and cheap labour, stabilizing and supporting the development and wealth of the centre in a traditional colonial format.

3   Immanuel Wallerstein introduced the semi-periphery in his ›World Systems Theory‹, claiming that a far more complex and shifting relationship between colonizer and colonized exists, with the semi-periphery playing an increasingly significant role as the balancer of the system and the disguise of the wealth gap between the ›developed‹ and the ›developing‹ in globalism.

areas draws from those economic models in order to better understand effective methods of protest.

The commodification and homogenization of knowledge and education are grounded in a long history of international structural ›development‹ policy that was conceived and installed by the US in order to ensure its position as the centre, dominating and exploiting its peripheries. The Bretton Woods system, which was implemented during WWII, established the US as the economic superpower in order to provide short-term development aid for a devastated Europe. This would allow Europe to return as a competent competitor in the capitalist market in the aftermath of WWII, remaining indebted to the US in the process. Structural Adjustment Policies would be the extension of Bretton Woods, imposed onto the ›developing‹ world, primarily in the Global South. They would provide criteria for opening and privatizing markets, including complete educational and medical reform packages, and a corporatization of resources and goods, such as crops, water, energy, etc. What was and still is referred to with these policies as the ›liberation‹ of territories and a salvation mission of bringing ›democracy‹ and ›development‹ to the oppressed world, merely echoes colonial salvation missions, fashioned for the expropriation of wealth and resources from outlying territories and the appropriation of everything that produces it.

After the economic boom following WWII, Europe would begin a process of emancipation from the economic dominance of the US, in which education would take on an increasingly significant position. This strategy would allow Europe to ultimately elevate its global economic status from a semi-periphery to a centre of power, through the processes of enlargement and integration of the European Union, supplementing other political interests such as economic, legal and military intentions with educational restructuring, producing its own peripheries and semi-peripheries in the process.

Knowledge economy areas

Europe would invest in a growing engagement in Research and Technological Development (RTD). In order to increase its competitiveness with the US, it would enhance intra-European academic mobility and promote Europe's profile as a study and research destination for non-European students. This intra-European academic mobility would be structured through the establishment of the European Higher Education Area, which was supported by the launch of the Bologna Process in 1999, whose joint primary focus is the development of a European Research Area (ERA) supporting the aforementioned aims of Research and Technological Development (RTD).

This flexible, yet regulated mobility arrangement of the EHEA and ERA has introduced the same terminology and logic of ›areas‹ into education as used in economic trade. In these ›areas‹, maximal mobility of goods, services and capital allow an unlimited production of profit.[4] It is also significant to maintain the difference here between mobility, which is protected by law, and migration, which is punishable by law.

Zones of suspension

The outlying regions of Europe, in which movement can be sanctioned, are defined by Étienne Balibar as *zones*.[5] They function to replace traditional national borders and are regulated through a permanent state of suspension or exception.[6] Those zones can never be integrated into the EHEA or EU, such as the entire region of sub-Saharan Africa, which is not considered to be ›civilized‹ enough to enter bilateral or multilateral trade, but should instead support the ›developed world‹ as resource-rich bargain bins.[7]

A system of detention camps and *zones* of suspension fortify the borders of what has been criticized by some ›No Border‹ activists as ›fortress Europe‹, a term originally coined in reference to the Nazi occupation of Europe. However, applying the Nazi propaganda term to current conditions becomes problematic as it likens the methods of the German *Wehrmacht* to those of the contemporary EU border and migration regimes. Therefore, we propose the use of the term ›fortified Europe‹ instead.

The establishment of the EHEA not only closely relates to the fortification of Europe by utilizing the same centre and buffer zones, but its function depends on the disfranchisement of excluded and included individuals. So it is necessary to not only refer to ›fortified Europe‹ in terms of its migration politics and border regime, but to understand the fortification as a transgressive logic being gradually applied to every sphere of life regulated by EU policy. The centre-periphery model must be viewed as a territorial strategy of dominance, based on the control and regulation of mobility and migration. We therefore, use the term ›fortified knowledge centres‹ to refer to how

---

4   There are ›four freedoms‹ protected by the EU, consisting of the free (or deregulated) mobility of goods, services, citizens and capital (which the first three elements constitute). The Lisbon Agreement of 2000 proposed including education, or knowledge, as the fifth freedom of the EU; see, for example: Richard L. Hudson, »A ›5th Freedom‹ for Researchers«. In: Science‖Business Special Report: »The 5th Freedom: Research in Europe. A Special News Report on the European Commission's R&D ›Green Paper‹«. www.sciencebusiness.net

5   See Marina Gržinić, »Analysis of the exhibition ›Gender Check—Femininity and Masculinity in the Art of Eastern Europe‹«. *European Institute for Progressive Cultural Policies*, Vienna, 12/2009; http://eipcp.net/policies/grzinic/en

6   According to Giorgio Agamben, the ›state of exception‹ describes increased state power in purported times of crisis with indefinite *suspension* of the law characterizing the ›state of exception‹.

7   This term is expanded by Khadija Sharife in »DRC's Magic Dust: Who Benefits?« http://www.pambazuka.org/en/category/features/61992

this relates to the fortification around the knowledge economy areas, as the EHEA and EU are congruent with the EU border and migration regime supporting the necropolitical[8] border defense projects of Frontex, not only accepting the consequences of drowning boat refugees, but enforcing it.[9]

THE FORTIFIED KNOWLEDGE CENTRE

When examining the development of the Bologna Process leading to the EHEA, the creation of the centre and its peripheries becomes clear. The signatories of the Bologna Declaration are congruent with the Member States of today's EU[10] and form the core of the EHEA or its centre. Being inside the borders of the Schengen area, the countries' citizens purportedly increase the intra-European academic mobility as they enjoy the freedom of movement and are therefore enabled to study, research and teach in any location within the Schengen area. As EU citizens, they are additionally protected from discrimination based on their national origin and cannot, for example, be charged higher tuition fees than residents; scholarships are available to them; and they have the right to work and make a living—principles that are guaranteed by the EU judiciary.

Its semi-periphery

The part of the EHEA outside of the EU forms its semi-periphery. This includes the Western Balkans, Turkey, Russia, the Ukraine, Moldova, the Caucasus Republics, thereby all non-EU countries on the Eurasian landmass west of the Caspian Sea[11] and (since March 2010) Kazakhstan. The semi-periphery is defined through all signatories of the European Cultural Convention[12] and the Member States of the Council of Europe (the only exception is Belarus who signed the previous, but not the latter). Its citizens benefit from the comparability of the national education systems, therefore, they can transfer credits and easily continue their studies in the centre in case they are selected and permitted to enter the Schengen area where they

---

8   Achille Mbembe defines ›necropolitics‹ as »the subjugation of life to the power of death« in Mbembe 2003.

9   See, for example: http://www.proasyl.de/fileadmin/proasyl/fm_redakteure/Flyer_PDF/FRONTEX.pdf; http://www.youtube.com/watch?v=kOuFo5egBqE; http://www.youtube.com/watch?v=zAAPNkBKrzo

10   Except for Cyprus, which entered the Bologna Process two years later in 2001.

11   Except Belarus, Monaco and San Marino.

12   The European Cultural Convention was signed by the members of the Council of Europe in 1954 to achieve a greater unity between its members for the purpose »[...] of safeguarding and realizing the ideals and principles which are their common heritage«. http://conventions.coe.int/Treaty/en/Treaties/Html/018.htm

are subjected to a number of (nationally-varying) discriminations such as the obstruction to work for money and the simultaneous obligation to prove the possession of an amount of money, which exceeds the maximal allowed annual income.[13]

Its periphery

The periphery of the EHEA is comprised of the countries of Northern Africa,[14] the Middle East[15] and Central Asia,[16] all of them participating in Tempus, »a vehicle for the promotion and exchange of Bologna ideas to countries surrounding the EU«.[17] According to the Bologna Process Conference Berlin 2003, there is no perspective to integrate these countries into the EHEA, because they are not signatories of the European Cultural Convention, therefore, they are not considered to share the »common cultural heritage of Europe« and »safeguard and encourage the development of European culture«.

EMERGING FORTIFIED KNOWLEDGE CENTRES

The elevation of Europe from a semi-periphery to a centre, influenced by the successful knowledge economic model, has caused the export of epistemology and ›braindrain‹ of the peripheries. Australia followed Europe's example and entered the race by initiating the Brisbaine Communiqué in 2006, targeting an *Asia Pacific Higher Education Area* for competition with the US and aspiring EU models. Australia has subsequently gained significant economic success, based on incoming students, seen as *guest consumers* (Rosenzweig 2010), statistically considered an ›educational export‹, repre-

---

13 To have a student visa prolonged in Austria, for example, the applicant must prove possession of 7,055 euro (as of 30 March 2010, with the quantity constantly being increased). At the same time, the monthly income for the respective students is limited to approximately 300 euro per month, thereby being less than the aforementioned quantity and less than a woman's lower-level annual income in Austria after taxes which was, according to statistics, 6,491 euro (in 2008, see: http://www.statistik.at/web_de/static/nettojahreseinkommen_der_unselbstaendig _erwerbstaetigen_1997_bis_2008_020055.pdf).

14 Algeria, Egypt, Libya, Morocco, Tunisia

15 Israel, Jordan, Lebanon, Palestine, Syria

16 Kyrgyzstan, Tajikistan, Turkmenistan, Uzbekistan

17 See *The World Education Services*, 20(4), April 2007, http://www.wes.org/ ewenr/07apr/feature.htm

senting the third highest export industry after coal and iron ore in Australia, according to 2006–2007 statistics.[18]

The area comprised of the Brisbane Communiqué signatories includes the 52 countries, which compose Australia's periphery. Interestingly, there is no country which is part of both the EHEA or its periphery and the Australia-dominated Asia Pacific Higher Education Area, with the exception of Turkey. This precise apportionment of the territories can be seen as a continuation of the territorial demarcation processes that the colonial empires carried out with their colonial conferences until the twentieth century.

So what is at stake is that the centre of the First Capitalist World (USA) dominating its peripheries (Western Europe and the ›developing‹ world) was ruptured within the last two decades into three centres—with the emerging EU and Australia—who established structures for education and research areas in order to compete with the US and create their own profitable peripheries. The model has allowed Europe and Australia to rise from (semi-) peripheries to centres and shows that other territories of rapid economic growth can potentially do so as well, such as India and China for example.[19] In times of crisis, education reforms and the corresponding spatial regulations have supplied a major territory for increased profit production, exploitation and consequent oppression.

Transgressive resistance

In October 2009, the Vienna Academy of Fine Arts was occupied, snowballing to the rest of Austria, linking to and sparking other protests worldwide.[20] Over the following months, the protests advanced and continued to expand, taking on different forms and mobilizing large quantities of people. Many of them were seen as an extreme threat and were reacted to with police violence and oppression. Varying levels of brutality have depended on geopolitical locations, economic status, class and segregation. Several universities in Germany were immediately evacuated by police with teargas and beat-

---

18 See: http://www.isana.org.au/files/AEI%20March%20sshot%20expt%20income. pdf (sourced from the Australian Bureau of Statistics).

19 China and India are members of the BRIC nations—Brazil, Russia, India and China—the most rapidly developing economies in the world and those with the greatest investment in Africa (their periphery). Goldman Sachs argues that by 2050, the combined economies of the BRICs could eclipse the combined economies of the current richest countries of the world; http://www2.goldmansachs. com/ideas/brics/index.html

20 See, for example: Lina Dokuzović and Eduard Freudmann, »Squatting the Crisis: On the Current Protests in Education and Perspectives on Radical Change«, *European Institute for Progressive Cultural Policies*, Vienna, 11/2009; http:// eipcp.net/n/1260352849

ings.[21] Assault and arrests have taken place in Vienna. A student was severely beaten and eleven were arrested at the University of Zimbabwe, following arrests in Harare and Bulawayo the week before.[22] In Melbourne, Australia a demonstration of 4,000 Indian students, protesting against racist assault, was violently broken up by police.[23] Water cannons were used to disperse protesting university students in Johannesburg demanding free tertiary education for the poor.[24] Six students were arrested for distributing flyers against neoliberal education at Hosei University in Korea.[25] 17 activists were arrested for anti-racist demonstrations at the University of California Irvine,[26] the ›Open University‹, established by protestors at UC Berkeley was raided by police, with 65 activists detained;[27] and a Ghanese immigrant, PhD student, and teaching assistant was brutally shot in the face in his own home by on-campus security at the University of Florida.[28]

In March 2010, a transnational Bologna Counter-Summit resulted from the linked international struggles. It was conceived as a protest against the meeting of the European Ministers of higher education in Vienna for the ›inception‹ of the European Higher Education Area. The Counter-Summit lasted for several days with presentations, protest actions and a blockade intended to complicate the arrival of the Ministers to the Hofburg Palace in Vienna, where the Summit was to be held. Protestors from several countries affected by the Bologna Process reforms announced their statements and demands there, increasingly taking the form of declarations, sabotage and seizure, rather than previous clearly articulated demands.[29]

---

21 Among others in Frankfurt, Jena, Heidelberg and Stuttgart.

22 http://wozazimbabwe.org/?p=626

23 http://www.wsws.org/articles/2009/jun2009/stud-j02.shtml

24 http://www.reuters.com/article/idUSLDE6230F4

25 http://www.edu-factory.org/edu15/index.php?option=com_content&view=article &id=284:six-students-were-arrested-on-hosei-university&catid=34:struggles& Itemid=53

26 http://www.huffingtonpost.com/2010/02/24/uc-irvine-protest-17-arre_n_475903. html

27 http://www.edu-factory.org/edu15/index.php?option=com_content&view=article &id=258:uc-berkeley-open-university-raided-by-police-65-arrested&catid=34: struggles&Itemid=53

28 Stanfill, Andrew: »UF Student was Shot in Head by Police«, 2 March 2010; http://www.gainesville.com/article/20100303/ARTICLES/100309832?p=1&tc= pg

29 Lina Dokuzović, »Lessons Learned: Struggles Against the Commodification of Knowledge, their Appropriation, Oppression and Knowledges of Dissent«. In: *creating worlds,* a web-journal of the *European Institute for Progressive Cultural Policies,* »an-academy«, December 2010; http://eipcp.net/transversal/1210/ dokuzovic/en

The examples of blockade in Europe, international uprising, transnational meetings and solidarity show a significant realignment of protest methodology. They show a struggle that transgresses national borders, expanding to question all of the spheres of life appropriated by capitalization and privatization. By including »demands, criticism and claims that go beyond the immediate context of education and universities, expanding to the identification of how the neoliberal capitalist market logic has infiltrated all parts of life,«[30] the global education protests proved to be transgressive—a crucial characteristic considering the transgressive character of the opposed system. However, this must include the protest movement itself. Therefore it is essential to be vigilant about all exclusionist strategies that are reproduced within the protests. Sexism and racism were not sufficiently attacked and led to some of the affected individuals breaking away from the protests.

Within the protests in Europe, it was alarming, for example, to see anti-Semitic stereotypes reproduced by a group of students from Weimar's Bauhaus University without being called out and contested by other protestors. Thousands of flyers of fake dollar bills were distributed, displaying a photo of Milton Friedman and a claim criticizing Bologna on the back, identifying a Jewish economist as the root of all evil, reproducing one of the most dangerous anti-Semitic myths about Jews and their economic dominance. As the only personified supplement for all possible claims against the commodification of knowledge, the banknote can be downloaded as a template to fill in *ANY* claim,[31] therefore *ANY* claim criticizing the commodification of knowledge is supplemented with ›the Jew‹ as the universal scapegoat. It is also remarkable that this action came from a university just ten kilometres away from the Buchenwald concentration camp. It is the same university which received public attention for censoring an art project dealing with the Shoah,[32] while concealing its own cruel history of anti-Semitism.[33]

Translocal struggle against the perpetuation of the nation-state

No matter what the protestors intended, the reproduction of sexist, racist, anti-Semitic and other exclusionist elements must be critically confronted with uncompromising rejection regardless of any wrongly intended restric-

---

30 Lina Dokuzović and Eduard Freudmann, »Squatting the Crisis: On the Current Protests in Education and Perspectives on Radical Change«, *European Institute for Progressive Cultural Policies*, Vienna, 11/2009; http://eipcp.net/n/1260352849

31 http://m18.uni-weimar.de/protest/uploads/BildungsgutscheinA4.pdf

32 See Ronen Eidelman, »The Neues Museum saga«, http://medinatweimar.org/2008/06/15/the-neues-museum-saga/

33 See the »history« section of the university's website: http://www.uni-weimar.de/cms/index.php?id=3886&L=1

tive thoughts, supposedly done »for the sake of the protests«. As increasing levels of oppression are the response to resistance, protestors cannot accept a reproduction of such ideologies within their articulated demands and actions. In a fight against the commodification of education, its subservience to capital and colonial strategies, and education's role as reproductive machinery, the link between capitalization and nationalization—supranational or transnational—must be observed and fought against as well. Transnationality has the danger of accepting, perpetuating and reproducing the logic of the nation-state. The expansion to transnational struggle and transnational networking of protests is key, but perhaps this is the moment to envision a *new vocabulary* of worldwide resistance.

This broader interlinkage of local implications of oppression and struggle describes what Subhabrata Bobby Banerjee terms ›translocality‹ as »[...] local communities living in democratic societies that are engaged in conflicts with both the state and the market, and sometimes even with ›civil society‹, while also making connections with other resistance movements in different parts of the world,« continuing with:

»The ultimate challenge of a theory of translocal resistance is to conceive the inconceivable: an extension of the democratic that transcends nation-state sovereignty, perhaps even transcends citizenship,« because »the nation-state then is a fundamental building block of globalization, in the working of transnational corporations, in the setting-up of a global financial system, in the institution of policies that determine the mobility of labour, and in the creation of the multi-state institutions such as the UN, IMF, World Bank, NAFTA and WTO. [...] So the translocal emerges at the intersection of political society and civil society where groups of people comprising the political society in different parts of the globe are fighting similar battles over resources against market and state actors« (Banerjee 2009).

Struggle and solidarity must not only take place within and across the centres, uniting the nations of Europe or states of the USA. The conditions of the centre are both connected to and complicit in the conditions of oppression worldwide, therefore, solidarity and struggle must extend to, for example, the struggles in non-Christian nations, the manifold protests taking place throughout the Global South, and zones subjugated to erasure. The protest cannot legitimize that erasure! Such zones receive brutal sanctions against the movement of people, the very movement necessary for transnational union.

This is where translocality comes into play. It is an international mode of struggle which simultaneously resists the links between capital and nation-state, which does not acknowledge the privilege of those within the centre, and does not reproduce the colonial ideology of salvation through education or the complex structures composing the knowledge economy. It takes the understanding of one's own involvement in global processes into actions of resistance. This model must be considered in future summits and meetings, in order to expand future protests beyond the centre, to establish exchange and collaboration on a translocal level with resistant forces across all regions, extending and challenging the regime of fortified knowledge.

BIBLIOGRAPHY

Banerjee, Subhabrata Bobby (2009): »Histories of Oppression and Voices of Resistance: Towards a Theory of the Translocal«. *Reartikulacija* 9, Ljubljana, 2009, http://www.reartikulacija.org/?p=612

Mbembe, Achille (2003): »Necropolitics«. *Public Culture* 15(1), winter 2003, p. 11–40.

Rosenzweig, Ben (2010): »International Student Struggles, Transnational Economies, Guest Consumers and Processes of Restructuring«. *Mutiny* 48, 2010, http://jura.org.au/files/jura/Mutiny%2048%20WebV3.pdf

Disrupting the Visual Paradigm

AMILA SIRBEGOVIC

In the Bevo Area, South City in St. Louis, a Bosnian community in search of its own post-Yugoslav identity has quietly contributed to this city's renewal. St. Louis is the second largest city in the US State of Missouri and has an estimated population of over 350,000. It is the principal municipality of Greater St. Louis, population 2,800,000, the largest urban area in Missouri, the fourth largest urban area in the Midwest, and the fifteenth largest in the United States.[1] Like many other US cities, St. Louis was formed by migration, especially in the late nineteenth and twentieth centuries by immigrants from Germany, Ireland and Italy. They helped to shape the cuisine, religious expression, music and architecture of the city.[2] In 1993 a new major wave of immigration from Europe began. These immigrants were war refugees from Bosnia and Herzegovina, who almost immediately started reshaping the city by creating better living conditions for themselves.

This article provides insight into the current situation in this particular mid-city, questions the impact of positive discrimination and racism on its development and shows how a post-9/11 minaret is impacting on the homogeneity of this area. Going forward and backward along the immigration and geographical time line‹[3] I compare three different urban areas, each of them renewed by local immigrants but also directly and indirectly connected through historical and immigration events. Highlighting the potential of the latest developments helps to explain these events and to find answers to the following questions: Considering current political developments in Europe

---

1   US Census Bureau 2009, http://quickfacts.census.gov/qfd/states/29/29510.html
2   Wikipedia, http://en.wikipedia.org/wiki/St._Louis,_Missouri [accessed 15 February 2011].
3   In order to understand migration development in Vienna, Austria, I tracked migration back to the former Yugoslavia, to Bosnia and Herzegovina. There I found on the one hand a vivid Chinese community and on the other hand rumors about a successful Bosnian community in St. Louis, USA. By following these ›tracks‹, a new space connected through migration was created.

such as the ban on minarets in Switzerland or the rise of right-wing parties with anti-immigration and islamophobic platforms in the Netherlands or Austria, what can we learn from an immigration country such as the USA that traditionally cultivates religious freedom? Or rather, is there anything that we can learn from »American society, which continues to appreciate whiteness?« (Matsuo 2004).

My research is focused on the *visible phenomena* of the transnational way of life of migrants, such as the social construction of transnational space and its connections and possible relations to the constructed environment. The transnational migration practice changes urban areas and leads to neighbourhood development without involving city planners. The essay focuses on active, self-organized participation and mostly informal networks in the urban quarters of migrants from Bosnia and migrants in Bosnia, concentrating on three cities in particular: Sarajevo (BiH), Vienna (Aut) and St. Louis (USA). In order to understand migration and its phenomena, this research has to be conceived beyond national state borders.[4] Migrants do not live in two different worlds; instead, through their transnational lifestyles, they create another space that they themselves define, limit and expand. According to Daniela Ahrens (2001) these transnational spaces are not only the sum of different locations in different countries; they are characterized by the »stacking of different social spaces over several surface areas« (Ahrens 2001: 148).

Living and working in exile in London, Duska Zagorac, director of the documentary *Patria Mia* (2008), made a movie about the growing Chinese community in Bosnia and Herzegovina. She came to realize that these people are a mirror image of her own migration and the dislocation of Bosnian people.

»The role of emigrants [and immigrants] is important in a sense of defining the identity of a country, which functions as an almost imaginary picture of those who have left and as a space for struggling for survival of those who have stayed or returned«.[5]

The documentary *Patria Mia*, which invited artists to create works on the lost identity of Bosnia and Herzegovina, grew out of this project. One of the issues was that these artists live all over the world while they »are the citi-

---

4   »... concepts such as transnationalism—and transnational spaces, fields and formations—refer to process that transcend international borders and therefore appear to describe more abstract phenomena in a social science language. By transnational space we mean relatively stable, lasting and dense sets of ties reaching beyond and across borders of sovereign states« (Bauböck/Faist 2010: 13).

5   See: »Bosnia and Herzegovina—Searching for Lost Identity« 2008, http://www.pro.ba/en/bosna-i-hercegovina-u-potrazi-za-izgubljenim-identitetom-bosnia-and-herzegovina-searching-for-lost-identity/

zens of this country, no matter where they live«.[6] My own constantly shifting migrant identity, personal experiences, and self-reflection are an integral and important part of my work. This research concentrates on issues that are interrelated. What I do is to comprehend migration from different point of views. I take on different roles, switching from me as an architect to me as a researcher and also to me as a migrant. As a migrant, reshaping one's own environment is part of the search for one's own identity. In particular, the second and third generations of migrants are creating a new, hybrid draft of their own lives, made of different elements and assembled together, where their own history of migration needs to be rethought. Erol Yildiz talks of ›postmigration‹, which is a new way of understanding the processes and projective past of migration (Yildiz 2009: 12).

The international movement of people affects and changes space, recreating, redefining and reshaping it and every individual involved. Migration simultaneously recreates the new seized space and the space left behind. Migration results in the creation of a new, vibrant, ever-changing identity for individuals as well as for cities embedded into the newly created transnational space.

How is the constructed environment modified by this transnationalism? How can architectural practice react to this ›socially dense‹ space? Could or should it be transformed by planners and how can we visualize its qualities? Can immigration be seen as a tool for reshaping the city, opening up new possibilities and visualizing the unplanned, inconceivable and unregulated city?

URBAN QUARTERS—SOMEWHERE IN THE MID-CITY

Working migrants (*Gastarbeiter*) who immigrated to Western Europe in the early 1960s settled mostly for economic reasons in the so-called ›mid-city‹ (Sieverts 2008: 14). According to Sieverts, the ›mid-city‹ lies between »the single, special place as a geographical-historical event and the everywhere similar establishments of the world's economic division of labour« (Sieverts 2008: 14). These districts are a result of the historical development of cities in Europe in the industrial nineteenth century. They are mostly former working class quarters, forgotten and neglected by urban planning for decades and now rediscovered, redefined and redesigned by migrants. It is precisely these parts of cities—wrongly labeled by populists and the media as ›ghettos‹, dangerous and parallel societies—that have a potential for lively urban development. Teddy Cruz sees in the US mid-city a potential for ›critical

---

6   See ibid.

engagement‹[7] with the prevailing architectural practice. Urban life with all its processes happens there (Cruz 2004).

The area around Ottakringer Straße in Vienna, the boundary between the sixteenth and seventeenth districts, is a former suburban workers' area, with a high density of buildings from the period of promoterism and a lack of green areas and public space. More than 25 per cent of residents of the sixteenth and seventeenth Viennese districts are not Austrian citizens.[8] Here is where I started my research on the potential for urban development and other visible phenomena of migration inside the European Union. A comparison with other political systems (regarding migration issues) was crucial, especially with a country on the border of the EU and an immigration country with an official immigration history such as the USA (in contrast to Austria, whose politicians still don't dare to proclaim officially that it is an immigration country). Therefore, I have expanded my research to Sarajevo in Bosnia and Herzegovina on the border of the EU and St. Louis in the classic immigration country USA in order to explore the causes and effects of the global issue of migration from different points of view.

(Un)planned urban renewal by Bosnian immigrants in St. Louis—Bevo Area/South City

The area around the Bevo Mill in the South City of St. Louis is a part of the city that has been changed and ›renewed‹ in the last two decades by immigrants from Bosnia and Herzegovina in particular. The first immigrants from Bosnia and Herzegovina came in 1993. The International Organization for Migration (IOM) organized and managed the immigration of 13 families (Matsuo 2004). An estimated 50,000 to 70,000 people from Bosnia and Herzegovina now live in and around St. Louis. Some of them came directly from Bosnia and Herzegovina; others arrived from Germany in the late 1990s when they had to leave because their ›Duldungsvisa‹[9] had expired. Most of them came from other parts of the United States because they expected better opportunities for a new beginning here, and they indeed found better conditions. How did these ›better conditions‹ come about?

In the early 1990s, the area around Bevo Mill was abandoned and left to deteriorate. The majority of buildings were vacant and had boarded-up ground floors. According to the current residents of South City, the area was

---

7   »[...] instead, the most experimental work in housing in the United States is in the hands of progressive, community-based, non-profit organizations, as well as small communities across the continent. These engage the social dynamics of unique neighbourhoods daily, mediating their histories and identities and the planning policies that shape their destiny« (Cruz 2004).

8   Magistrat der Stadt Wien, MA 17—Integrations- und Diversitätsangelegenheiten (2007): *MigrantInnen in Wien 2007—Daten, Fakten, Recht*, info sheet, p. 7.

9   *Duldung* (German) = acquiescence (English)

characterized by low rents and poor or non-existent infrastructure. At first, Bosnian migrants rented the houses and stores; later on they started buying, restoring and selling them. Because they were given the opportunity to obtain loans from the local bank without the usual required bank history, new possibilities opened up that allowed this development to occur. The trust of the mayor made this possible. Today, you can safely walk the streets where small cafes, restaurants and supermarkets are very popular. These changes were not backed up by local city planners but were initiated by the people themselves as bottom-up renewal. Beside gastronomy services, a Bosnian Chamber of Commerce, a newspaper editorial office of a Bosnian diaspora newspaper and lawyers are also located in the Bevo Area. The existence of these services demonstrates their transnational identity, which continues to unfold.

Figure 11.1: A postcard of the Islamic Community Center in St. Louis showing the minaret (built in 2002) beside the well-known Arch

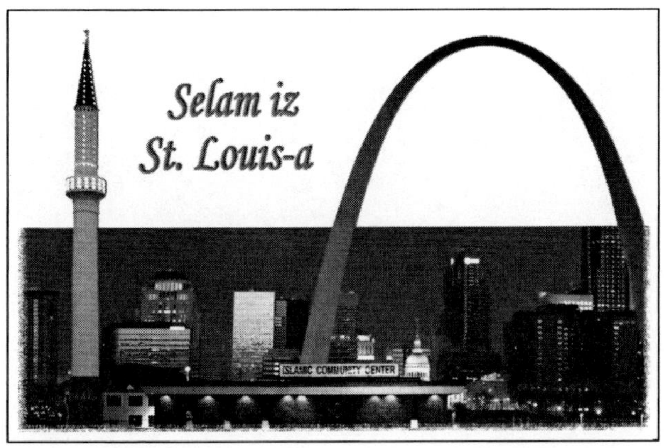

Source: author's archive

»Although many Bosnians experienced occupational downward mobility, an economic boom in St. Louis coupled with Bosnians' strong family ties have created an opportunity to capitalize on family human resources. A large ethnic enclave also provides an information network, through which Bosnians seek educational and financial upward mobility for their children. Although many Bosnian refugees in St. Louis are Muslims, they have never experienced prejudice and discrimination, unlike Middle Eastern Muslims. Being Europeans and also secular Muslims have reinforced each other, rendering Bosnians racially ›invisible‹ in American society, which continues to appreciate whiteness« (Matsuo 2004).

In 2002 an Ottoman-style minaret was built beside the Islamic community centre. This empty former bank office building was bought by the community centre and restored as a house of prayer. In spite of a small protest, good relations to the mayor and confidence on both sides have enabled the construction of the minaret, which can be found at most Bosnian mosques. I see this minaret as fulfilling two functions: First, it disrupts the visuality of this typical American mid-city, providing an element of surprise situated between townhouses and a shopping mall. Second, it is an embodiment of lived and acknowledged transnational identity.

Erol Yildiz (Yildiz 2009: 9) sees the difficulties in understanding migrational processes in the fact that in Europe racism still must be dealt with ›as everyday normality‹ (based on Foucault's hegemony-dispositive, 1978) and it seems at first glance as if this is not the case in an immigration country like the USA. The paradox is that the same problem must be dealt with here, except that everyday racism points in another direction. In the case of immigrants from Bosnia and Herzegovina, it functions as ›positive discrimination‹.

Figure 11.2: Europa Market, one of the first Bosnian supply stores in the Bevo Area of St. Louis, opened in 1993

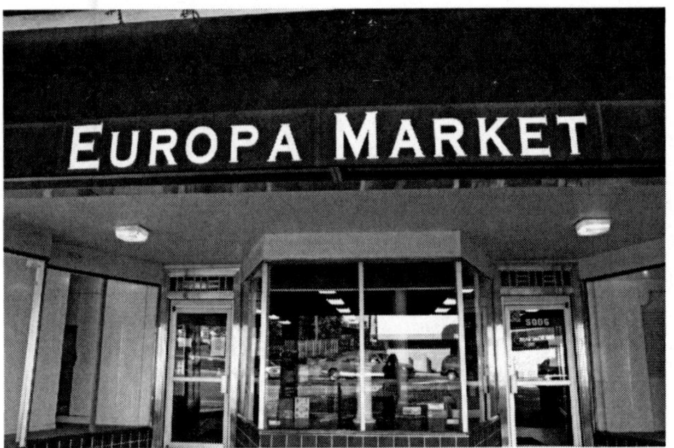

Photo: author

As white Europeans, they don't stand out individually. Because of the prevailing non-white racism, they receive preferential treatment when searching for a job and an apartment. Since this increases opportunities in American society enormously, it also increases their impact on the city and the visibility of the changes in the city.

Chinese shopping area on the outskirts of Sarajevo—Rajlovac

Fifteen years after the end of the war, Bosnia and Herzegovina is still a country in transition. Corrupt and politically unstable, it is affected by the politics of former war enemies. A country bordering the EU, Bosnia is making an effort to stabilize politically and economically in order to join the EU.

As a member of the Stability Pact for South Eastern Europe, the country is taking part in the stabilization of the region, working together with the EU and other Balkan countries where Stabilization and Association Agreements (SAA)[10] are being made. Regulated and thought out migration policies and legislation on migration issues are only fragmentary and are determined by these agreements. The country continues to work on regulating its own political system, transitioning from the former communist system and recovering from the consequences of the war in the 1990s. At the same time, it borders the EU and is therefore forced to deal with the migration policies of the EU.

According to unofficial numbers, about 10,000 to 12,000 migrants from China live in Bosnia and Herzegovina. They have student, work or tourist visas, but their period of residency is limited and they don't have a settlement permit. The development of Chinese migration to the countries of the former Yugoslavia is directly related to the EU and its expansion. After the fall of the Iron Curtain in 1989, Chinese migrants settled in Hungary, mostly in Budapest. With Hungary's candidacy to the EU, the visa regime was intensified. As a consequence, many Chinese left and settled in Serbia in the mid-1990s. During the NATO intervention in 1999, many of them left Serbia and settled in Bosnia and Herzegovina and Croatia.

Figure 11.3: Kineska prodavnica, Chinese store, warehouse and residence in Rajlovac, Sarajevo

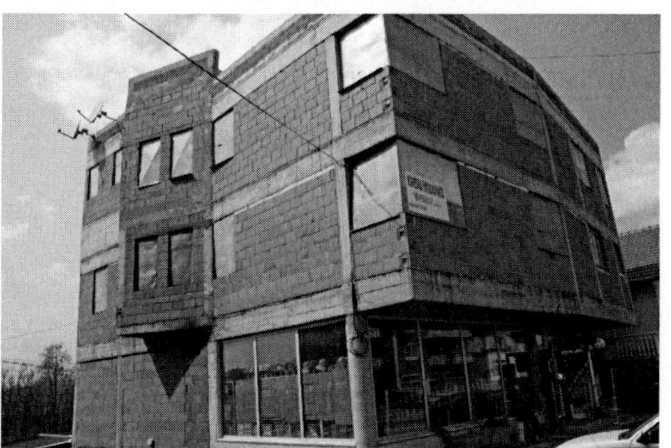

Photo: author

Rajlovac is located in northeast Sarajevo at one of the main entrances to the city. The main street is full of Chinese shops with red Chinese lanterns hanging above the shop entrances. During the war, this area was the line separating the two different sides. After the war, it was dominated by de-

---

10 See: http://europa.eu/legislation_summaries/enlargement/western_balkans/index _en.htm

stroyed and demolished houses. Most of the former house owners left during the war and didn't return. As a result, these houses remained empty and were left to deteriorate. Today there are newly built three and four story buildings with large parking lots in the front. The ground floors are usually used for shops selling cheap products from China; the windows of other levels are usually boarded up on the street side and the space is used for storage. Satellite antennas and clothes drying in the backyards give away that these houses are multifunctional and also used for living. Located on the outskirts of Sarajevo, Rajlovac is also a ›mid-city‹ as defined by Teddy Cruz and Thomas Sieverts. According to the UNHCR, 800,000 people were displaced in 1998 within Bosnia and Herzegovina,[11] and over 100,000 people are still displaced in 2010.[12] Only in devastated areas like these migrants from the outside could settle down. Here they also had more possibilities for adjusting the space to meet their needs. Simultaneously, an urban quarter is being revitalized by migrants without architects and urban planning. The public space in front of the shops is being occupied and used depending on individual needs with the result that the limits between private and public are blurring. The shopkeepers and distributors and their families play cards inside and outside the shops, drink coffee, eat, study and sell their goods. There is no clear arrangement of functions either on the ground floor or in the vertical space. Where does the business start, where does the storage end and where does the private living space begin? As expressed by Teddy Cruz, this is an example of »three-dimensional zoning, based not on adjacencies but on juxtaposition, as dormant infrastructures are transformed into usable spaces« (Cruz 2004).

Ex-Yugoslav neighbourhood with cafes and other places to go out in Vienna—Ottakringer Straße

At the border between the sixteenth and seventeenth Viennese districts on Ottakringer Straße, migrants from the former Yugoslavia have created a lively area with cafes and other places to go out that has a Mediterranean flair. While former commercial streets have gone to rack and ruin and empty shops have become a common sight in streets in Vienna and across Europe, the exact opposite is the case on Ottakringer Straße. Small, medium and large businesses run mostly by migrants supply residents during the day. In the evening, this street is transformed into an area where the second and third generations—young people whose parents and grandparents were working migrants and war refugees in the 1990s—go out.

---

11 Migration-Info.de, »Migration und Bevölkerung 1998«, *Newsletter* 06, July-August 1998, http://www.migration-info.de/mub_artikel.php?Id=980608

12 UNHCR 2010, »2011 UNHCR country operations profile—Bosnia and Herzegovina«. http://www.unhcr.org/cgi-bin/texis/vtx/page?page=49e48d766

During the 2008 European Football Championship, the city of Vienna organized public viewings of all games in the inner city. These places were among the most secure public spaces in Europe for two weeks during the championship. Visitors were checked when entering these areas, and their movements were regulated and limited. At the same time, local cafe owners on Ottakringer Straße spontaneously organized unofficial ›public viewings‹. At first, visitors could watch the games inside cafes and celebrate in front of the cafes. Visitors spontaneously seized the public space for themselves so that police were forced to close the streets to traffic for fear of security problems. As more and more people started coming to Ottakringer Straße to watch the games, cafe owners reacted by putting their TV screens in the cafe windows. At the beginning, these ›public viewings‹ were meant for the regular customers of these cafes, but very soon people from all around gathered to watch these games together, independent of community, migration background and age. For two weeks, a new space opened up, showing all the possible uses of public space, sidewalks, facades and streets. This spontaneity caused further actions such as the projection of games on makeshift structures. This unordered situation made the integration of different social classes and generations visible. Migrants stopped being observed as ›them‹ and were suddenly accepted by the local media, who turned the ›most dangerous‹[13] street in Vienna into the ›Croatian football mile‹.

TRANSMIGRATION

Beside their unique historical development, there are other similarities between urban quarters in St. Louis, Sarajevo and Vienna. One of the most important ones is the transnational identity and lifestyle of their residents that first of all assures their existential survival and additionally contributes to urban regeneration and to an improvement in the quality of life for all residents. Given different opportunities, the new residents—the immigrants—can contribute to the society and thus help influence, shape and reshape it. While the former working migrants in Vienna are still impacted by the ›policy of rigid motion‹[14] (Holert/Terkessidis 2006: 46) and are sometimes still considered to be ›guests‹, Bosnian immigrants in the US can de-

---

13 Ottakringer Straße is often demonized by the local media as one of the most dangerous street in Vienna.

14 The ›paradox of rigid motion‹ was already created within the *Gastarbeitersystem*. The fiction that the workers would return someday was kept alive in all countries of immigration for a long time by both sides, by the state and by the migrants. This created a population that lived here and there, which was both present and absent. Under these difficult conditions the migrants created something new: they spanned their own territory, a networked, transnational space (Holert/Terkessidis, 2006: 46).

velop their transnational identity as part of the community. According to Karakayali and Tsianos the transnational social space exists in a conflictual relation to the integration paradigm and its practical implications. By responding to the conditions of the nation state space, migrants transform the regulatory and integration efforts of immigration countries into their own ›clandestine‹ form of migration, thereby creating a ›drifting‹ social space (Karakayali/Tsianos 2007: 10). The common trait uniting all three sites whose migration practices were researched is the active ›responding to conditions by ›disrupting‹. In the example of Ottakringer Straße, it is the practice of informal networks that disrupts public space. In Rajlovac, it is the appropriation of housing units and the usual arrangement of functions that is a disrupting migration practice. In St. Louis, it is the cooperation between the community and the city administration that disrupts the visuality of this mid-city. However, it is not architectural practice acting here, although the areas affected are part of it. Migration practice bears a potential for renewal because unlike architecture, it occurs out of a state of exception, it is uprooted and eventually more dynamic.

BIBLIOGRAPHY

Ahrens, Daniela (2001): *Grenzen der Enträumlichung. Weltstädte, Cyberspace und transnationale Räume in der globalisierten Moderne*, Opladen: Leske + Budrich.

Bauböck, Rainer/Faist, Thomas (2010): *Diaspora and Transnationalism: Concepts, Theories and Methods*, Amsterdam: Amsterdam University Press.

Cruz, Teddy (2004): »Border Postcards: Chronicles from the Edge«, http://www.cca.qc.ca/en/education-events/259-teddy-cruz-border-postcards-chronicles-from-the-edge

Holert, Tom/Terkessidis, Mark (2006): *Fliehkraft: Gesellschaft in Bewegung – Von Migranten und Touristen*, Köln: Kiepenheuer & Witsch.

Karakayali, Serhat/Tsianos, Vassilis (2007): »Movements that Matter. Eine Einleitung«. In: Transit Migration Forschungsgruppe (eds.), *Turbulente Ränder*, Bielefeld: transcript, p. 7–17.

Matsuop, Hisako (2004): »Bosnian Refugee Resettlement in St. Louis, Missouri«. In: Peter Waxman and Val Colic-Peisker (eds.), *Homeland Wanted: Interdisciplinary Perspectives on Refugee Resettlement in the West*, Hauppauge: Nova Science Publishers.

Sieverts, Thomas (2008): *Zwischenstadt. Zwischen Ort und Welt, Raum und Zeit, Stadt und Land*, Basel: Birkhäuser.

Yildiz, Erol (2009): »Von der Hegemonie zur Diversität. Ein neuer Blick auf die Migrationsgesellschaft«. *dérive*, Zeitschrift für Stadtforschung, 37, p. 8–13.

Space Complicities

Towards Strategies of Inhabiting Exception,
Wars and Parks

KARIN REISINGER

>Before maps the world was limitless.«
(Abdulrazak Gurnah 2001: 35)

*Figure 12.1: Idyllic landscapes in Eifel National Park,
April 2010*

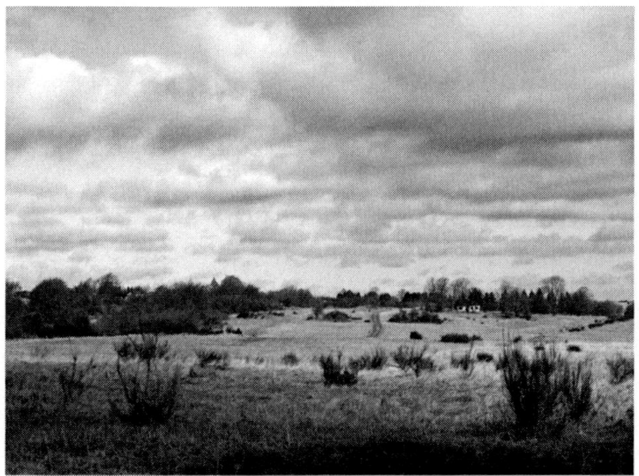

Photo: author

In order to contemplate politics of current space complicities, I will look at a
wide range of material. After considering idyllic parks and their inherent
violence I progress to the strategies of the literary figure, Bartleby the Scrivener, and his impact on the theories of Giorgio Agamben and Gilles
Deleuze, returning to an understanding of specific current space complicities

emerging from inhabiting exception. For these complicities I use the example of national parks, because the concept is being adopted steadily throughout the world and leads to a remarkable inhabiting based on various cultural surroundings. When you research national parks online, at first you only see proud tourists' photos, but then you come across a map, a picture of national parks as they are located around the world.

Figure 12.2: Sketch of national parks greater than approx. 1,000 square kilometres

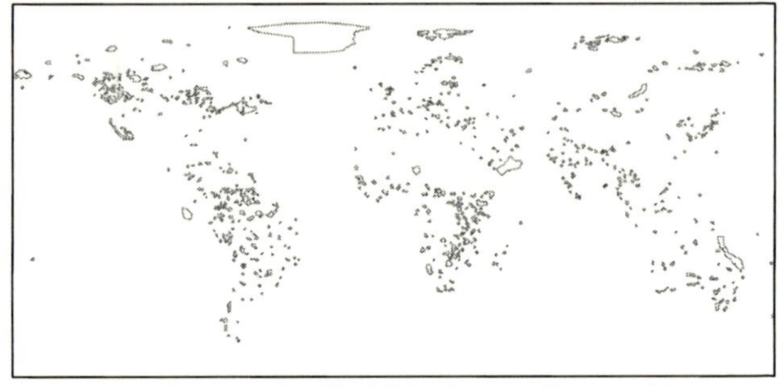

Map: author, based on the World Database on Protected Areas (http://www.wdpa.org/WDPAMapFlex.aspx), September 2010

The number of national parks is steadily increasing, so the map is only a snapshot. It shows global connections from the professional perspective of the cartographer and the archive. The basis of the map is the *World Database on Protected Areas;* »a foundation dataset for conservation decision making«[1] is how the organization describes itself. The parks are connected through the IUCN (International Union for Conservation of Nature and Natural Resources),[2] the headquarters of which is in Switzerland. It is the world's oldest and largest global environmental network with more than 1,000 governments and NGO members. In light of these spatial similarities of exceptions there are clear separations of who is serving, who is served and who is able or allowed to enter, and who remains outside the doors. These divisions are mainly determined by the logistics of resorts for Western tourists with all the service requirements: food, accommodation and the fulfilment of the desire for nature and adventure. But in addition to background organizations and divisions, space has to fulfil the requirements of idyllic pictures for tourists' photos, videos, archives and films:[3] the picture

---

1   http://www.wdpa.org/

2   http://www.iucn.org/

3   According to *The Internet Movie Database* (http://www.imdb.com/) movies that play in national parks include: Karl May films (Plitvice Lakes National park, Croatia), *Crocodile Dundee* (Kakadu National Park, Australia), *Lord of the Rings* (New Zealand's national parks) and *Indiana Jones* (Arches National Park, USA).

of an innocent and idyllic space that has always been there and will stay in its specific *natural* form.

BECOMING[4] PARKS

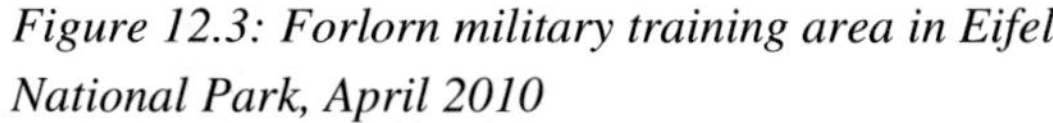

Figure 12.3: Forlorn military training area in Eifel National Park, April 2010

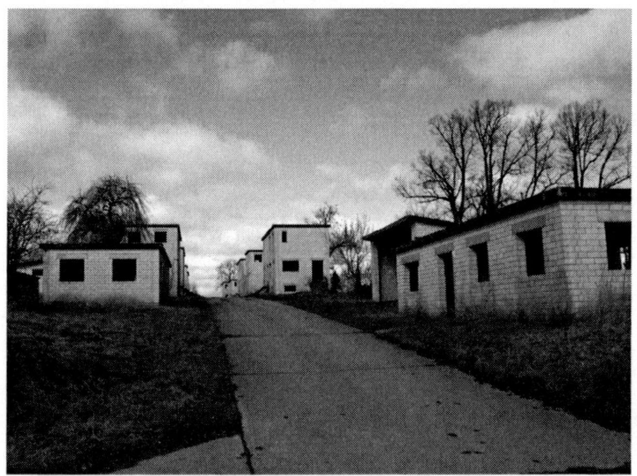

Photo: author

One specific case is Nationalpark Eifel with a size of 110 square kilometres.[5] It was opened in 2004 after a Nazi elite school, Ordensburg Vogelsang, had operated there in the 1930s, followed by a British take-over and a long period of use by the Belgian military for their field exercises. The area was called camp Vogelsang and restricted for locals—except for the open house events organized by the Belgians (Heinen 2007). Of all functions, specifically military uses have created the foundation for enormous nature preservation areas. This use of space seems ideal to be appropriated by natural conservation; both share a common typology, but this is not the only reason. In Nationalpark Eifel for example, the red deer stock—one of the most important arguments for turning the area into a national park—was connected to military field exercise, so that following these exercises and the military, a substantial part of the red deer stock migrated along with the Belgian army across national borders.[6] For the animals, tourism turned out to be more invasive than the military. Another national park that has under-

---

4 *Becoming* refers to Deleuze' becoming of animals and men of war. (Deleuze/ Guattari 2004: 256–292).

5 http://www.nationalpark-eifel.de/

6 According to an employee of the national park forest management.

gone radical transition is Gorongosa National Park in Mozambique with a size of about 4,000 square kilometres. Between 1920 and 1940 the area was a hunting reserve for visitors and politicians. During this time Jose Ferreira lived in a thatched hut in the park and worked as a first guide. By 1940, a tourist centre was built near the Mussicadzi River, but it was soon washed away by a flood. In 1951 Chitengo Camp was opened to tourists, and by the end of the 1950s, 6,000 tourists per year visited the camp. The national park was established during Portuguese colonialism in 1960 as a resort for European tourists, who arrived in the next city, Beira, where direct flights from Britain were planned. By the late 1960s the camp had grown into a small town. In the restaurant 400 meals were served a day. After these *Golden Years* in the language of colonialism, when Mozambique was on its way to independence, civil war broke out and continued until 1992.[7] During the latter phase of the war, the national park was occupied as headquarters of the military camp of the RENAMO (Mozambican National Resistance)[8]. From 1982 on, the national park was an area of conflict; the infrastructure of the park and vast parts of the animal population were destroyed. In 2008 the park was reopened.[9] A tourist guide writes that the employees of the overcrowded camp seem unmotivated (Hupe/Vachal 2006: 218).

BECOMING EXCEPTION

To understand what is going on spatially I would like to look at national parks using the theories of Giorgio Agamben's *State of Exception*.[10] The organization and genealogies are especially important to understand national parks and further similarities as *sites of exception*, the spatial product of a specific history and (in)globality, a situation of connectivity and disconnectivity. The understanding has emerged from reflections on camps and other inclusions, also in National Socialism. Some connections are extremely helpful to understand the whole process of how the spatial apparatus of exception works and what possibilities local actors have in order to inhabit or even deconstruct the closed-ness and finished-ness of such strong exceptions. These are the questions that I want to apply to some specific national parks, the gardens of Western society. The concept of the national park emerged from the late colonization of North America in the nineteenth century. An important figure in the development of the concept is Frederick

---

7   http://www.gorongosa.net

8   http://www.kkmosambik.de

9   http://www.gorongosa.net

10   If not otherwise cited, I refer to *Homo Sacer* (1998b) and *State of Exception* (2005). Both books are closely intertwined concerning the notion of exception.

Law Olmsted.[11] His involvement in the process was motivated by his personal life circumstances and by green spaces overseas, such as parks in Paris and London, which were opened to the public after having being the preserve of royalty for centuries. He was particularly impressed by Victoria Park in London and Birkenhead Park in Liverpool, which, from his perspective, were »entirely, unreservedly, and forever the people's own« (see Heacox 2001: 118). The idea of the common became very important in the development. But how common are national parks today? Another important factor in the motivation was a personal crisis: Olmstead was diagnosed with an enlarged heart and found nature to be healing (Heacox 2001: 118–122). A crisis makes great changes possible by necessity. What sounds like a platitude is a process towards radical decisions: »The concept of necessity is an entirely subjective one, relative to the aim that one wants to achieve,« Agamben writes and ends with Balladore-Pallieri: »For this reason, the principle of necessity is, in every case, always a revolutionary principle« (see Agamben 2005: 30).[12]

When looking at national parks, we should consider the influence of crises in nature and health. As situations of uncertainty and instability, crises lead to heated conflicts, resolved by extreme decisions.[13] The simultaneous occurrence of financial crises and crises in nature, such as environmental and natural disasters, definitely has an impact on the production of space. This *intersection of crises and emergencies* influences the production of architecture and regional planning by speeding up the decision processes, making them even more unpredictable and opaque. The IUCN, for example, combines NGOs and governments and due to natural crises, it decides on large segments of the world's landscapes. A second anchor between these specific spaces and sites of exceptions is the notion of nation. National parks have become transnational, but remain a strong identification point present in the mere denotation as *national* (park). Referring to the nation, every single country is proud of its *own* national parks although the concept includes foreign influences—even in the United States. The notion is like an identification label that is applied to every single example. And at the same time, a suspension of several national surrounding factors must be taken into consideration: special laws apply; tourists from the entire world come specifically to these places and special organizations like the National Geographic and the IUCN interact closely but not in terms of nationality, rather of transnationality. This ambivalent set of connections is instrumentalized to sustain nations. The suspension of law and replacement by an ›Environmental

---

11 The creator of New York City's Central Park and other parks, opponent of slavery, co-founder of *The Nation* magazine, chaired the first Yosemite Park Commission from 1864 to 1890.

12 Agamben quotes Giorgio Balladore-Pallieri (1970), *Diritto Costituzionale*, Milan: Giuffrè, p. 168.

13 On decisions: see also Agamben 2005: 30.

Law‹[14] produces new spaces in order to reconstitute a natural state of environment under the claim of a crises, the emergency of saving nature. Agamben even calls the natural state a state of exception: »The state of nature is, in truth, a state of exception, in which the city appears for an instant [...] *tanquam dissoluta*« (see Agamben 1998b: 118). Therefore clear borders emerged to sustain an apparatus of *including exclusion* (Agamben 1998b: 17–19). In national parks, it is explicitly defined who is allowed to get in and who not and in what function.[15] This clarity is a further step to the maintenance of closed-ness and finished-ness. Sites of exceptions are not only dependent on their naturalness, but also on the idea or at least the camouflage of remaining the way they are forever, in terms of set borders and temporal finished-ness. The same applies to the definition of restricted sites: wilderness zones, completely left to nature are the highest category of environmental protection. Often they are parts of national parks that people are only allowed to enter with very rare permission. *The World Without Us* is a successful (well-sold) vision from Alan Weisman (Weisman 2007), in which he imagines a world without humanity.[16] »We, humans, are reduced to a pure disembodied gaze observing our own absence.« (see Žižek 2008: 48) This is the maximum suspension of human inhabiting. As Agamben writes, suspension leads to *zones of undecideabilities* (Agamben 2005: 2–3), *zones of indistinction* (Agamben 2005: 26), which means, we have a corset of strict spatial perimeters, but the zone in-between is undefined. What is defined is what it is not—logic of negativism. The basic architecture is the typology of the camp (Agamben 1998b: 20, 153–180), but the whole concept of exception has the potential of a typology for different current spatial phenomena. They are transferable to different concepts of large-scale exceptions like tourist resorts and further camp-like structures. Not without mentioning *Homo Sacer,* Keller Easterling points out that the structure of the camp can be seen in many different innocent forms, like boats or golf courses (Easterling 2005: 14). Even Agamben considers nondescript sites like lobbies at airports or hotels (Agamben 1998b: 174) when reflecting on the *camp-and-more-typology.*

There is a contingency between exceptions, between solutions besides radical transitions, a contingency that transcends different space solutions. Therefore, I consider different genealogies of national parks like Gorongosa and Eifel in relation to their architectures: architecture organizes and makes possible the camp-like everyday life. In addition, I ask the question of how these formalities and functionalities can be appropriated, entered or used; anything that locals can do. How these static, predictable and authoritarian spaces can be inhabited or even de-territorialized? In this I consider a liter-

---

14 http://www.eli.org/

15 The different functions include, amongst others, service, tourism, science, site preservation and guidance.

16 http://www.youtube.com/watch?v=XJVQowigxFM

ary figure that is very basic for further works by Agamben on contingency, Herman Melville's *Bartleby the Scrivener*, a long, short story from 1853 (Melville 1985). It is important to look at the background of the story. First, it is set in a very specific time. In 1853 in North America, exploitation and changes of ownership structures are observable during the Gold Rush, westward expansions and the Civil War era. This period created a foundation for the genuinely American concept of the *pioneer*. The setting of the story involves the first urban agglomerations and ongoing land seizure in the West. Herman Melville's biography also offers informative background material (Delbanco 2007). His mobility was incredible and the flop of *Moby Dick* resulted in a personal crisis. In *Bartleby the Scrivener*, Melville described strategies of inhabiting North America in the nineteenth century. The complicity between him and his employer is essential in building a relationship and in deconstructing formal constraints at the same time. This complicity helps Bartleby claim space and remain without fulfilling formal tasks, thus changing functions of spaces. »I prefer not to« becomes a central phrase of negation in times of land seizure, maintaining specific conjunctures. I will try to illuminate pragmatic strategies along the way to this complicity using the plot. Bartleby did not make a great play of going to a lawyer's office and asking for a job as a copyist on Wall Street. Precisely because of his *normalcy*, his *un-particularity* he becomes interesting for the lawyer's office and is finally hired. He seems to be a perfect balance, contrary to his very oppositional and particular colleagues. At first Bartleby's work is tireless, silent, pale and mechanical. But suddenly, even surprisingly the formula »I would prefer not to« comes into play. First as a response to additional jobs like going to the post office, but soon it becomes a way of refusal for every job instruction (Melville 1985).

BARTLEBY'S SPACE OF COMPLICITY

Like a ghost Bartleby slinks into view of the lawyer. His invisibility is supported by very specific spatial circumstances. The rooms of the lawyer's office are divided into two parts by a folding glass door: one zone for the lawyer, one for the employees. The lawyer decides whether the door is open or closed. He places Bartleby in his own half of the office, in the corner beside the folding door, so as to have the silent man beside him. It is obvious who creates the spatial situation and who has the right to see. Bartleby's desk is put next to a small window, but there is a fire wall in front of it. The little amount of light comes from far above. And in addition, the lawyer is separated from Bartleby by a high green folding screen. So he is invisible to the lawyer, but he can be heard, hidden behind the innocent greenness of the wall. It does not only hide Bartleby, but also the lawyer, who wants to maintain community and privacy at the same time (Melville 1985, 16–17). Agamben sees the green folding screen encompassing a laboratory, where the experiment is prepared (Agamben 1998a: 46). This sensitive mode of uncertainty is necessary for the formula »I would prefer not to« to operate later on (Reisinger 2011: 133–134). In this spatial manifestation of power dynamics, Bartleby starts working very hard. The situation is already full of contradictions: a shared room, but a screen; a window, but without a view. This is why it is so surprising when Bartleby, in this situation of uncertainty that Melville has painted in detail, suddenly speaks up and refuses to work. He continues to react with indecision:

»In this very attitude did I sit when I called to him, rapidly stating what it was I wanted him to do—namely, to examine a small paper with me. Imagine my surprise, nay, may consternation, when, without moving from his privacy, Bartleby, in a singularly mild, firm voice, replied, ›I would prefer not to‹« (Melville 1985: 19).

To investigate the relationship between strategies and spaces of complicities I use two specific situations with two different examples. One is a spatial coexistence in Eifel National Park in Germany—more precisely, it lies within an exception of the national park—the swimming bath of Ordensburg Vogelsang, and the other one is a carefully arranged interior space of a provisional safari hut in Gorongosa National Park in Mozambique. These pictures describe two juxtapositions which have emerged from space complicities. They are the results of inhabiting exception. The orange plastic watch next to the largest well-preserved Nazi mosaic is a trace of taking over a specific space: *Within* Eifel National Park the National Socialist education camp, Vogelsang, was inhabited by the local sports and swimming association. They invested an enormous amount of free time and extra skills to appropriate this space.[17] The members of the association positioned the orange plastic watch—most likely from IKEA—next to the mosaic with a Catholic reference to walking on water. In official publications the scenery is shown in black and white (Herzog 2007: 74) or without the watch. In the other example, a comfortable interior in an apparently improvisational tourist hut in Gorongosa National Park is a further case of different interests. One fulfils the image of nature and asceticism on the outside; the inside reflects the needs of Western tourists.[18] Both examples show a high ambivalence inwardly.

INTO

According to Deleuze, what is inherent in Bartleby's formula is the function of a border (Deleuze 1994: 8). Because of its not-finished-ness (*I would prefer not to...* but *not to* what?) Bartleby is standing on a threshold between different possibilities: acting or not acting; *prefer* is a word that Bartleby's

---

17 http://www.schwimmbad-vogelsang.de/

18 http://www.naturalhighsafaris.com

colleagues call *queer*: »Oh, *prefer*? Oh yes—queer word. I never use it myself. But, sir, as I was saying, if he would but prefer—« (see Melville 1985: 40). The word *prefer* itself is not definitive. Grammatically the formula is not correct; it is an *anomaly, atypical* (Deleuze 1994: 8, 10) and names rather what it is not. Also, it is versatile and encroaches upon other people to survive, so it is not fixed to one body. It produces a *growing zone of indecisiveness, a zone of the undetermined* (Deleuze 1994: 14). Because of its lack

Figure 12.4: Video INTO *shows the way along the transition from the national park into an exception, Ordensburg Vogelsang, filmed April 2010*

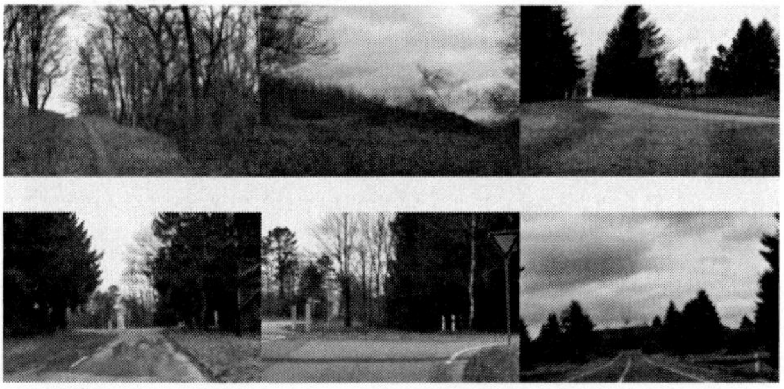

Video stills: author

of reference the formula becomes timeless and dislocated; it creates spaces without functions: it does not only empty language by decoupling words and things (Agamben 1998a: 36), words and action, but also decouples space and function and opens it for new functions. Bartleby, a fictional figure from the period of nineteenth century American settlements could also provide some important insight for the current migration, speaking with Kafka, Deleuze writes that Bartleby has no more ground than his two feet need (Deleuze 1994: 20)[19] and that he could operate the way he did in Melville's short story anywhere in the world; he is *momentary* (Deleuze 1994: 21). The decoupling of biography and site and the lack of rootedness make it possible to appropriate space, which would usually not be accessible. It develops a useful emptiness, a starting point for something new. Agamben even calls this process *decreation* (»Ent-Schöpfung«, see Agamben 1998a: 47–55). Bartleby is a scrivener, who refuses to write copy. When we consider that he works for a lawyer, his refusal of the copy can be interpreted as a denial of law (Agamben 1998a: 71). Law uses the logics of copying, transferabilities, but Bartleby uses logic of negativism, which is able to suspend and deconstruct predetermination of space. In consideration of current spatial manifestations, in which transnational and transcultural spaces are repeated at

---

19 Deleuze quotes Franz Kafka (1983), *Tagebücher 1910–1923*, Frankfurt/Main: Fischer, p. 18.

different locations in the same form—copied and pasted—the refusal of creating further copy gives hope. As the lawyer specializes in transferring real estate, Bartleby's refusal of work leads to a further consequence: the transfer of the possession of land and accumulation are undermined.

Politics of complicity

Deleuze focused on Bartleby's formula in a spatial, but also political way. He sees Bartleby from the perspective of a collective issue, a community of anarchist individuals, a political programme. Further on Deleuze writes that this programme is comparable to two different forms of class struggle: the universal immigration in America of the nineteenth century and the universal proletarization of Bolshevik Russia (Deleuze 1994: 48–50), and I argue that it is also valid in current complicities of global and local players. In *By the Sea,* Abuldrazak Gurnah refers to *Bartleby* in the story of a refugee from Zanzibar seeking asylum in Great Britain (Gurnah 2001). With the simplicity and clarity of those stories from everyday perspectives, we can see complicities more critically. Politics of usurping space open an understanding for the possibility of crossings and inhabiting of the closed-ness of exceptions, but at the same time, it is important to see sensitive states of uncertainty with all their masquerades critically, to risk a glance behind the high green folding screen and consider the possibility at the same time. Bartleby's ›ascetic land of milk and honey‹ (Agamben 1998a: 43–44) has cancelled the logic of reason and underlies the will of a *Homo Tantum* (Deleuze 1994: 50). This state of uncertainty, caused by preferring, leads to sensitive complicities, whose enduring is not warranted (Reisinger 2011: 135). Because of unclear requirements they find themselves in steady changes, a steady process of becoming. In the set of connective geographies of national parks and further exceptions, I followed constructed as well as lived complicities by considering genealogies, logistics and risks of examples that emerge in a liaison of exception and lines of de-territorialization, regulation and deregulation.

Aporia: professionalization of resistance

»I never feel so private as when I know you are here,« (Melville 1985: 51) the lawyer thinks while Bartleby stands silently and stiffly in the middle of the room. The lawyer has come to an arrangement, but what disturbs this arrangement is professionalism. The lawyer's clients and colleagues wonder about the peculiar man who does not work. Eventually Bartleby has a negative influence on business in the lawyer's office. If visitors speak to Bartleby, sometimes he does not even react; the lawyer is afraid of disreputability (Melville 1985: 52).

»›The time has come; you must quit this place; I am sorry for you; here is money, but you must go.‹

›I would prefer not,‹ he replied, with his back still towards me« (Melville 1985: 43).

Finally the lawyer is forced to relocate his firm. When the next lawyer moves in, Bartleby is still there. Without the premise of complicity he evicts Bartleby, who lives in the staircase afterwards. The story ends as such: Bartleby, who refuses to move, is accused of vagrancy and brought to the ›Tombs (the Halls of Justice)‹, a jail in Manhattan, a mausoleum for the living. He dies in the yard of the institution, between heaven and earth (Melville 1985: 64–65). The ongoing complicity that Melville has described between Bartleby and the lawyer is above all a coexistence of the stationary and the migrating. As soon as Bartleby is forced to leave the site he has selected, he dies. Without freedom of movement he cannot survive. The resistance comes to an end, stops being resistance, if he has to face the consequences of professionalism (Reisinger 2011: 135). »The deterritorializations remain relative, compensated for by the most abject reterritorializations [...]« (Deleuze/Guattari 2004: 314). The founding of Eifel National Park—probably the most relevant inhabiting of the military camp Vogelsang—is not least of all due to volunteer work by the development association, a grassroots organization that was founded in 2002, only two years before the park was opened.[20] This NGO consists mainly of local people: teachers, retired historians, a captain, artists, people who shape their direct environment. Its members explicitly fought for to keep the buildings of Vogelsang to make history tangible, although ANTIFA Cologne or nature conservation societies suggested leaving the buildings to nature. But after the official opening of the national park, the organization became institutionalized and all financial support for the development association was cancelled, because their tasks were taken over by institutions.

Finally, two main questions on the responsibility of research are still open before grassroots organizations disappear. If we research informal, marginalized implications, how can we deal with the danger of contributing to institutionalization by making things public? And: Informal strategies profit from its invisibilities. So, how do we talk about a ›silent man‹ (see Melville 1985: 64) like Bartleby standing opposite manifestations of exception and exclusion? Spaces of complicity mainly exist as conjunctures of different layers of site productions, of the formal and the informal, tradition and change, the global and the local. Each use specific architectures, scales and politics. A map with national divisions is not helpful, nor is a fixation of a certain scale; the contingency of different scales crushing into each other has to be regarded and requires differentiated methods of research that have to be combined. For example, Bartleby's office and the geographical and urban backgrounds of North America's nineteenth century pioneers show

---

20 http://www.foerderverein-nationalpark-eifel.de

such cases of different scales that we re-find in the local context of transcultural concepts like national parks. The lines of deterritorializations (Deleuze 2004) are not only spatial facts in the shape of traces, but as processes they also extend to the question of research methods, of how to look. A further contingency that interweaves with spaces of complicities are spatial settings that connect radical exchanges of meanings and functions. This does not only ultimately disqualify essentialist modes of architectural perceptions but forces us to deal with spatial and temporal contingencies at the same time, with instability and unpredictability, but also with the concept of faking stability and predictability.

BIBLIOGRAPHY

Agamben, Giorgio (1998a): *Bartleby oder die Kontingenz*, Berlin: Merve.
—— (1998b): *Homo Sacer. Sovereign Power and Bare Life*, Stanford, CA: Stanford University Press.
—— (2005): *The State of Exception*, Chicago, IL: University of Chicago Press.
Delbanco, Andrew (2007): *Melville*, Munich: Hanser.
Deleuze, Gilles (1994): *Bartleby oder die Formel*, Berlin: Merve.
Deleuze, Gilles/Guattari, Félix (2004): *A Thousand Plateaus. Capitalism and Schizophrenia*, London and New York: Continuum.
Easterling, Keller (2005): *Enduring Innocence. Global Architecture and its Political Masquerades*, Cambridge, MA: MIT Press.
Gurnah, Abdulrazak (2001): *By the Sea*, London: Bloomsbury Publishing.
Heacox, Kim (2001): *An American Idea. The Making of the National Parks*, Washington, DC: National Geographic Society.
Herzog, Monika (2007): *Architekturführer Vogelsang. Ein Rundgang durch die historische Anlage im Nationalpark Eifel*, Köln: Biermann.
Heinen, F. A. (2007): *Vogelsang. Von der NS-Ordensburg zum Truppenübungsplatz in der Eifel*, Aachen: Helios.
Hupe, Ilona/Vachal, Manfred (2006): *Reisen in Mosambik*, Munich: Hupe.
Melville, Herman (1985): *Bartleby,* Stuttgart: Reclam.
Reisinger, Karin (2011): »Bartleby, the Scrivener. Räume, Strategien, Komplizenschaft«. *trans* 18 (politics), p. 130–137.
Weisman, Alan (2007): *The World Without Us*, New York: Thomas Dunne Books.
Žižek, Slavoj (2008): »Censorship Today. Violence or Ecology as a New Opium for the Masses?«. *Volume* 18, p. 42–54.

Boundaries of Practice

Employing Social Art Practice

Exploring New Methods for Research and Geopolitical Realities

APRIL BOJORQUEZ AND MATTHEW GARCIA

It is another hot day in a desert metropolis of nearly five million residents. As cars speed up and down major streets, drivers and passengers are easily disconnected from the place they are traversing. The landscape is merely a meaningless blur occupying the commuter's time and space until they finally arrive to their destination.

Within the blur exists the site we refer to as *Elote Blanco*. The site is little more than a rusty trailer in a vacant lot. Along its perimeter are various plywood boards with »Elote Blanco de Mexico« (*White Corn from Mexico*) hand-painted in black. Occupied by one or two men sitting under the shade provided by a tarpaulin cover, the site often appears to be empty. Sounds of polka-like rhythms common of Northern Mexican regional music project from the owner's truck radio and compete with the bustle of the speeding cars.

Elote Blanco is also located in Phoenix, Arizona, within a US state undergoing geopolitical crisis. As a border state, Arizona is at the intersection of opportunity and tension. The modern US-Mexico border is now little more than a militarized industrial complex. The security infrastructure spans the entire border region, comprised of various walls and fences, including ›virtual fences‹ of cameras and sensors monitored by border patrol agents. There are more than 20,000 federal border agents patrolling the US side of the border, in addition to hundreds of armed volunteer vigilantes.[1] Although these fixed structures and mobilized forces suggest the border is a hard and permanent line of division, its boundaries are in other ways blurred. For example, one can easily place a telephone call from a cell phone from a Mexi-

---

1   Erin Kelly, »Arizona Republic. Southwest to get 1,000 more Border Patrol agents«. 23 June 2010, http://www.azcentral.com/news/articles/2010/06/23/20100623arizona-more-border-agents.html#ixzz1GhLUK9F3

can border town to the US without dialing internationally. The separated border is thus in some ways transparent and is often crossed and transgressed.

Figure 13.1: Project Elote Blanco site

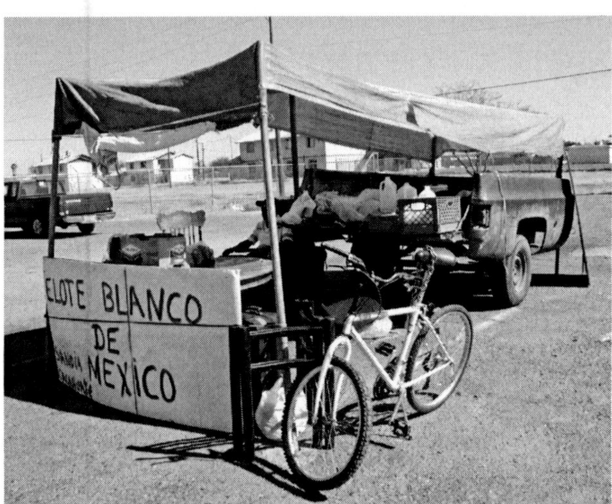

Photo: authors

Place is often defined by structures and borders, however, the countercurrents of globalization, the networked society, hybridization, and even privatization, have blurred traditional notions of how place is created and maintained (Dear/Leclerc 2003). But the power of separation in the region is strong and the border is its most enduring symbol, with thousands of miles of walls and fences separating people and communities. The border serves as a monument to a structuralist concept of classification, where everything is assigned a single place of belonging. Néstor García Canclini has classified borders as boundaries that separate two countries; an area to cross over; an area that is impossible to cross; a territory in which each adjacent country risks losing its identity; and a territory that allows each country to rediscover the importance of its identity (ibid.). In Southwestern United States the border has become identity. The border should be thought of not only as a schism into two countries, but also a single place with a single ecology and cultural history.

GEOPOLITICAL REALITIES

In the United States, particularly in Arizona, the word ›border‹ has become highly politicized; the phrase ›protect our borders‹, has become a rallying cry against so-called ›invaders‹ or ›illegals‹. These phrases have successfully branded those who are Mexicans or look Mexican as undocumented criminal opportunists, consequently legally and socially stigmatizing those who are or appear to be Mexican. Additionally, this anti-immigrant message has developed into a war-like rhetoric mobilizing conservative, right wing activists against a perceived enemy invasion. The following comes from an editorial in the Arizona newspaper, *The Payson Round Up*, on 21 May 2010 written by Arizona State Senator Sylvia Allen titled, »Being on the front lines of illegal immigration«:

»[...] People who live within 60 miles of the Arizona/Mexico border have for years been terrorized by the daily invasion of foreigners who cross their property. [...] The Border Patrol is not the border. [...] I do not blame the Border Patrol—I blame Washington. [...] The border can be secured. We have a responsibility to protect our citizens and to protect the integrity of our country. There can be no talk of amnesty. We are being overrun to the point where we are becoming a North American Union rather than the United States. [...] Maybe it's too late to save America. Maybe we are not worthy of freedom anymore.«

This passage uses immigration and border issues to attack the federal government, sentiments that have increased with the rise of the conservative Tea Party Movement established in 2009.[2] The state of Arizona is thus a microcosm of national demographic and political shifts taking place in the country connected to a strong distrust of federal government.

Currently, two million (30 per cent) of Arizona's residents are Hispanic. Historically, the region now called Arizona was inhabited by Native Americans, followed by the Spanish, and was briefly a part of the Mexican state, Vieja California. Cities such as Santa Fe, in present day New Mexico, were established prior to the English colony of Jamestown, Virginia. Other cities such as Tucson, Arizona, were established shortly after and inhabited by indigenous people and mestizo's, people with both Spanish and indigenous ancestry, today referred to as Hispanic. Following the Mexican-American war of 1848, the state became a US territory and briefly proclaimed itself as the Confederate Territory of Arizona. A majority of the territorial population was Hispanic, although revisionist histories often exclude their numbers. In 1912, Arizona became the 48th state to join the Union, the last territory of the US mainland to be colonized. In many ways, the current political turmoil is part of a continuous effort to establish Arizona as an Anglo-American colony.

Contemporary Arizona has attracted many migrants, a notable number from the eastern and midwestern regions of the United States, California, and Mexico, fundamentally changing the socio-ecological landscape of the state. As the region has become increasingly pluralistic, it no longer resembles the colony it was meant to be, according to its Anglo ›pioneers‹. As a

---

2   United States President, Barack Obama assumed office January of 2009.

consequence, a recent wave of anti-immigrant legislation was enacted, encouraging ›attrition through enforcement‹ of Mexican immigrants. Various legislative measures have been passed, aimed at restricting employment and public services to the undocumented, targeting the Hispanic community, specifically Mexicans and Mexican-Americans.

The majority of Arizonans (over 60 per cent) live in Maricopa County, in the south-central region of the state, where Hispanic/Latino communities make up 40 per cent of the population. For several years Maricopa County Sheriff, Joe Arpaio, has conducted ›sweeps‹ in largely Hispanic/Latino communities. ›Arpaio's sweeps‹ typically take the form of police raiding workplaces or surveillance stations at intersections, stopping people for minor traffic violations. Any driver or passenger suspected of being an illegal immigrant is detained and processed under Arpaio's authority and, if necessary, handed over to federal immigration authorities for deportation. Raids have also led to the arrest of US citizens suspected of being ›illegal‹, found without ›proper identification‹. Arpaio is currently under investigation by the US Justice Department for civil rights violations and abuse of power. Many political pundits suggest indictments may be brought against the sheriff.

On 23 April 2010, Arizona Governor Jan Brewer signed the ›Support Our Law Enforcement and Safe Neighborhoods Act‹ also known as SB 1070 into law, placing Arizona in the international spotlight. The law, sponsored by state Senator Russell Pearce, »[...] allow[s] a law enforcement officer, without a warrant, to arrest a person if the officer has probable cause to believe that the person has committed any public offense that makes the person removable from the US.«[3] The law requires local law enforcement agencies to attempt to determine the immigration status of anyone reasonably suspect of being an unlawful alien in the United States during any legitimate point of contact. Key provisions of the law were blocked, ruling, »race, lineage, or national origin discrimination was a motivating factor in the enactment of S.B. 1070«.[4] Critics of the bill believe the »[...] law implicitly sanctions racial profiling against Hispanics,« both legal and illegal in the state of Arizona.

Additional legislation is currently under construction. Planned initiatives would require hospitals to verify the legal status of patients, encouraging the deportation of patients who cannot provide proof of citizenship. Other bills challenge ›birthright citizenship‹ and include an immigration omnibus bill, requiring proof of legal status to drive a car, enrol children into schools, at-

---

3   Arizona State Senate, Forty-ninth Legislature, Second Regular Session. Fact Sheet for S.B. 1070, 2010. http://www.azleg.gov/legtext/49leg/2r/summary/s.1070pshs.doc.htm

4   Nick Wing, »Federal Judge Rejects Jan Brewer's Challenge to Arizona Immigration Lawsuit«. *Huffington Post*, 2010, http://www.huffingtonpost.com/2010/10/12/arizona-immigration-law-1070_n_759334.html

tend a community college or university, and to obtain any sort of license, including a marriage and food-vending licenses. For non-white residents, Arizona is becoming a modern police state.

PROJECT ELOTE BLANCO

Project Elote Blanco was initially an attempt to employ social art practice for the exploration of quotidian and alternative public spaces in Arizona. Through this work we have encountered the complexities of place and the realities of the local. Social art practice has become a tool to explore place within the everyday and a means to interact and occupy it as artists, researchers, and community members. For the purpose of this essay we are defining social art practice as an artistic process which contributes, creates, and questions social and community engagement. Therefore, the value of the artistic process that constitutes *Project Elote Blanco* rests in the social relationships created between the artists, the *Elote Blanco* proprietor, and the site itself.

The site thrives off the street trade of raw white maize, imported from the Mexican state of Sinaloa. A single vendor can sell up to one hundred dozen ears of maize daily. This site has been in operation for 17 years as a centre for the exchange of this maize that journeys across the border and into warehouses throughout urban Arizona. From there, the corn is sold to various streets vendors for resale. From the pre-colonial Mesoamerican markets to contemporary Phoenix, the activity of *Elote Blanco* reveals that maize continues to provide a livelihood for its producers and consumers.

Figure 13.2: Man sitting under tarpaulin and Elote Blanco trailer

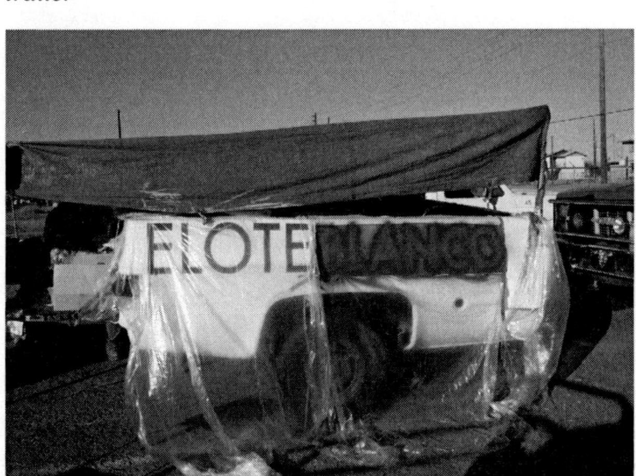

Photo: authors

Figure 13.3: Completed typographic mural

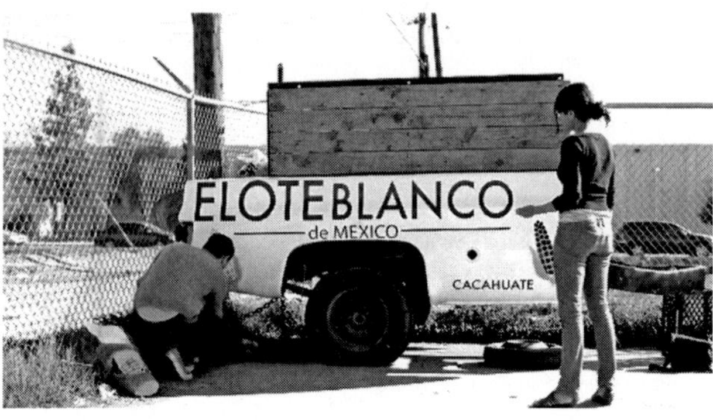

Figure 13.4: Typographic mural with graffiti

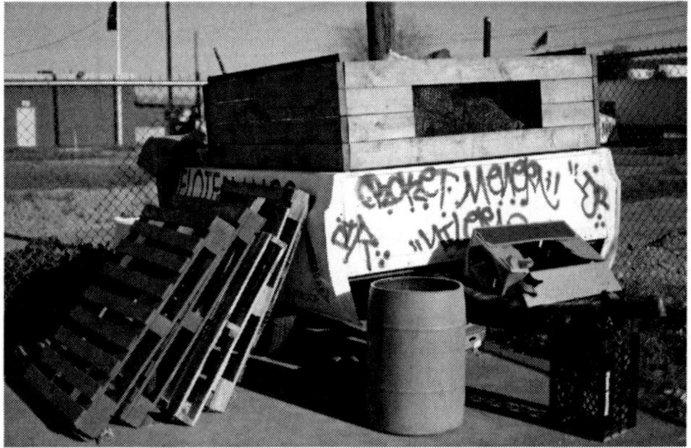

Photos: Bojorquez/Garcia

We have chosen to refer to the project as *Elote Blanco*; *elote* stemming from the indigenous *nahuatl* word for maize and *blanco* the Spanish word for white. The site is demonstrative of an active Mexican community who rely on *elote blanco* for cultural and economic subsistence in a political environment where it is illegal for many to earn a living. Maize from this site is transformed into various food products for personal consumption and commercial distribution. Through its various forms, such as the ubiquitous *tortilla* and *tamale*, maize serves as a cultural monument to the Mesoamerican civilization, which first cultivated this botanical giant approximately 8,000 years ago. Today, maize plays a significant role in Mexican popular culture and on the streets of Phoenix. Although the predominant activity at the site is the exchange of maize, many patrons use it as a social space, where information sharing plays a significant role. Patrons often visit the site to share electronics and tools, locate cheap auto parts, or for information concerning other local resources or community events.

Figure 13.5: Elote Blanco site prior to the completion of the typographic mural

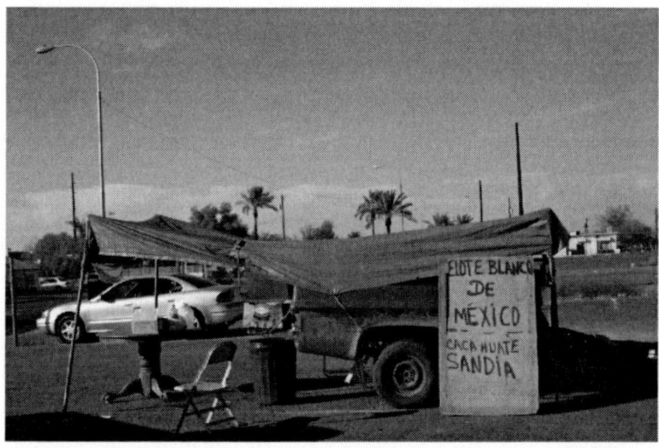

Figure 13.6: Elote Blanco site after the completion of the typographic mural. Photo of the proprietor's typographic mural, which remains at the site

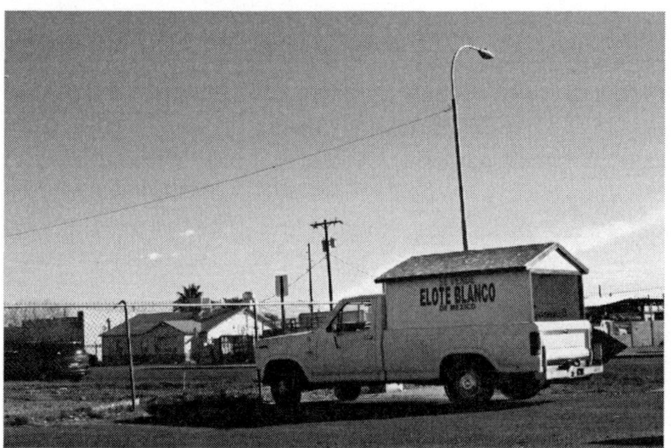

Photos: Bojorquez/Garcia

As Arizona politics have become increasingly anti-Mexican under an anti-immigrant guise, the collaborative social art project also became an exploration of geopolitical realities and its affects on place and community. As artists, we have experienced the instability caused by the current political situation. Local businesses have been destroyed and the people connected to them displaced.

The project began as collaboration between two artists, one of whom is being trained as an anthropologist. The practical goal of the project was to embed art practice and discourse into community space by executing a site-specific visual intervention. The principal artist chose to create a site-specific installation intended to create social connections with the owner and patrons.

Informed by the visual vocabulary of the site, the artists created a typographic mural on a storage trailer, the central feature of the site. The mural was intended to serve as a promotional tool for this small business, while contributing to the aesthetics of the urban landscape. Both the owner and the artists received benefits for their participation. The owner received a free paint-job of a rusty trailer he had been meaning to paint for several months, while the artists received access to a site of personal interest.

The media used to complete the project was informed by an online tutorial of a *fifty-dollar paint job*, a product of the popular Do-It-Yourself movement. The process included sanding the trailer, one coat of primer, eight coats of paint, and finally the application of a design using laser-cut stencils created specifically for this project. The project was conducted over the course of three months and was finally completed after fifteen visits.

Following the completion of the mural, the proprietor executed his own typographic mural on his personal truck, complementing the original project. The proprietor's mural demonstrates the social and aesthetic contribution of the original typographic mural at the site. Unlike Nicolas Bourriaud's notion of *relational aesthetics*, the artist and proprietor were not participating in a shared activity but were both acting within a shared space, demonstrating the significance of place and its impact on cultural production (Bishop 2006). Unfortunately, the trailer (along with the mural) was graffitied and eventually stolen several months later.

Although the trailer is no longer present, the mural has made an aesthetic contribution to the site, which remains visible today. The proprietor's mural serves as an artifact of the project and is indicative of the aesthetic and social exchange that took place as a result of the intervention.

DISCIPLINARY BORDERS

Project Elote Blanco offers various entry points for the exploration of broader cultural and disciplinary processes. Since its inception, the project has been shaped by our disciplinary and geopolitical situations. Complexities have surfaced as a result of this collaborative process, though through this experience we have come to understand our disciplinary and geopolitical borders as intersections of meaning, practice, and place. These intersections are the sites where we reinterpret the processes and products we produce as artists and anthropologist.

The exploration of new methodologies for research is important to further understanding of place and its relationship to the production of knowledge. Through the execution of *Project Elote Blanco* we attempt to reconstruct and reconstitute borders as intersections through socially embedded art. Dislocated from terrain, these intersections act as new territories for the exploration of practice, research, and geopolitical realities. It is at these intersections where »something original [can be] created in a new place, combining cultural and material forms from multiple origins,« or what has been referred to as *hybridity* (Dear/Leclerc 2003: 10). Thus, these peripheral sites, or borders, are now situated at the core due to their situation at the centre of the intersections. It is at these intersections we believe art can become anthropology.

Anthropologist Russell Bernard has stated that »from the earliest days of the discipline, right up to the present, anthropologists have been prodigious inventors, consumers, and adapters of research methods« (Bernard 2006: 2). Therefore, the insertion of art practice within the ethnographic process should be welcomed as methods continue to adapt and respond to changing human relations. In the Elote Blanco example we argue that social art practice can play an instrumental role in the development of ethnographic research. By inserting social art practice into ethnographic methodology, researchers can engage in an alternative immersion into place and a community, allowing for participatory knowledge construction. This process challenges traditional objective approaches to knowledge construction—a linear format for investigating phenomena common of positivist science.

Much like ethnography, the arts generate knowledge and ideas from experience, therefore both share the objectives of seeking understanding, provoking thought, and inspiring ideas. Both practices compliment each other and produce innovative approaches to both the arts and sciences. The project produced various artistic products: a typographic mural and the documentation of the site, currently in the form of a short digital video. Consequently, the product of this project has been pre-determined as art, ultimately belonging to the artist. This created several investigative complexities for both the artist and anthropologist. How do anthropologist and artist negotiate their roles, their practice, and the presentation of their collaborative work? How will the work be best used? Are there additional sensitivities artists need to acknowledge when working with anthropologists? Could these anthropological sensitivities censor the artists? Is the product art or ethnography?

Unlike traditional ethnographic investigations *Project Elote Blanco* began as socially embedded art, resulting in an ethnographic exploration of place, community, and maize food systems in the Southwest.

As the project continues, further understanding of the modern industrial food systems will be explored through the small-scale social, economic, and cultural exchange, taking place at this site. Although industrialized global food systems have been determined to have deleterious environmental, social, and economic consequence, this site reveals positive social, cultural and economic outcomes for its consumers.

INVESTIGATIVE URGENCIES

When the project began during the autumn of 2009, the site was experiencing economic and commercial growth. During this time, the proprietor purchased an additional pickup truck, car and large commercial truck to assist with the expansion of his business. He spoke of opening additional locations, hoping to expand his client base and serve other communities.

Following the completion of the typographic mural, a neighbourhood artist requested permission to create a graffiti mural on the large commercial truck recently purchased. The artist left a sketch of his design, committed his services free of charge, and requested the purchase of materials, expected to cost 200 US dollars. Excited by the proposal, the proprietor agreed to purchase materials as soon as he could acquire the extra money. The project never happened. Anti-immigrant politics in Arizona began to make their mark on the economic, social, and cultural landscapes of the state.

Local politics created several uncertainties and ultimately affected the development of the site and the project. The proprietor was forced to downsize his business and sell his commercial truck. Many of the site's patrons fled Arizona or choose to stay indoors, fearing harassment by police and neighbours, who were encouraged to report anyone suspected of being undocumented to local authorities. Due to the sites rapid economic decline, the proprietor himself contemplated moving to New Mexico. At any moment the site could cease to exist.

As local artists and researchers, we have been forced to respond and adapt to urgencies created by our geopolitical realities. These realities remind us that despite globalizing phenomena the local is territorialized and therefore still exists. The project revealed social art practice as a useful tool for responding to investigative urgencies with immediacy. As local community scholars we are met with the challenge of responding to such urgencies. Although the project demonstrates the impact of socially embedded art, the need for new research methodologies, and the complexity of globalizing food systems, the site also reveals the vulnerability of research and communities within particular socio-political environments. We conclude that in a time of such uncertainty and tension, research and socially embedded art practiced by local scholars is of increasing importance.

BIBLIOGRAPHY

Allen, Sylvia (2010): »Being on the front lines of illegal immigration«. *The Payson Round Up*, 21 May 2010, p. 4A.

Bernard, H. Russell (2006): *Research Methods in Anthropology: Qualitative and Quantative Approaches*, fourth edition, Lanham, MD: AltaMira Press.

Bourriaud, Nicolas (2006): »Relational Aesthetics«. In: Claire Bishop, *Participation*, London and Cambridge, MA: Whitechapel Gallery and MIT Press, p. 160–171.

Canclini, Néstor García (2003): »Rewriting Cultural Studies in the Borderlands«. In: Michael Dear and Gustavo Leclerc (2003): *Postborder City: Cultural Spaces of Bajalta California*, London and New York: Routledge, p. 277–285.

Dear, Michael/Leclerc, Gustavo (2003): *Postborder City: Cultural Spaces of Bajalta California*, London and New York: Routledge.

Kelly, Erin (2010): »Southwest to get 1,000 more Border Patrol agents«. *Arizona Republic*, 23 June 2010. http://www.azcentral.com/news/articles/2010/06/23/20100623arizona-more-border-agents.html#ixzz1Gh LUK9F3

Wing, Nick (2010): »Federal Judge Rejects Jan Brewer's Challenge to Arizona Immigration Lawsuit«. *Huffington Post*, http://www.huffington post.com/2010/10/12/arizona-immigration-law-1070_n_759334.html

Demands on Education

Things, We've Learned ...

The exhibition 2 or 3 Things, we've learned *explores, by way of a subjective collection and discursive as well as performative interventions, the demands that art, education and social movements make on each other. The central issues are those of space, image and collectivity. The search is focused on the eruptive moments and the consequences of ongoing interventions and change over a long period of time, as well as changes and interventions that last.*

EVA EGERMANN AND ELKE KRASNY IN CONVERSATION:

[0:00:04]

In our discussions the connections were always key. We talked about connectivities, but also about conflicts and contradictions between the fields of art, of education and of movements of protest. Herewith we refer on one hand to the protest movements at universities in Austria and in Europe during the 2009 winter term and thereafter, but also movements making demands on other forms of education. Our research is a collaborative journey along these sometimes conflicting yet connecting lines. Institutions of teaching and learning can be seen as spaces of possible change, as soon as one starts to reflect, to desire and to demand things from an intervening and activist's point of view.

[0:02:29,7]

We were interested in projects and discourses actively dealing with the educational system, offering educational criticism or intervening into mainstream educational contexts. What approaches can be found, offering a different reflection upon education or proposing educational alternatives and self-organization? Which projects cover the topics of teaching and learning? In addition to these issues, the criticism by the protest movements and the eruptive moments created during the universities' occupation became important. These situations created a potentiality, an extraordinary situation where other ways of learning were possible.

[0:05:18,6]

An impressive collective agency was manifested. On one side, there were demonstrations. For example 50,000 people demonstrated on one evening and 40 universities all over Europe were occupied. On the other hand, normality returned quickly. How could we create another kind of permanence, another kind of lasting moment, out of such intense political activity, collectivity and discussion? How can we translate these eruptive learning activities and shifts into long-lasting, permanently altered circumstances? The title of the exhibition project should therefore not be understood in the sense of a lesson, but in the sense of a discussion on the intersection of artistic production, critical pedagogy and protest movement.

After the politicization that students and tutors experienced through protests, there appeared also de-euphoric moments: What have we really changed? What has remained? Just a few things changed. It was a moment to pause and reflect, an interim time to take stock, reflecting other extraordinary situations ranging from the recent strike to former protest movements.

[0:07:26]

The project pursues the perspective of protest and functions as a kind of collection in multifold ways. The exhibition space becomes a place where objects, artifacts, photographs, videos, processes, workshops and discussions meet. Artworks confront contradictions in the debate. On the one hand, this will open up space for confrontation, and on the other it will create a collection, which documents the artistic projects and the processes of educational critique.

[0:09:07.2]

This subjective collection is not an archive in the classical sense, or a finalized documentation, but an (educational) method. It is a gathering of collective experiences. The question of what a collective could be or how collectivity could be organized expresses itself as an unresolved desire. The exhibition format we are creating is again a space, where collectivities meet each other: on one side through collected things, through works of art and artefacts, on the other side through different positions. In the documents, magazines and materials of AG Hexenpower, Art Work, of the seminar Zwischen Kunst & Bildung of the Free Class Frankfurt, Rosa Kerosene, of Manoa Free University, Meine Akademie, W...WirWissen, the School for Nonproductive Learning, of rum 68 or <reformpause> long-lasting debates within art as a form of educational criticism become traceable.

Figures 14.1 and 14.2: 2 or 3 Things, we've learned.
Intersections of Art, Pedagogy and Protest, *storefront with wall-newspaper. IG Bildende Kunst Gallery Vienna, 2010*

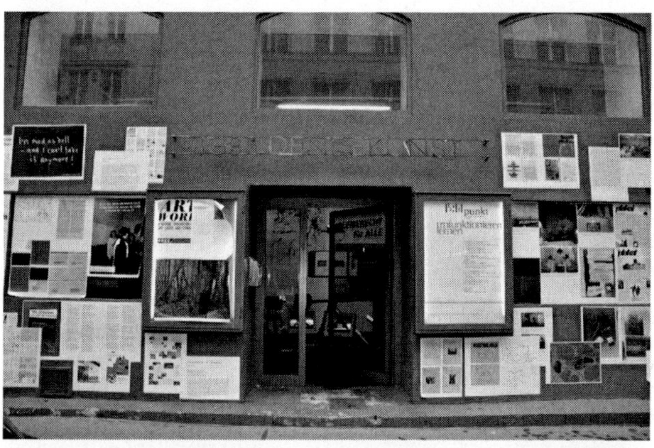

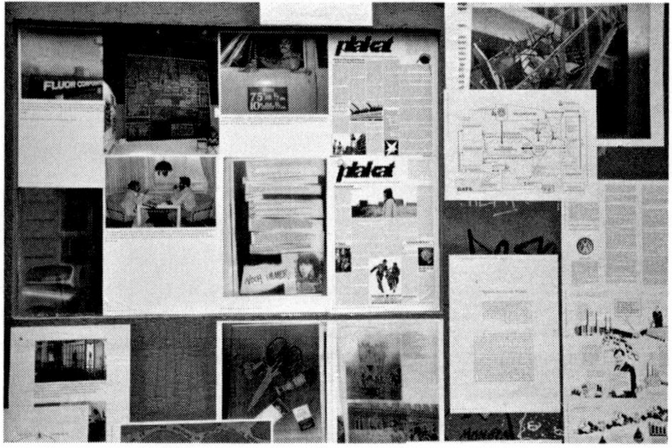

Photos: Eva Egermann

The spatial intervention of Julia Wieger is working with reproductions of this collected material on black and white posters on the façade of the IG Bildende Kunst building. This creates an expansion of the exhibition space into the street and the collection is made public/accessible in the most literal sense. The façade becomes a wall newspaper. Citations chosen from the archive material are presented in new neighbourhoods and contexts.

[0:15:03.1]

The various thematic lines within the exhibition can be described as following. First: the fundamental connection between the fields of education and art as well as interferences, interventions and transfers between them. The project *Hidden Curriculum*, for example, deals with hidden curricula in educational institutions. The term ›hidden curriculum‹ refers to rituals and habitually practiced patterns, rules and norms, which are conveyed as the hidden agenda in schools and universities. In collaboration with students from three different schools, Anette Krauss asked about these practiced patterns.

The field of art is also a system with coded patterns, manners and rituals, comparable to a socialization process. Rainer Ganahl uses art spaces to organize reading circles within. Texts written by Karl Marx, Antonio Gramsci, Rosa Luxemburg and Franz Fanon are read collectively in the White Cube, in a gallery or in a limousine during an Art Fair. Which role does the respective context play for the reading and how are collectivities and situations created?

H.arta Group (Maria Crista, Anca Gyemant and Rodica Tache) situate their work in the contexts of processes of the civil society, spatial formations, different publics, conception of history and gender relations. The ›transitionality‹ marking Romanian everyday life becomes the initiating moment to create other escape routes in history and other educational concepts.

H.arta Group drafted an alternative schoolbook for art classes, which defines the starting points for teaching art in a completely new way.

Sofia Olascoaga works in various contexts and is part of the School of Panamerican Unrest. She is dealing practically and theoretically with contexts of experimental pedagogy and artistic practice in Mexico. One reason for the critical debate with the connections of artistic strategies and alternative education methods is the reduction of resources for public education in Mexico. Another motivation is the interest in alternative educational history with historical references to collectivity and collaboration, artist groups like Proceso Pentagono, No-Grupo, Grupo Suma or TAI Art and Ideology Workshop.

[0:20:54.5]

The second thematic line leads to works of art, but also to material, dealing with educational protest movements in the past. What were the historical struggles for education, their discourses in other times and in other places? What did people learn and un-learn from this and what could we build on today—how could we apply the knowledge of former struggles—in the sense of a genealogical practice—to present debates and arguments? The projects pose the question: whose history is documented and whose is not? What will remain? We want to examine other historical processes, amd show the continuity and discontinuity of protest movements. A broken continuity that is leaving traces...

In her work, Heidrun Holzfeind interviews activists in Mexico, who occupied the UNAM (Universidad Nacional Autónoma de México) in 1968. The former students of the University of Mexico drafted a programme against the prevalent repression and called for strikes and occupation. In interviews, they point out the importance of this movement for Mexican society, politics and culture. Sabine Bitter/Helmut Weber examined the archive material at the Simon Fraser University in Vancouver from the 1960s. In their series *Events Are Always Original* they demonstrate through photographs taken one day after the end of the protests that these documents can also be perceived as an archive of tracing movements, as an archive of the traces of a production of space in the sense of Lefebvre. The archival materials were the material basis for a change in the contemporary perspective. On one hand they were looked at from a contemporary perspective and their meaning for us today. On the other hand, which is equally important, the materials were also re-read and used to reveal the traces of the production of protest from an emancipatory perspective. Originally these photographs had been taken in order to comply with the necessities of insurance and damage assessment. The contemporary reading in the work of Sabine Bitter and Helmut Weber constitutes an intervention into the archived representation turning the representational logic of the assessment of damage into a representational logic of the assessment of empowerment, change and the traces of the production of another possible space within the university.

Marion von Osten and students and tutors of the University of Lüneburg researched within their project <*reformpause*> the history of educational reforms from the 1960s to today, and the tradition of criticism within university spaces. The research resulted in posters and a newspaper discussing how universities should be reformed and on what kind of historical traditions this argumentation is founded. These materials were included in the exhibition; copies of the newspaper were made available for the visitors to take home with them. Madeleine Bernstorff presents the screening *En Rachachant* by Daniele Huillet/Jean-Marie Straub based on the narrative *Oh! Ernesto* by Marguérite Duras. The relation between classroom, pupil, mother and teacher is shifting. Marijan Crtalic examines the present meaning, reception and presence of sculptures, which were made in the workers' settlement of the Croatian steel factory Sisak in the context of a factory-run educational programme. The processes, which Crtalic documents artfully, bear witness upon a period of over 40 years of the making of these educational sculptures.

Cecila Wendt and Emma Hedditch rediscovered a forgotten document of a self-organized situation establishing an alternative form of learning. They came across the Free Women's University Project that was founded in Italy in the 1970s. It was documented cinematically by Adriana Monti and photographically and in text form by Paolo Melchiori. The desire for learning broke every time limit and spread from the metal workers and chemical workers to the housewives and the unemployed: Scuola senza Fine/school without end ... From the initial 150 Hours of Courses emerged the Free Women's University.

[0:33:11.5]

Compared to these historical and documentary works other projects operate in a fictional or half-fictional/docu-fictional form. This is the third thematic line.

The O.T.K. Crumpers dancers, depicted in the drawings of Petja Dimitrova, demand non-violent education and self-determination and connect post-colonial theories with the practice of a critical, non-hegemonial form of image-production, but also the specific local reference to Vienna-Ottakring. The Factory of Escape by the Copenhagen Free University criticizes a neoliberal educational machine through the production of images as a visual and spatial strike. With connecting theory and performance, Dolce & Afghaner interact, react and intervene into real situations of demonstrations or occupation of spaces and create new fictional situations with real criticism and real demands within these exceptional situations of protest.

Fourth, we come to the question: What are the promising, alternative forms of education/learning? How can eruptive protest and learning activities, with regard to their settings, be transformed into changed relations? How can the disturbance within thinking be used for movement to facilitate collective involvements that last? What could queer education be?

[0:41:12.8]

During the Anti-Bologna-Summit at the Vienna Unicampus in March 2010, we participated in a workshop, dealing with feminist/queer demands on education and the sexism within the educational protest movement. This was organized by students (some from the group Kollektive Involviertheiten/ Collective Involvements*).*

Following the stories on the spaces and the speaking positions within the occupation, we got the impression that gender egalitarianims is still not to be taken for granted in the context of educational situations. The history of feminist movements is one of discontinuity. The creation of continuities, spaces and interventions or for example Women's Movement for everybody *is a practice of the group* Collective Involvements *(Moslam, Pfingstl, Wag-*

ner, Weissman, Schasiepen), who discuss, practice, improvise and work on queer-feminist education concepts in collaboration with the Büro für fremde Angelegenheiten, Vipfek und Schwere Schwestern *in the context of the exhibition.* Treat me right! *was a party performance at Marea Alta which took place in conjunction with the exhibition.*

> *Figures 14.3 and 14.4:* 2 or 3 Things, we've learned. Intersections of Art, Pedagogy and Protest, *inside the project space. IG Bildende Kunst Gallery Vienna, 2010*

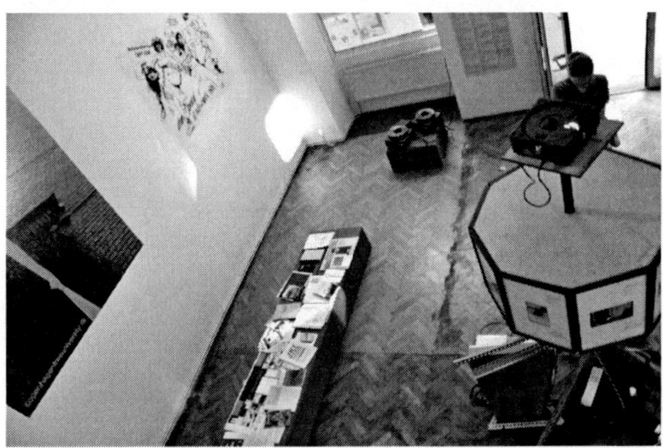

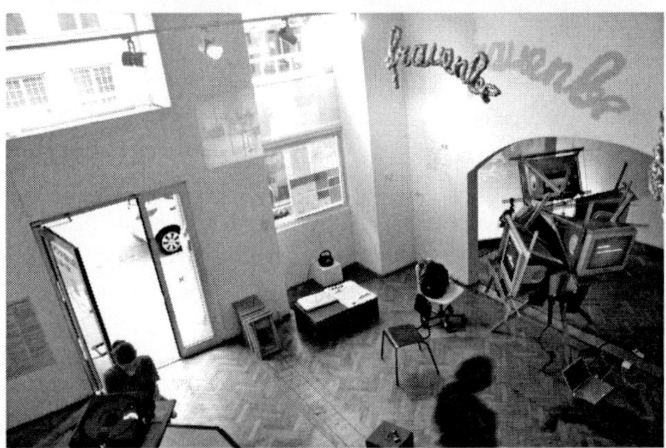

Photos: Eva Egermann

Share a skill step by step is the instruction for the event Show & Tell, *which was hosted by Marthe Van Dessel. The pedagogical format of* Show & Tell *was turned into a collective production of learning from each other. Katharina Strubers' visual work deals with the situation of protests, public lectures, held on the streets as part of the strikes, on Piazza Navona in Rome. On 29 October 2008 in Italy, a resolution was passed about new educational laws. Behind the protesters, occupying public space, we can see the ministry down the lane, the workplace of Berlusconi and minister Gelmini. Struber challenges the limits of documentation.*

[0:45:38.2]

What all these projects have in common, apart from questioning the organization of collectivity, is the level of possible interventions and shifts. They initiate something. The artworks in the exhibition and collection create other images, visual experiences: imaginations on education and learning activity as well as possible shifts in predefined spaces of education or of educational contexts.

The spatial intervention of Nanna Neudeck and Titusz Tarnai translates the eruptive moments, displaced and distorted situations into an opportunity of action for visitors to the exhibition. The monitors, traditional slide projectors as well as digital projectors were installed on tripods made out of steel supporters and euro palettes as platforms. Steel handles made it possible to turn the projecting devices placed on the tripods. Each turn made by visitors created new perspectives within the exhibition. Each turn created new shifts, alternative constellations, sometimes even a layering of projections. Each new position created by the turns of the visitors changed the exhbition as a whole. The neighbourhoods reflect the contexts. The installation of the display created the potentiality of visitors' intervention.

The blog by bolwerK http://www.ooooo.be/2or3thingswevelearned is a growing space for debate, controversy, shift, intervention, discrepancy and links.

Space is educating, space is formed, space is forming.
The social production of space, as Lefebvre is pointing out, can be taken a step further through conceptualizing space as the third educator. Who else is educating? What educates oneself? What forms oneself? To put it as a question: We walk past the previously occupied auditorium of the Academy of Fine Arts Vienna. How do we perceive this space? Do we see it as occupied with all these bodies, their inscriptions and volatility? This disposed imaginary leads us again to the relation of moment and duration ...

Whereas before the strike, the auditorium was not seen as or associated with a place of self-organized intervention and inhabitation, this has changed. It is now a place with possibilities. This happened with many places and is a substantial shift. Additionally, the protests led to the founding of new structures, of networks and magazines, to the formation of political consciousness. These accomplishments, be they newly created spaces or political structures and projects, however, are mostly fragile and precarious. They will always have to be re-established and re-claimed, over and over again.

Figure 14.5: Email from the Camel Collective, January 2011

Betreff: 2nd World Congress of Free Artists

Greetings to the 2nd Congress,

We wanted to once again send thanks to all who took part in making the congress such an enjoyable and enlivening event. It was a great success in terms of collecting together a brilliant variety of perspectives, claims, and demands on Art, Pedagogy, and Political Agency.

It is our intention that the conversations and consequent network of relations it has instigated continue beyond the presentation in Århus. Certainly the necessity of politicizing methodological discussions on art and pedagogy, i.e. the "educational turn" in art, will not cease to be urgent. This will be accomplished by consistently framing the desire to reassess art education with analyses of power relations, by linking general questions of teaching methodology to the privatizing enclosures of universities and academies, and to contesting the extortionate fees demanded of students and their families. It should also include solidarity with student protests against the effects of the Bologna Process in the EU, and with the occupations and protests in the UK (see http://london.indymedia.org/articles/6092 and their list of related links).

The Århus performance is one instance of our activities around this Congress, the next will consist of a book we intend to produce in the coming year. We will be in further contact with authors regarding language, bios, and all of the other logistical details that arise when committing speech to print. Thanks to those who have already sent updated bios.

Video clips from the 2nd Congress will be online at http://congress.camelcollective.org.
We plan to have a selection available by the end of the month.

Warm Regards,
Camel Collective

This text derived out of the project *2 or 3 Things, we've learned*, an exhibition project in the IG Bildende Kunst Gallery in Vienna, autumn 2010, in which the *space RE:solutions* conference was happening and was translated, with the help of Anne Elizabeth Moore, in the course of the preparation of the 2nd World Congress of Free Artists, November 2010 in Aarhus, organized by the Camel Collective.

Access to Interfaces of Expression

A Workshop with Women Artists in Syria

STEFANIE WUSCHITZ

In the last five years, Syria has experienced an increase in Western imports and considerable growth within the IT field. While Syria's one party socialist system is adapting neoliberal economic strategies that encourage repression, young female artists use the opportunity to examine new tools of artistic expression. My research focuses on the application of new technologies by young women artists in Syria. During a field trip beginning in June 2010, I collaborated with eleven female Syrian artists in Damascus. The collaboration involved a workshop aimed at developing interactive stories, which articulate individual narrations in public space. How do women artists make use of open source technology in public space? How is it transformed and which conflicts arise in the process? The participants of the eight-day workshop came from theatre, media, and sculpture backgrounds, but also computer science and software development. My research method of a site-specific art workshop served as a vehicle to translate different forms of agency and observe nuances of self-representation, including my own. The theory of the open source movement clashed with a reality of failing Internet access in Syria, as well as censored websites and the problem of restricted downloads from US hosted websites. In this article I will describe the participant's particular working conditions concerning their access to tools of expression outside mainstream culture.

Ever since the online platform Wikileaks gave the public access to data kept secret by the US military, the term *access* has become a key phrase in Western media. What will the political impact of access to information and software be? On the one hand, access can trigger unforeseen waves of productivity (Shirky 2008), productivity by thousands of users (the multitude) continuously developing free software and content. These developers do not get paid for their work, yet the multitude collaboratively creates products in the scale of the Linux operating system. Clay Shirky calculates that since 2001 it took 100 million cumulative hours of human thought to write Wikipedia's content (Shirky 2010). On the other hand, giving access means giving up control of the product and its responsibility. The largest IT companies in the world are now negotiating the limits of access to their devices. These debates are mainly concerned with commonly used software, such as applications created for smart phones. But the battle over the concept of access also includes commercial hardware products. It has been a battle between forces that want the exclusive statutory right to exercise control over copying and other exploitation of a technology and those who want to offer the right to distribute hardware design (i.e. schematics, bill of materials, and PCB layout data), in addition to the software that drives the hardware.

Artists living in liberal capitalist states often felt the economic need to join communities in order to afford the tools for their means of production, such as musical instruments, video cameras, or, in recent history, software for personal computers and laser cutters. They created peer-to-peer networks that provided peer-to-peer learning environments and room for work in peer production (Kleiner 2010). Decentralized, free, inclusive networks served as a strategy to work autonomously from centralized enterprises and governments. The work in peer production served as a strategy to face issues of limited, restricted, or censored access (Zer-Aviv et al. 2010: 88).

Liza Bear is a New York-based writer, filmmaker, and activist, who has adapted these strategies since the very early stages of her career. The collaborative work she has created since the mid 1970s deals with the use of commercial media and the way it disempowers the public in communication policy. In comparison, she documented the role of alternative media and how it challenges the way means of production (technologies) are tied to reasons for production, such as capitalist advantage or national ideology. She was co-founder and editor of the magazine *Avalanche*, which built a platform for critical conversations on conceptual art. This way, the networks she built allowed her to create the work she intended on content she chose.

There, of course, were always privileged individuals who used the opportunity to work for powerful agents, such as aristocrats, international corporations, or religious leaders. These authorities granted access to tools and networks only to selected artists. An example of one of these influential facilitators was the IT company Bell Laboratories (today AT&T), which supported a group of artists in realizing their artwork from the 1960s on. The artists were encouraged to enter Bell Laboratory's premises to experiment with cutting edge technology. Women artists such as Carolee Schneemann, Betty Beaumont, and Lillian Schwartz, who later became pioneers in interactive art, were initially using Bell Lab's facilities. One of the results of opening the premises to artists was Carolee Schneemann's project *Snow*. This interactive anti-war performance could only be realized with Bell Laboratories' technology to speed up and slow down the projected film according to the way the audience was moving in their seats. In an interview she said:

»I worked with a technician from the telephone labs, Bill Klüver, so I was able to design an SCR switching system [...] I wanted the audience to influence—to some extent—the media without their knowing it. And because the imagery was volatile and suppressed, it was imagery that I felt the crowd needed to see, but would not welcome [...] And as you know, there is explicit censorship, and then there is invisible censorship, which meant that I wouldn't have a gallery represent me, I wouldn't have articles reviewing the work, I wouldn't have support from the museums.«[1]

However, artists who wanted to use Bell Lab's facilities for critical work or articulate dissent were discouraged by the corporation. Today companies are cautious about whom they grant access to their products, facilities, and know-how. User generated iPhone applications, e.g. need to go through a strict selection process before they are published and available for other users.

Syria looks back at a history with close political ties to the former Soviet Union. While positive features like the tuition-free university system‹ still stem from this era, even today filmmakers, writers, and intellectuals are kept from distributing their work or presenting it to an international audience. The extreme growth of Internet usage in Syria (from 0.2 per cent of the population in the year 2000 to 17.7 per cent in the year 2010) has brought about changes. This caused the Syrian government to maintain even more rigid control, specifically over the entire flow of information sent over the Internet. Internet censorship of political websites is pervasive and includes popular websites such as blogging engines, Facebook, and YouTube (Human Rights Watch 2011). Human Rights Watch claimed that

»Authorities continued to broadly violate the civil and political rights of citizens, arresting political and human rights activists, censoring websites, detaining bloggers, and imposing travel bans. Emergency rule, imposed in 1963, remains in effect, and Syria's multiple security agencies continue to detain people without arrest warrants, holding them incommunicado for lengthy periods.«[2]

Syria's president Bashir al-Assad took over power from his father Hafiz al-Assad in 2007 and has gradually opened the Syrian market to Western goods. At the same time, Syrian law assists Syrian security services with extensive immunity for acts of torture. The markets are more liberal, but the regime is as rigid as it was before Bashir al-Assad came into power. This is why self-organization is a very common tactic in Syria to sustain social and economic structures that would otherwise break down.

The symbol of counter-movement and subculture in the ›West‹ is the stereotype of the *hacker*. This male agent supposedly moves between nation states and digital empires without leaving a trace. Hackers seemingly access

---

1   Author's interview with Carolee Schneemann, 30 September 2010, New York.

2   See: Humanrightswatch, 2011, country summary Syria

and change data they desire, orient themselves within information society, and actively participate in international hacker networks. The meaning of the word hacker can be interpreted as criminal, terrorist, or thief. It is a myth generated by mainstream media (Pfaller 2002), yet hacker culture forms a productive and well organized subculture. Hacker spaces are representations of hacker culture in physical space. These public workspaces provide a solution to the isolation so many computer experts face. In most urban areas on this planet, hacker spaces can be found, created by a critical mass of individuals who share knowledge, skills, equipment, tools, and the costs for the space. The space is dedicated to tech-related, collaborative practices located at the intersection of the real and digital world. Some members are only in their teens. They learn how to programme from older members of the hacker space and are socialized in this form of community.

The peculiar thing about a hacker space is its white male dominance that becomes obvious the moment one enters. Hacker culture is a culture informed by a code of behaviour, a style, and a habitus that implies maleness. The *nerd*, a person whose life is absorbed by technophile practices, is respected and a valued exception within the already male dominated IT field. Roland Barthes describes the monk in the fourth century as an individual in a state of exception, who is economically unproductive, but leads an intellectually rich life that serves the rest of society. The monk, even in a community of monks, is marginalized, but is a symbolic necessity for the public. It is comparable to the role of the Shaman (Barthes 2007: 156). Most members of hacker spaces are white middle class males. Only 8 per cent of all members in Vienna's hacker space Metalab[3] are female. Although facilities and WI-FI are open to non-members, and although it claims to be inclusive, the community evolving around hacker spaces practices invisible censorship. Although informal, accessible, and open, it is a highly self-selected community. A very specific kind of individual spends time in these places. Some who have learned to master one or several programming languages do not hesitate to try their skills on high-level engineering tasks and do not shy away from spending a night playing computer games. Mostly individuals in hacker spaces *hang out*—a contemporary form of ›otium‹ (Arendt 1967: 24–25). As it is described in Hanna Arendt's *Vita Activa*, ›playing‹ becomes mixed with the concept of gaming and working (ibid.: 138, 144, 182). The unique situatedness of the hacker space as a workspace without any need to be economically effective opens an atmosphere ideal for artistic, ludic, intellectual, and scientific endeavours: Exploring and playing with IT structures, software, hardware, rules and networks, interfaces, and new forms of communication empowers its members to make technology of their own.

To adapt this kind of strategy to the needs of women and transgender people, a group of women and queer persons met regularly at Metalab, a hacker space in the heart of Vienna. Eight to ten participants organized

---

3   http://metalab.at/

workshops for each other and shared their skills. They partly tried to find new, gender sensitive terms for the electronic parts and tools, experimented with new techniques and started a network of female users. All these practices were tolerated by the people of Metalab—sometimes with an irritated look, sometimes encouraged through announcements on the public wiki.[4] Yet each woman coming to the bi-weekly meetings felt exotic, like she was in the wrong place, did not belong. It was comparable to visiting a foreign culture. The environment, as welcoming as it was supposedly arranged, felt strange and impossible to adapt to one's own preferences. The reason was the effective and temporary use of the space by the group. This assiduous and focused use contradicted the hacker culture's *working mode* of playful and aimless presence.

The male dominated hacker culture, and the technologies it cultivates cannot be made accessible for females by merely securing physical access to the social space, just as you do not become a monk by visiting a monastery. The determining factor shaping the social space of technology is partly the timeframe and aimlessness, but most of all the male centred culture evolving around it and the practices performed within a hacker space. To be exposed to the male dominated culture of the space as a woman or transgender person diminishes the otherwise supportive conditions that a hacker space can offer. The feeling of not belonging overrules the anticipation of aimless and playful exploration. As an experiment we wanted to create a setting, which would foster women's access to technology in a similar way as hacker spaces do, while at the same time making technology their own territory (Lazzarato 2002).

During an expanded timeframe in an aimless atmosphere in which technology was not yet interpreted by male connotations, the working space was set into a place that was not dominated by white middle class *Western* man. This place was an old house in the centre of Damascus, Syria. In May 2010, eleven women and transgender persons from a wide variety of backgrounds including computer science, architecture, photography, video, and graphic design came together to *hack* tools, think of new interfaces, and design interactive stories. Kyrah Kosina, an excellent programmer from Austria, and I introduced two tools to the group, which helped to create interactive applications. We tried to introduce the tools without gender bias (e.g. the Free Hardware Microcontroller *Arduino* was simply called *Arduina*) and assist every participant with the installation. The other tool was open source software, which helps visualize data and interface the screen with the physical world via web cam or sensors. Although the software is free, downloading it was restricted. A US embargo dating back to the Reagan administration made it difficult. The sanctions include banning the sale of sophisticated technology, such as computers, aircraft, and related spare parts. The restric-

---

4   Wiki is an editable form of website, to which any person can contribute.

tions made it hard to conduct our workshop, since our access to open source software was much more limited than we had expected.

Figure 15.1: Workshop with women artists, Damascus, 2010

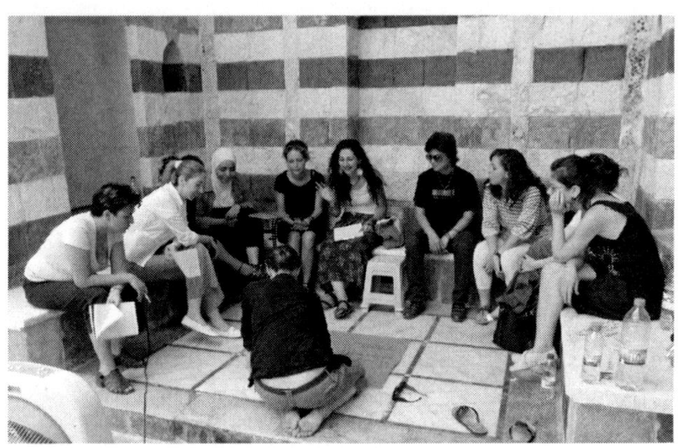

Photo: Karin Kosina

On the first day we were confronted with many limitations on several levels. The gallery that had offered a room to us cancelled last minute. Some women articulated that they had expected a very different kind of event. The format of a workshop was unfamiliar; it seemed awkward to some participants that we would all meet at the same time in the morning, since it was not an actual course or school. Over the next days some came at the agreed time, some three to four hours later. The next challenge was the microcontroller. Even open source hardware seems to be configured to ›Western‹ standards. The microcontroller usually only needs to be plugged into a laptop via USB cable in order to be programmed via PC, but suddenly none of the microcontrollers were detected as new hardware by the computers. Each of the Syrian PCs had a different Windows operating system installed, each of them a cracked version, which was extremely unstable and slow. After hours of challenges using the restricted Internet, downloading from the restricted website, and installing the stubborn hardware on a ›stolen‹ operating system, we finally had the tools we needed. We then started our collaboration.

It began with a general first round of experimenting with interfaces to computers other than a mouse or keyboard. The group developed concepts about what could be done and would be interesting for individual participants to explore.

There is generally a higher interest in studying engineering and computer science in Syria than in Austria. Not many women actually work in their profession after they get married, but the tendency has increased. Yet honour crimes and forced marriages cast a shadow on the issue of gender equality in Syria (at least ten honour crimes were documented by Syrian women's rights groups in 2010). The opening of Syria's markets to Western goods has widened the gap between different income groups. Yet the prospering IT field in Syria has created many new jobs, producing for markets in the Emirates and Asia. Women who develop websites or who work in animation and graphic design will find jobs easily. The growth of the IT sector has strengthened the economy. At the same time, the rising prices on the housing market have made it necessary for women to work full time in order to afford an apartment. In many families being able to afford an apartment still counts as the ticket to marriage. Syria hosts more Iraqi refugees than any other country, with 210,000 registered with the UN High Commissioner for Refugees (Human Rights Watch 2010). This was radically changed by Iraqi refugees trying to find apartments and shelter. The economic pressure created by the housing market determines when young Syrian couples receive their family's permission to get married and move out. This is why young women are encouraged to find work; the rent would otherwise usually be too high for the husband to pay alone. There are a growing number of people rebelling against these traditional marriage agreements. Students are sharing apartments, and there is a growing LGBT community. Still, most young Damascenes wait until their early thirties to move out of their parents' home and get married, due to the high housing prices. In private houses or private companies there are spaces of freedom in which critical thinking and contemporary art is cultivated. Alternative lifestyles are experimented with, and even a hacker space was established. None of the above is accessible to the public or an official institution. However, there are a growing number of unofficial platforms for critical discourse.

Since copyright licenses for media do not exist in Syria, the open source movement is not very significant. Generally, every Western mainstream film or software can be bought for one dollar at the street markets. Musicians will not make money selling CDs since people are not accustomed to paying more than 70 Syrian pounds (about one US dollar) per CD, and the government allows alternative music industries that could serve as a source of income to musicians. Software and media is ›free‹, meaning that one can buy it cheap on every street corner. Yet it is not ›open‹ in the sense that someone could look at, develop, and change the source code. Women graduating from the fine arts departments usually work in the enormous restoration business, since many old houses were bought and are now being renovated to become hotels and restaurants for the storm of expected tourists. Advertising was not allowed until 2005, when hundreds of billboards were suddenly built, and the markets became more and more deregulated.

Our participants had not heard of the open source tools we introduced and were surprised about our political and strong opinion about them. During the brainstorming phase we sat in a circle and tried to think of ideas worth exploring. Some ideas focused on new forms of visual, tactile, or audio interfaces the visitor could respond to; others focused on the conceptual layer—the kind of experience into which the visitors would be immersed. The artists in the group agreed that they wanted to create spatial installations that filled up an exhibition room and elicited visceral reactions from visitors. They wanted to use light, sound, touch, and video tracking in their installation and create a whole series of interactions. The ideas were merged so that the form of interaction and interface would match the concept idea. Within a short time three projects crystallized, and teams of four were built around each project. We sat together like women have been sitting together knitting or weaving for thousands of years in many cultures, except that we were soldering to LEDs, assembling wires, and weaving videotape to carpets. It was not like the sweatshops of electronic corporations in Mexico or Malaysia. We all sat on the floor, sang, chatted, smoked cigarettes, and joked. It was almost a women's hacker space atmosphere. Bibi, an avid photographer, soldered 150 LEDs to wires in only one day, and we made a lot of progress.

Working late into the night in the cooler temperatures made the group become closer. The next day, almost all the projects were finished and functional. Ninar, a musician and singer, had organized a number of old, conductive video tapes[5] from the Syrian TV station, where her father worked. We were able to weave three carpets out of this old video tape. Bibi, Rania, and Massa soldered long wires that hung from the ceiling and were connected to 150 tiny ping-pong balls with LEDs. Another 150 wires hung down in the same manner and height. A brown, dusty stone was attached to each one. Bibi and Ninar called the installation *Please Touch*. When the wires with ping-pong balls attached (which had a negative charge) touched the ones with stones attached (which had a positive charge) the electrical circuit between the two wires was completed. The electricity caused the lamps to go on for an instant. Interacting with the circuit provoked the visitor to formulate a performative gesture, which generated a feeling of emergence. Through the visitor's playful response to the dangling wires, the artists intended to create interaction and subjectivity (Kozel 2007).

The second project was mainly created by Rania, Kyrah, and Waroud. A webcam tracked the silhouettes of people in the room to project their video image in transformed colours. When a person was moving, a fortune cookie phrase appeared attached to the projected silhouette. Rania invented meaningful, subversive, and ironic fortune cookie phrases, so each visitor had the chance to receive an individual phrase. If someone in the room was moving faster than the silhouette, the phrase would slowly slide to the faster person. This way, people could try to catch fortune cookie phrases from others, creating small collaboration between the phrase and silhouette, mutually altered by one another (Lazaratto 2002: 15).

---

5   Old video tape is conducting electricity. It can be used within electric circuits to generate variable resistance in order to make low cost touch sensors.

The third installation triggered three different videos and sounds according to the visitor's position in the room. If a user stepped on one of the three video tape carpets, she caused a specific sound and projection on the wall representing phases of a personal crisis.

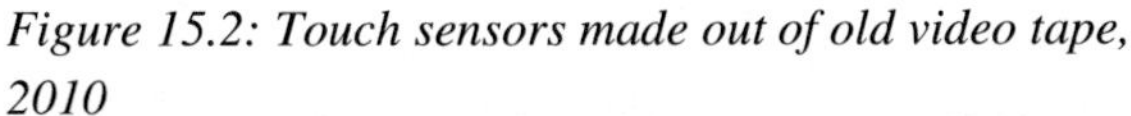

Figure 15.2: Touch sensors made out of old video tape, 2010

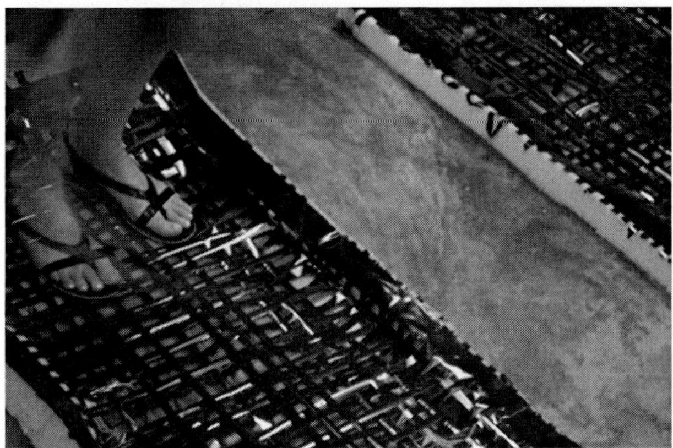

Photo: Karin Kosina

The next day everything stopped working. The group was fragmented and under stress. In this situation, on the last day, Bibi and Ninar told their boyfriends to come and help repair the projects. The young men had trouble helping, since the problems were complex and demanded specific skills like e.g. programming in Java. Bibi and Ninar were surprised they could not help. The boyfriends left again and the group joined forces to find a solution for the video carpet project. With a lot of patience, coordination, and an enormous amount of time, Kyrah managed to create a second video tracking system. When the first visitors arrived for the final presentation, all women artists had put on fashionable cocktail dresses and make-up. Five different ambassadors visited the opening and dominated the space with their presence, re-establishing gender roles. The quiet workshop had become framed as a high society fine arts event. For many visitors it was the first time they were confronted with an interactive art piece. After two hours the wires were helplessly entangled and a short circuit had ended the responsive character of the light installation, but the other two installations worked. Ecstatic with success, Abeer started to envision gigantic kinetic sculptures of screens and motors. Nisrin described how, in the future, videos on a video blog could help fight honour crimes in Syria. Rania planed interactive installations for her dance company's next choreography. Massa and Nisrin gave several interviews to explain what they had created.

In their book *Commonwealth*, Hardt and Negri describe how the process of collaboration generates singularities. They quote the story of orchid and wasp in Deleuze and Guattaris' *A Thousand Plateaus* to illustrate how the meeting of singularities leads to a new continuously changing common character. From my perspective, the experience of the workshop, the collaboration, was a constant metamorphosis and continuous creation of new singularities. The concepts and projects themselves mirrored this experience.

Figure 15.3: Please Touch, *installation view, 2010*

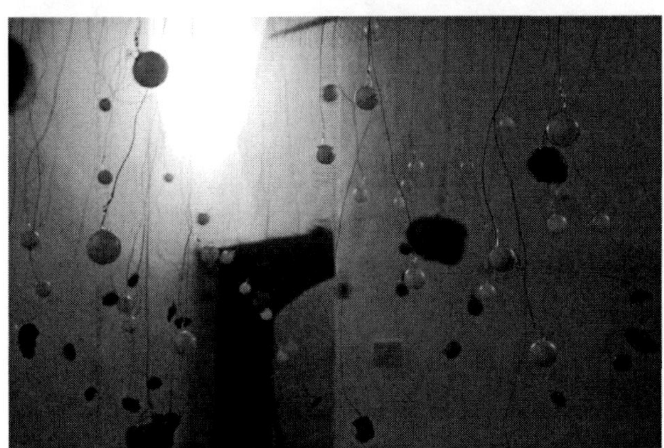

Photo: Karin Kosina

In a workshop I held in New York in September 2010, the well-established media artists participating in this women-only event, had similar conversations to the young media artists in Damascus. For both groups, the impression of working in collaboration like this was profound and therefore most influential to project ideas.

What we had hoped to accumulate in knowledge with this experiment was how strategies of access can be adapted and changed by agents in a site-specific manner. The question we could not answer was, whether, through performative practice, it was possible to intervene in existing and established sets of meaning as a women-only workshop in Syria, trying to influence how events and tools are signified for members of the group. However, the way male connotated objects were re-named and re-read opened new frameworks for collaborative networks. These networks could become important pre-conditions to future productions. The space the group occupied, shared, and re-shaped with their interactive spatial installations created the foundation to adopt new practices. The dominant codes of technology could, to a certain extent, be infiltrated by performative rules, which the group generated within this space. This was done not only through the use of technology, but also through its placement within female connotated semantic domains and the skills the artists had acquired during the communicative process of this collaboration.

BIBLIOGRAPHY

Arendt, Hannah (1967): *Vita Activa*. Munich: Piper Verlag, (original: 1958. *The Human Condition*, Chicago, IL: University of Chicago Press).

Barthes, Roland (2007): *Wie zusammen leben*, Frankfurt/Main: Suhrkamp.

Günzel, Stephan (2007): *Maurice Merleau-Ponty*, Vienna: Turia + Kant.

Hall, Stuart (1973): »Encoding/Decoding«. In: Roger Bromley et al. (eds.), *Cultural Studies: Grundlagentexte zur Einführung*, Lüneburg: Zu Klampen Verlag.

Hardt, Michael/Negri, Antonio (2009): *Commonwealth*, Cambridge, MA: Harvard University Press

Human Rights Watch (2011): »World Report«, http://www.hrw.org/en/world-report-2011/syria [accessed 19 February 2011].

Internet World Stats (2010): »Internet Growth and Population Statistics«, http://www.internetworldstats.com/me/sy.htm [accessed 20 February 2011].

Kleiner, Dmytri (2010): *The Telekommunist Manifesto*, Amsterdam: Institute of Network Cultures.

Kozel, Susan (2007): *Closer. Performance, Technology, and Phenomenology*, Cambridge, MA: MIT Press.

Lazzarato, Maurizio (2002): *Videophilosophie. Zeitwahrnehmung im Postfordismus*, Berlin: b_books.

Pfaller, Robert (2002): *Die Illusionen der anderen. Über das Lustprinzip in der Kultur*, Frankfurt/Main: Suhrkamp.

Plant, Sadie (1997): *Zeroes + Ones: Digital Women and the New Technoculture*, New York: Doubleday.

Shirky, Clay (2008): *Here Comes Everybody: The Power of Organizing Without Organizations*, New York: Penguin Press.

———— (2010): *Cognitive Surplus: Creativity and Generosity in a Connected Age*, New York: Penguin Press.

Zer-Aviv, Mushon et al. (2010): *Collaborative Futures*, http://collaborative-futures.org

»... but we have always been here«

Visible and Invisible Representation of Heteroglossia and Minority Languages in the Alpe-Adria Region

NADA ZERZER

The topic of visible heteroglossia has recently taken on a new urgency in my homeland of Carinthia, Austria. Politicians of both minority and majority parties have once more started to negotiate the question of bilingual topographic signs in the area. The issue of putting up a bilingual sign at the entrance to a village is being discussed in such a grave and religious manner that the importance of representation, the importance of visibility and invisibility, the inclusion and exclusion of public symbols/iconography is starting to take on a new significance.

For this reason, every time I get the notion that my field of research is becoming a partially historical topic or that it might be of less importance than the economic development and the stability of our currency, it is actually becoming more and more relevant.

In this essay I aim to present results from field research on the issue of how heteroglossic people in the three regions of Carinthia (Austria), Primorska (Slovenia), and the Trst/Trieste region (Italy) experience their multilingualism and its representations in everyday life.

The research focus is on space—created by people using more than one language in their everyday life and by the representations of the languages in their living environment—the towns and villages. I want to take a closer look at life with—or in—heteroglossia and at the possible integrative handling of it. First, I will introduce the general topic, the focus and the area and social context of the research. Then I will introduce one participant in the field research and outline her point of view in relation to the leading questions.

Language—talking, writing and communication—is not singular and monofunctional but works on many levels, has several ways to transport meaning and even different ways to work. Language is partly descriptive, it is a way of reproduction and a means of saying what we think about the world around us. But it is much more—language is also a way of creating and producing the world we live in. Language and speech is a possibility to form and to change the reality of our lives. This becomes evident in examples such as marriage when the words of a priest or a registrar change the legal status of two people (Austin 1975).

When we deal with heteroglossia this becomes more and more evident because this creative potential is being put to use by all individuals involved.

Basically, this essay asks the following questions: How can questions of multilingualism be approached in a political/pluralistic/democratic way? How can negotiations of space and representation in a society constructed as minority and majority be approached? What is the living experience of the minority speakers—their views of their multilingual environment and how much importance do they place on visual representation? And how can research of a multilingual environment be carried out with a focus on the visual experience?

The aim of this research is not to discuss multilingualism of minority contexts from a juridical point of view, i.e. reflecting on minority rights and laws, or even to compare the legislation of different European countries. This text neither wants to define ›good‹ or ›bad‹ nor to evaluate laws, administrations and politicians; there are already enough experts in all of these fields.

APPROACHING THE FIELD

Central Europe, particularly the Alpe-Adria Region, is very rich in culture and languages and is highly diversified. Here, Romanic, Slavic and Germanic languages and cultural areas meet, intertwine and occasionally merge, which is a very special situation in itself. The permanent contact with one or more neighbouring cultures leads to permanent reflection of common interests and differences, of bonding and separation, of the familiar and the alien. Theoretically, areas of cultural contact are spaces of imagination, of untold cultural riches and infinite potential: where cultures and languages meet, circulate and merge, new forms of culture can emerge, i.e. individual compositions of these very components, of this very situation. In fact, this idealistic image is not particularly realistic and can be shattered very easily due to the reality of border regions. A look at a neighbouring language, culture or country very often arouses more suspicion than interest, more disapproval than intrigue. Instead of overcoming the obstacles and cooperating, instead of creating a shared culture of this area, belonging, classification and differentiation, the distinction between *we* and *they*, between *one's own* and *the other's* seems to be more important here than anywhere else.

The tension between imagination, the idea of potentiality and the pessimistic view of reality that manifests itself in Carinthian society, is the source of this work.

Figure 16.1: Koper/Capodistria is a small town on the Slovenian coast, very close to the Italian border. It belongs to the official bilingual area, where the bilinguality of all public affairs is regulated by law. This concerns education, media and all inscriptions in public space

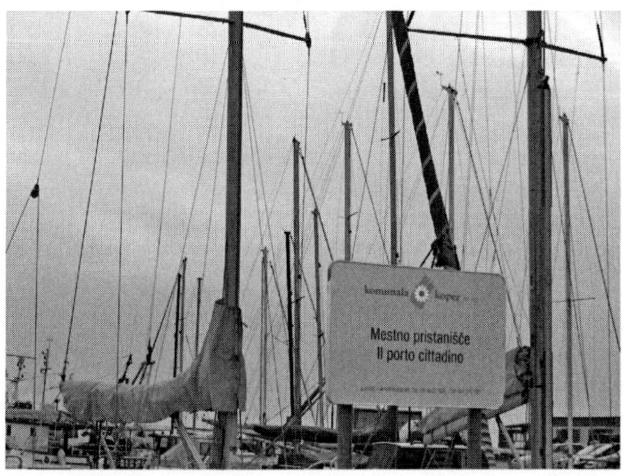

Photo: author

Theoretical approach:
political dimensions of language in public space

The concept of this research is political: the issues addressed are *public* and *power*, which are both present in the field of politics. The issue is furthermore political in the sense, as explicated by Chantal Mouffe (Mouffe 2005), that many of the positions in question are contradictory, and concurring, and can therefore not be reconciled. There is no possibility to unite the different positions into one position shared by everybody and often there is not even a compromise. To mention a popular issue relating to this, which is further discussed below, there is no compromise over monolingual and bilingual topographic signs, it has to be either one or the other. The actual sign is the result of the prevalence either of the advocates of bilingual or of monolingual signs, and the defeated group has to cope with the result. Contrary to the ideas of Chantal Mouffe, a democratic society needs to withstand such contradictions and needs to find a procedure that enables proponents of both positions to live side by side without one position being repressed or eliminated and without negating the contradictions. The political task is the aim of recognition of the legitimacy of the other, of being adversaries but not enemies, of having no solution, no common ground, but being able to live with this.

In the wider understanding of architecture, which is the basis of my research, the field of interest and research is space. As architecture, being the art and science of space, it knows far more ways to create space than by merely building houses, rooms, walls and decorating them. It starts with the fact that architecture is more than the physical-material aspect of space, and more than something static, predetermined, or unchanging. It is not the idea of some space that would be defined by three dimensions and confined by borders. It is much more, it is a construction of the idea of space being provided through people inhabiting it. By living, working, feeling, thinking, interacting, people produce space and at the same time they formulate/configure/create its character. When carrying this to the extreme, one could say, space is a social function.

When the ways of living and interaction of people are established as constitutive elements of producing space, communication and language as means of interaction become crucial in their contribution to the evolvement of space. This can be said about private as well as public spaces. They can be connected to memories of single people but also to the collective memory of a group or a whole society. The more people share these memories or have singular/personal memories connected to one place, the stronger the characterization of the place becomes.

In heteroglossic regions, the existence of more than one language, the representation thereof and the resulting social and emotional entanglements contribute significantly to the social constructions of space. Focusing on the inhabitants' social practices as constituents of space, I have concentrated on the relations of speakers and languages and their representations in heteroglossic regions. The representation of heteroglossia and its importance for social constructions of space is discussed using multimodal material from the three regions, collected by myself and other research participants.

Field research

As the most important part of this research, I see the inclusion of the views of minority speakers in the process of gathering material and in producing a set of knowledge about heteroglossia. The way I chose to achieve this was to ask heteroglossic people in the research areas to share their views in a multimodal way, provided by cultural probes.[1] Cultural probes were chosen

---

1   The method is adopted from Gaver et al. 2004. Cultural probes were developed for participative and integrative design methods in urban planning. The idea was to enable the participants to contribute to the process without being design experts themselves. Therefore, people who usually don't think about the design they would wish for their environment and who are not used to finding the right words to say what they mean, a bundle of tools, containing e.g. cameras, sketch

as they have some advantages important to my approach. They enable me and the research participants to gather/give information in many different ways—an interview, photos, sketches, maps, notes etc. As the probe is not limited to the time of the interview itself, it provides time for reflection, thereby enabling a research participant to include information that maybe did not come to mind during the interview. This seems even more important as some people mentioned that their participation in the research triggered new reflections on their heteroglossia and on the representation of their own language. An important aspect of using cultural probes is that they enable me to include contradictory information without making a hierarchy or compensating between them.

On the interviews

The interviews about the ways to live and experience one's own heteroglossia contain narratives of what comes naturally and what is controversial or contested, they tell us about structures of power and majority relationships, and of political practice in everyday life. They offer a possibility to phrase questions about a society's dealing with cultural plurality.

The people interviewed expressed the importance they attach to heteroglossia and to their belonging to a certain group or minority as an element of their biography. Often this is constructed as a crucial element, guiding decisions throughout their lives.

Figure 16.2: Bilingually labelled herbs sold on the green market in Koper/Capodistria

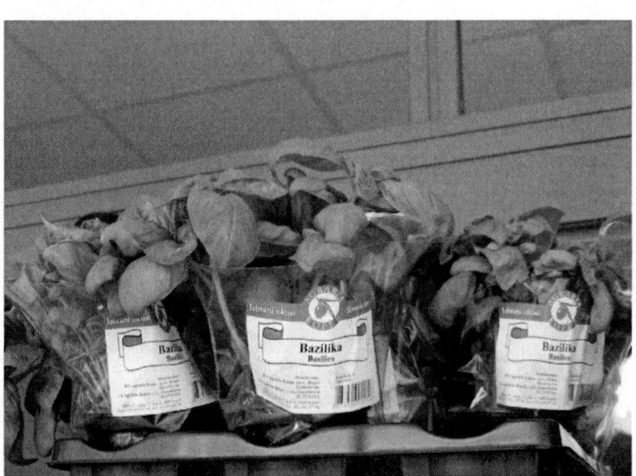

Photo: author

pads, maps or postcards was developed. In addition, the probe is not to be used under supervision but on its own in order to grant freedom of thought and action.

On reviewing the interviews, it was important for me to connect the personal language narratives with the regional and broader historical narration because the speakers move in an area of transition where the past few decades and the past century have seen dramatic changes. In the interviews, narratives of personal or family history interweave with broader history. They are marked by disruptions and antagonism and very often become connected to the language biography. Being heteroglossic, being part of a minority, is a special kind of being pluralistic within oneself and research methods should take this into consideration. In our research group[2] we work with biographies as multimodal narratives—they are not only told verbally, but in a holistic sense, which contain impressions of all of the senses. The construction of sense, of meaning in one's own biography often happens emotionally and intuitively. Very often I use pictures as starting points for memories and the constructions of identity and social or structural connections.

ANNA

In the following, one example from the research is presented. With the material that was gathered by or with a participant, the working method is explained and results that have already emerged from the research are introduced. The gathered material indicates that visual aspects of representation of minority languages contain a significant importance for the speakers. The visibility and visual representation are read as a confirmation of their own history and even of their own existence. On the other hand, they recognize manifestations of problems and deficits by considering visibility. The relationship between minority and majority and the status of the minority language within the whole society are negotiated by means of representation.

The participant introduced here in more detail is a 62 year old retired teacher for Italian and History at the Italian high school in Koper/ Capodistria in Slovenia. Let me call her Anna. The interview was conducted in Slovenian, which is not Anna's first language although she speaks it very well.

Right at the beginning she embeds her personal observation in the broader historical context while at the same time recommending herself as a useful interview partner for me:

»Posebno vidim, globoko vidim te stvari, ker sem se tu rodila, in poznam to kulturo.

---

2   Forschungsgruppe Spracherleben (http://www.cis.or.at/spracherleben/about.html) is a research group at the Linguistics department of the University of Vienna. The trans-disciplinary group works on questions around living and experiencing language(s), on societal and individual heteroglossia and on consequent discursive practices.

[I've observed this for quite some time as I was born here and grew up here, I know the culture [of the city].]« (Anna, 0:26).

Furthermore, some time later in the interview she once more emphasizes the reliability of her testimony and her knowledge of the history of the place:

»Tu je bilo vedno … veste, tu je bila Avstrija, potem je bila Italija, potem je prišla Jugoslavija, potem Slovenija, a mi smo bili vedno tukaj.
[There always was … you know, there was Austria [Habsburg, Austro-Hungarian Empire—author's note], then there was Italy, then came Yugoslavia, then Slovenia, but we have always been there]« (Anna, 5:05).

In the antipodes constructed between the durability of the person and her family's historical background and being in this place, and the ephemerality of borders and state constructions an important means of self-legitimization of a minority becomes obvious.

This statement, which appears in variations in several of the interviews, also contains the questions of territoriality. This territoriality is constructed on a very personal level, individually or on the basis of small collectives, and is opposed to nationality and state-territorial concepts. The discrepancy, or gap, between these concepts opens up questions for my further work.

Figure 16.3: Lack of respect for ancient architecture expressed by waste containers in the city square.

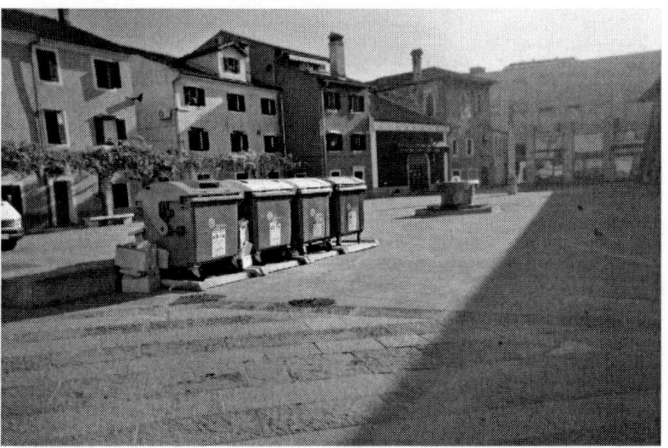

Photo: Anna

Anna also talks about the negligence that the majority renders to the culture and history of the minority, about ignorance, the reluctance to understand the language and about the representations of the language being rendered invisible:

»[...] čeprav določene stvari so uničili. [...] Čisto enostavno stvari, pisane stvari, so čistili, pa so tako mocno čistili, da besede se ne čitajo več... prav manjka ta sensibiliteta za zgodovino.
[... several things were destroyed. [...] there are things, written things that were cleansed so thoroughly that the inscriptions cannot be read any more. The sensibility for history is clearly missing there.]« (Anna 05:56).

Despite this often painful history, Anna describes the confluence of cultures as a special wealth and she expresses her wish that this wealth should be worn and shown with pride—for example in the form of bilingual inscriptions in public spaces, but also by using the Italian language.

»[...] ampak je bogastvo za vse. Mislim, da vsi prostori, kjer so konfluirale kulture, jeziki, in so to doživeli s težkimi trenutki, kar je normalno, so tudi bolj bogati. In vsi zgubijo, ne samo mi, vsi zgubimo, če odstranimo ali hočemo ukiniti, prikrajšati neke stvari.
[... but the wealth belongs to all of us. I think that in areas where cultures and languages come together like here and where people experience difficult moments with this, which is normal, these areas are wealthier. And we all lose, not only us [the minority—author's note], but we all lose something, when things [i.e. visible proof for the present and historical cultural diversity—author's note] are erased or destroyed]« (Anna 8:50).

Figure 16.4: Two street signs for the same street—in two different variations of the Italian name.

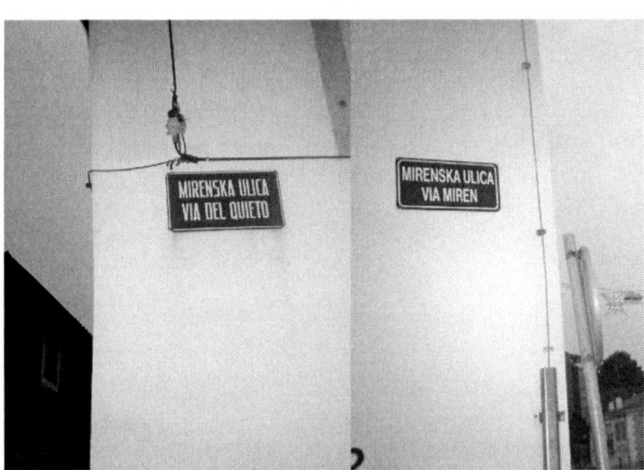

Photos: Anna, collage: author

Anna talked a lot about the bitterness and the impotence she experiences and also about the discrepancies between law and its implementation and realization. She describes her frustration about the carelessness, the unkindness, the thoughtlessness and her irritation about wrongly written inscriptions in public spaces, not only by private individuals, but also by authorities and public institutions such as the university or the administration. Of the disinterest, resulting senselessness or even disrespectful inscriptions, or the example of a sign on two different ends of the same street. The Italian name has been translated in two different ways.

Here, Anna draws a parallel between the carelessness that majority-speakers inflict on the minority language and the careless dealing with the history of the city and the architectural monuments. Like many Italian inhabitants of Koper/Capodistria, she connects the architecture to Italian, respectively Venetian, history and as Italian contribution to the town's history and development. This way, the negligent preservation of buildings and monuments is interpreted as negligence of the estimation of its Italian history.

»Tu na trgu imamo srednjeveški stolp. A ni mogoče, da na ta stolp daš potem aircondition gor. In tu pridejo drugi problemi, estetski, a kdo čuti neke stvari, a spoštuje ambient.
[Here on the main square there is a medieval tower. But on a tower like this you cannot install an airconditioning unit. Here you can see other problems—aesthetical, or if someone feels these things, if someone respects the ambience.]« (Anna 11:30).

The minority legislation in Slovenia is considered to be exemplary, but Anna judges its implementation to be wanting. As there are no consequences to the meaning of punishment to be expected when ignoring and neglecting the legal regulations concerning the minority language, Anna says, some parts of the administration tend to ignore the rights of ›the Italian language‹. This phrasing is a typical way of addressing minority rights, and the minority person is reduced to nitpicking and nagging when insisting on their rights. This was said in the context of the experience of Anna's elderly mother who speaks Slovenian only very badly and who had trouble explaining her condition to doctors. As the doctor—patient relationship is already hierarchical, and as medical problems make people feel insecure anyway, the feeling of impotence is increased by the language conflict. Anna criticizes the doctor's behaviour and goes back to her statement at the beginning—we have always been there.

The hierarchical situation of minority and majority language comes to the foreground when Anna talks about forms of social negotiation, in this case the topic is the size of the letters used for inscriptions. The size being equal to the grade of recognition the collective speakers might enjoy.

»Vidi se, da so [...] posebno jezikovne stvari, ker morajo biti pisane, ker mesto je dvojezično, niso vedno uopštevane. In če so, so velikokrat, napisi javni, ne samo veliko napake, in tudi ko človek gre tam notri in pove, da so napake, te osebe nimajo zanimanja, da se popravi te napake. Ampak dvojezično mislim da pomeni, da jeziki so paritetni, in ne da en jezik, slovenščina, ima večji napis od druge.

[One can see [...] that things need to be written, because the city is bilingual, but this is not always considered. And where they are, they are often, the public inscriptions, are often not only with many mistakes, but also, when you go in and tell them there are mistakes, the people are not interested to correct the mistakes. But bilingualism, I think, means that the languages must be equal, and not that one language is bigger than the other.]« (Anna, 1:48).

Figure 16.5: Anna talks about different sizes of letters and the resulting hierarchization of languages, this is her example

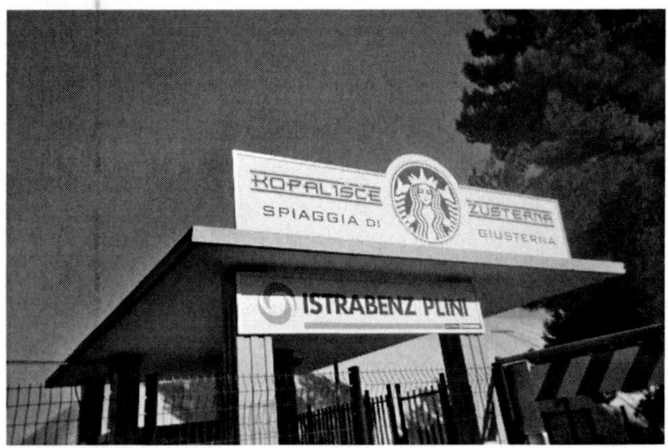

Photo: Anna

From these narratives of social interactions there is one thing that catches the eye—it is the feeling of impotence and the pain of being overpowered by a predominant rival. And this rival is mostly the comfort, the convenience of the majority language, of the bigger group of speakers and of the standard, not the least concerned about the pain Anna feels when she experiences the depreciation and disregard/irreverence for her culture.

BEYOND THE COLLECTED DATA

The multimodal biographical approach to the representation of minority languages brings results that would otherwise not be obtainable. Interviews, photographs, sketches and notes complement one another. So far, the bundle seems to be meeting the concerns of the complex questions in a very constructive way. The new kind of material being generated by the complex research method helps to gain new insights and interpretations as the narrative does not stand alone but has other material to be specified. The use of cultural probes to gather information encourages the research participants to think about their own and the social heteroglossia and to try to express their thoughts and feelings about them. There are indications of individual and collective constructions of identity that gather around the representation of language/languages. This not only surfaces in the presented interview and the accompanying pictures contributed by Anna but also in numerous other interviews.

In the visual contributions the negotiation of power relationships in the form of written language becomes especially evident. This can be seen in the relationship of majority and minority and their ability or non-ability to communicate, but also in social and political structures and the way they work as described in the example around the implementation of the minority laws. As described by Anna, the ambitious minority law that is not being executed produces a double-bind and makes her feel insecure and insignificant. Her reaction is to offer her help to the authorities to improve the implementation of the provisions and to keep pointing to the deficiencies. At this point it seems promising to adopt further methods to work with the gathered material as the research participants' reactions to the stated short-comings differ greatly. It is the contradictory and inconsistent moments in minority/majority relationships, which make evident the importance of further research in this field. The negotiation of the representation of cultural/language minorities is only one aspect of handling difference. The idea of equalizing the population to eliminate conflicts is not only an illusion but has proved itself a dangerous concept throughout history. Situations as described by Anna and other research participants indicate that this lesson has not yet been learnt. There are several areas of representation and of everyday use of a language that in the eye of minority speakers need to be taken care of.

For their results to have a perspective that can be put into practice, one point has to be beyond question: that diversity is of considerable social value, no matter whether ethnic, cultural, linguistic or otherwise. Then, it is a job for everybody, for all members of the society, to take the necessary measures. Considering this fact, Anna's communicative strategy to keep working on her (linguistic) living environment can be seen as promising. One visible result of Anna's efforts could be street signs with correct street names.

Oral source

Anna (2006), born in 1944, pensioner in Capodistria/Koper. Personal communication, recording at author's place.

BIBLIOGRAPHY

Anderson, Benjamin (1991): *Imagined Communities: Reflections on the Origin and Spread of Nationalism*, London: Verso.

Assmann, Jan (2000): *Das kulturelle Gedächtnis. Schrift, Erinnerung und politische Identität in frühen Hochkulturen*, Munich: C. H. Beck.

Austin, John L. (1975): *How to Do Things with Words*, Cambridge, MA: Harvard University Press.

Gaver, William/Boucher, Andrew/Pennington, Sarah/Walker, Brendan (2004), »Cultural Probes and the Value of Uncertainty«. *Interactions* 11(5), p. 53–56.

Gorter, Durk (ed.) (2006): *Linguistic Landscape. A New Approach to Multilingualism*, Bristol: Multilingual Matters.

Hall, Stuart (1997): *Representation. Cultural Representation and Signifying Practices*, London: Sage.

Kress, Gunther/Van Leeuwen, Theo (1996): *Reading Images. Grammar of Visual Design*, London and New York: Routledge.

Mouffe, Chantal (2005): *On the Political*, London and New York: Routledge.

Mörtenböck, Peter/Mooshammer, Helge (eds.) (2003): *Visuelle Kultur. Körper—Räume—Medien*, Vienna: Böhlau.

Phelan, Peggy (1996): *Unmarked. The Politics of Performance*. London and New York: Routledge.

Rogoff, Irit (2000): *Terra Infirma. Geography's Visual Culture*, London and New York: Routledge.

Scollon, Ron/Wong-Scollon, Suzie (2003): *Discourses in Place: Language in the Material World*, London and New York: Routledge.

Strauss, Anselm/Corbin, Juliet (1997): *Grounded Theory in Practice*, London: Sage.

Methodologies of Destabilization

KIOSKCOLLECTIVE

PREFACE

In her book *Enduring Innocence*, Keller Easterling articulates what she perceives to be limiting academic strategies, including: litigious corrective proof, academic ventriloquy or a three-part sermon; being journalistic, encyclopedic or totalizing (Easterling 2005: 10). Easterling's resistance to these traditionally academic means of mediating knowledge threatens to leave us suspended between action and stasis; she opens up a methodological minefield. We are driven and eager to proceed, yet Easterling's words stick with us and if not these strategies, then how do we begin, and what methodological tactics might we employ?

Our response to this has been to bring the issue of methodology into question. Moving away from a Deleuzian tracing of subject (Deleuze/ Guattari 2004: 14), and by adopting a productive, indefinitive and flexible mapping of such, we want to approach sites of knowledge production with a set of methodologies that go beyond simply voicing or theorizing our concerns in abstraction, but that instead allow intervention, conversation and new directions to emerge. Through our practise-based research we want to start new chains of consequence and contingency, rather than translating those that already exist into quantifiable figures. We hope to explore flexible ways of reading, processes of acquiring and methods of communicating knowledge.

We operate in an inherently awkward, post-institution space, a space that holds the potential to unravel the ground on which our theory of academic rote stands (Rogoff 2006). This unravelling has become a priority, and an exploration of methodologies that are born of destabilization has become our starting point. Casting aside the fool-proof to embrace the fool-hardy, the minefield of methodology has become a treasure chest of opportunity— and it is this that continues to unnerve and excite us, driving us in our exploration of critical spatial practices.

Capital Space

As an international centre of global finance, the Canary Wharf estate is fueled by airs (of acute, iridescent capital) and graces (of thick, historic rectitude and strength). It is both cultural and industrial melting pot and privatized, elite and territorial seigneury. First inhabited in 1991, this private estate was constructed on the site of East London's former dockyards. Now, at the centre stands One Canada Square, the landmark pyramid-topped monolith—a momento mori—a giant tombstone to London's heavy industry.

As a research project, Capital Space[1] is not based on a linear-structure, but is organized around a series of thematics explored through practice-led research methodologies. These aim to approach the subject from a range of angles, allowing nodes of interest to emerge and gather, configuring and reconfiguring the constituent elements into shifting constellations of once disparate ideas.

One such methodology is exemplified in the ›fisherman‹ fiction. This story, which was told to us, quickly transcended its capacity to be a singular strand of research. The ›fisherman‹ soon became a touchstone that would inform our reading, writing and critical understanding of the possibilities of alternative and experimental methodologies. The ›fisherman‹ as poetic counterpart to theory is a key-player, a pawn in the grand structural plan of capital. He embodies the workings of the micro-economy; the fictive knowledge; the site of knowledge; the anecdotal mapping of the terrain. The figure of the ›fisherman‹ exists in multiples, as the ›shoe-shiner‹, the ›economic astrologer‹, the ›dry-cleaner‹; and others like him, producing both anthropological diversity and affective clarity to the naturally complex structures and systems of this site.

The following lexicon derives from the relational clusters of thematics and methodologies that these multiple entry points create, drawing a retroactive framework for the project Capital Space. In this context, the lexicon serves to contest more traditional modes of reading and writing, drawing out the intricate theoretical matter that forms its base.

Although the definitive is unavoidably implicit in the compilation of a lexicon, it provides a method of drawing together the vast network of intricacies and disparate poeticisms that make up Capital Space. The lexicon becomes implicated through fiction and vice versa.

We arrived at the junction between the East India Dock Road and the Blackwall Tunnel Approach, where Billingsgate Market marks the clashing of territory between the East End and Canary Wharf, to realize that once again our fish-seller was not selling fish, indeed he wasn't there.

---

1   www.capitalspace.org

We were told of this man, the fish-seller, the ex-city worker who caught his fish early in the morning, to sell until he sold-out across the day. He stands there before Canary Wharf, in the shadow of his past, following his own shadow as the day cumbersomely chases the light. Meandering between junctions and basins alike, between import and export, as other. He isn't a renegade, nor is he part of the black market, he simply angles for pleasure, for an honest wage, to appease the fact that he no longer dictates the shadow to which he is now fastened.

Our man was not there the day that we ventured between the shadows that cooled and the highways that propelled one into the heat of the city. Maybe a day off, perhaps a self-entitled holiday.

APOCALYPSE

FUTURE-GAZING: The sci-fi, the futuristic, the entrenched post-present, the end of days; Canary Wharf evokes an apocalypse of the present. So forceful and captvating are the lines and reflections of Canary Wharf's architecture that it is easy to get swept up in its aspirational future-gazing. It speaks of a pre-occupation, pre-habitation and pre-taming of the future of finance. Through this gesture it waves goodbye to the archaic procedures of the present and past, signaling their demise with a nod to the future. It embodies an apocalyptic cheerio.

ANXIETY/APOCALYPTIC CYNICISM: This private estate feels at once ultra-threaten*ed*, ultra-threaten*ing* and ultra-safe—the blind eyes of its high towers and ostentatious displays of global capitalism seem threatening yet vulnerable. Terror is always looming. The fear of ›immanent‹ attack on this bastion of Western financial power pervades the shining glass of the gated metropolis. This perpetual state of crisis, proclaimed not least by traffic lights in company foyers, is managed and responded to via paranoid and preemptive gestures, symbols and structures.

CRISIS: As the headquarters of the financial crisis, with its fatally far-reaching financial decisions, Canary Wharf sealed the deals that sent ripples throughout the country and the world. Is Canary Wharf in crisis? The East India Dock Road fisherman embodies an alternative economy, born and played out in the vicinity of Canary Wharf's crisis. Lay-offs leave workers seeking alternative sources of income—the ex-banker sells fish from a bucket by the side of the motorway—an uncanny return to Docklands' past life in a quasi-folkish turn of events.

CAPITAL: Unable to physically contain the technological requirements of a wired-up, global banking world, the centuries-old architecture of The City relinquished its spatial monopoly into the larger and better equipped hands of its over-confident neighbour. With performance as it's mantra (of both its efficiency and theatricality), Canary Wharf eagerly took on London's banking responsibilities. Retaining a certain flavour of refined English power, The City masquerades as the face of English wealth—the hard-peddled image of the genteel English financier is strong currency in this intricate and ruleless game. While client meetings and networking events are performed in the plush elegance of The City, the functionality of Canary Wharf points to The City's ultimate defunctness.

PALIMPSEST: Canary Wharf by-passes the emotional register of the politics (Thatcherite privatization) and resistance (residents vs. privatization) that constituted the particular dynamic in which one industry gradually and literally re-placed another. The obsolescence of one global industry—shipping—is ossified by the existence of another—finance.

ELEMENTS

LIGHT/SHADOW: The elements shape, and are shaped by, Canary Wharf. They map a body of facts, stories and layers of information, revealing emotive and symbolic micro-economies. For example exploring the monetary value of light, in the context of urban development, the broader narratives of wealth and poverty, mobility and resistance start to emerge.

Daniel works on the 14th floor of the Barclays building, a 30-floor skyscraper to the east of the Canary Wharf development. In the winter the sun never rises high enough to take the adjacent social housing out of the Barclay's shadow. »We used to live at Canary Wharf in a low-rise block of flats,« he told me, »… but as more and more tall buildings popped up we felt the shadows looming over us. In the end we decided to move.«

MIRAGE: For those still swimming in the shallows of financial dependency on the state, overt images of corporate success and mobility can be as irrelevant and unobtainable as they are incomprehensible. And for an immigrant community that has moved into the shadow of Canary Wharf, gaze falls first onto the day-to-day means of provision and survival, and not toward extravagant symbols of excess and success. These are two seemingly unconnected worlds, fluctuating in turn as mirages on the same architectural horizon. They are non-confrontational, disengaged and non-contingent.

WATER: Water in the context of Canary Wharf—the river, the sea, the fishseller—facilitates a curious unravelling and refiguring of layers of history and anecdote. It offers a shifting surface on which to bring together disparate kinds of knowledge. The elemental-as-economy is recognized and utilized at Canary Wharf, exemplified in the presence of an unnaturally born natural environment shoe-horned into the Canary Wharf complex.

WIND: Canary Wharf is an architectural slice of the big apple. But transport this slice of downtown horizon to the exposed river estuary location of East London's West India Dock, and soon the divergent weather conditions make their presence felt. The architectural planning and structure of the estate is designed and manifests in such a way that the wind is channelled in a wind-tunnel fashion, with gusts so severe that it becomes almost impossible to move through the streets. For staff working in the main block of buildings, which are occupied primarily by international banks, as opposed to the ›second-rate, blue-chip companies‹ separated from the central hub by a five metre-wide water divide, all of the buildings are connected by underground walkways that minimize, if not eliminate, a need to venture outdoors. On the other side of the glass, and on the other side of the water, the wind howls aggressively. On the inside, in the centre, you may never need to feel it.

RIPARIAN LANDSCAPE: The wonder that is the communion between temporality, geography, water space and capital in Canary Wharf writes into the place, a poetry. The poetics of water space and the capital that informs its economic (née industrial) prominence, unifies in context to the overarching framework of London's Docklands. The Thames Head, Valley, Gateway and Estuary provide significant points of reference and context to Docklands; trade, connectivity and investment. This, as economy, balances the unnatural and natural flows in and out of the abstract systems of Docklands to which it contributes. Because of this, the economy of water draws an entire genealogy over both its physical and metaphorical surfaces.

Figure 17.1: Verena Schwarz and Anne Tetzlaff, Roothold, *performative essay (detail), 2010*

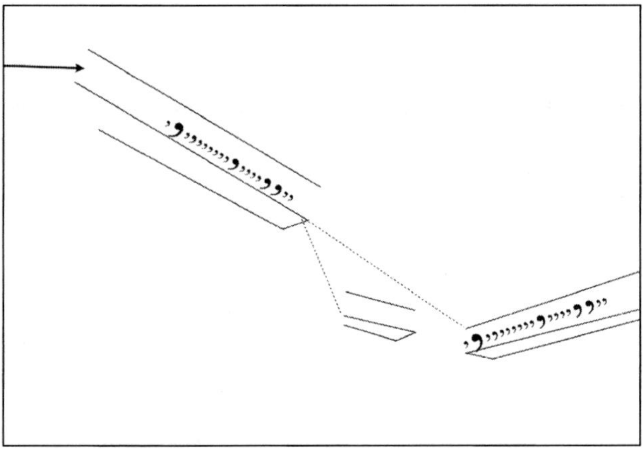

Drawing: Capital Space

TERRAIN: Measuring the city with bodies, steps and glances, the intuitive sense of the space of Canary Wharf begins to unravel. The Limehouse Link and Aspen Way form a white-noise sound barrier and physical obstacle to the pedestrian with measuring feet. The fisherman of our story patiently waits by the spaghetti junction, where no pedestrian was expected to tread.

NEEDS

DESIRE AND UNIFORM-ITY: The transient inhabitants of Canary Wharf's branded space reveal contingent dimensions of this economy. Canary Wharf has a working population of over 100,000 people and although it is a centre of global finance, only a small percentage of these people work directly in business and financial affairs. The rest provide services to fulfil the needs—actual, perceived and determined—of the operations of global finance. Offices are filled with IT staff, executives, mailroom workers, receptionists and cleaners. Outside the confines of the office are security guards, gardeners, builders, personal trainers, waiters, shoe shiners...

»[Canary Wharf] magnifies the feeling that I want to avoid when I work, [...] you become like a soldier going to work, everyone looks the same, there is no difference or diversity, everyone is wearing the same thing [...] all I could hear in the tube was the footsteps, everyone doing the exact same thing, going in the exact same direction, looking the exact same way, it magnifies all those things that in some way I am trying to avoid« (sales person, Canary Wharf).

Asking the peripheral majority about their experience of working at Canary Wharf, a web of desires, frustrations and forces come into play. Service operates in tense partnership with aspiration.

DREAMING ECONOMIES:

»Very few people talk to you, everybody is always too busy for that. I'm sitting on this chair for six hours but most of the time nothing happens, so I think about the future—I build in my own head a dream house, stairs, cupboards and corners« (toilet ›security‹ worker, Canary Wharf).

»I'm self-employed here, and between one job and the other I can do what I want. At the moment I'm reading this book about Mongolia; sometimes I kind of get lost in my thoughts—how good would [it] be travelling? And you know what? I'm actually trying to save some money with my partner, sort out everything and go for it. My dream is doing the Trans-Siberian« (shoe shiner, Canary Wharf).

»I prefer being outdoors rather than inside an office with artificial light and all of that. In winter it gets tough, Canary Wharf is very windy and there's little remedy for that. I've been doing this in The City before and I liked it mainly because there are lots of things happening in the streets. It's like magic. Here it's different though, not much going on, people rushing to their offices or to the shops. Every now and then I like to give false directions to people, make something happen« (flyer distributor, Canary Wharf).

From within the dynamic of a contemporary retail/labour market at Canary Wharf, dreaming economies are continually acted and rarely actualized. Dreaming becomes a rabbit hole through which to escape from the discontent of a mechanic and repetitive job, creating a numbness and oblivion. While at the same time they whisper hopes of resistance and exit. Dreaming economies counteract the discontent of a mechanic and ultra-efficient labour market, expanding endlessly into the ephemeral, before perhaps materializing in the physical. Hope and aspiration offer vehicles to navigate impossibility: »... nothing happens, so I think about the future«. It is this dreaming in the face of mundanity that births the poetic; poetics inspired by real limitations.

LOOKING* AND LISTENING**

* Looking: glancing, gazing, looking away, gawking, examining, watching, capturing
** Listening: paying attention to, asking, eavesdropping

RUTS/THE DAILY GRIND: The workers' movements in and around Canary Wharf are typically the same day-in, day-out. Each worker replays the habitual movements that constitute their daily commute. Routes to and from Canary Wharf are limited and are monitored by security checkpoints, signalling the ›controlled‹ and ›safe‹ character of the area. There is a certain repetitiveness surrounding and emanating from this ›neighbourhood‹. A shopkeeper or a banker has a routine, a routine that is typically Monday to Friday, early morning to late evening with a scheduled lunch or coffee break. People are performing a job, filling a role as consciously constructed as the space itself.

PERCEPTION: Codes of dress and behaviour are integral to the formation of one's perceived role in Canary Wharf. It is a place synonymous with banks, skyscrapers, and business suits. A uniform instantly places you in a category: suits—business; fluorescent jackets—maintenance; jeans and cameras—tourists. Clothes allow for the creation of a distinct identity, and with the precariousness that followed the financial crisis, image became more important than ever. It is a place comprised of comings and goings and dress indicates a role.

THE ORGMAN: London's financial centre is marked by wealth, safety and control. Emanating from the estate's aesthetic is the character of the ›orgman‹, who embodies the role of both ›architect and salesman‹ (Easterling 2005: 2). Keller Easterling's ›orgman‹ in her book *Enduring Innocence* is someone who sells logistics, management styles and networking protocols. The orgman knows every building, every public sculpture, and where the precise borders of Canary Wharf lie. Canary Wharf has been described as soulless, stale, and bland, a bubble separated from the surrounding communities.

PATROL: People rarely feel threatened in Canary Wharf, despite it being perceived as one of the world's prime terrorist targets. The many different forms of security include private security guards in uniforms, plain-clothed patrols, personnel on horseback, sniffer dogs and the thousands of CCTV cameras constantly surveying the area. Throughout this space there is a palpable sense of awareness of the surrounding environment. Everything in the area has a specific purpose and is meticulously placed accordingly. The estate's high standards of order and cleanliness are revealed by the organized flowerbeds and perfectly mowed lawns, all without a trace of graffiti. Its image is conscientiously constructed and any cracks are quickly concealed.

FICTION

STORYTELLING: The fisherman triggers a sentiment towards the poetics and relevance of figures like him, towards the micro-economy, and towards storytelling. This man stands for a strategy, which brings fictive knowledge, that which is not logically tangible, into physical space.

The application of fiction as a processual tool provides room for a speculative methodology, sewing together the residue and prospect, what is there and what is hidden. It preserves, it serves to elaborate and it becomes method through its ability to do just that. Fiction celebrates, respects and transcends temporality; yet it is fastened to time and stays alive in the present. It is situated.

FICTIVE KNOWLEDGE: Fictive knowledges inform and emphasize the palette of truths that appear and fluctuate within time and space. Fiction suggests, registers and methodologically theorizes anecdote against history. Fictive knowledge reveals not only a pluralism to place and territory, but also reveals place and territory as wholly susceptible to definitive strategies of knowledge.

Fiction-as-tale-as-truth-as-›method‹, writes into this work a narrative surrounding the micro-political, the micro-economic and the micro-regime. It becomes or acts all three. Fiction allows for the examination of the substrates of the physical territory and in turn this under-layer becomes pro-tagonist.

Situated Knowledge: Fiction-as-method questions *what* it processes by examining just *how* it is processed. It does not produce nor invent, but it presents. It presents access-points, it allows for the transversal manoeuvring between routinely veiled places, existences and sites of knowledge. By having access to these, the process of fiction enables a reading of the greater picture. As a method it is timeless; the fishseller and the shoe shiner transcend the fixed material realities and fiscal wizardry, they manifest as perpetual flows of consistency and bridge the progressively gaping causeway between human and capital. As such, the economic crash and Canary Wharf were affective machines—producers of fiction.

Mapping

As a form of knowledge production, mapping is traditionally both the illustration and product of a profound Eurocentricism. It alludes to the problematic possibility of understanding place in full and space in its entirety. By virtue of the very communion between knowledge and map, mapping perpetuates the oft-mistaken rigidity of place as defined by its physical and relative location, by the borders which contain it and by its physical characteristics. This in mind, a cynicism over cartography, allows for the teasing apart of mapping itself, bringing a plurality to mapping that extends beyond the inductive map itself.

Exploratory alternative mappings and cartographies permeate the grounds of otherwise fortified theory and method. Such mapping allows for an in-depth exploration of the attributes that constitute and define place and space, and so contribute towards finding other possible points of entry.

Counter-Cartography: Practicing variations of cartography introduces that which would ordinarily be omitted from the physical map and begins to examine and express otherwise hidden, shifting contingencies of a place. It allows alternative perceptions and imaginings of place to be aired and for factors, perhaps more unstable or operating on less translatable registers, to be acknowledged as equally valid means of approaching and gaining an understanding of space. By undoing any agency behind definitive knowledge, that which cannot easily be categorized or written emerges.

Off Mapping: Here mapping is not all-encompassing, it is not simply an alternative paradigm of knowledge categorization, and it is not another definitive trying to counteract the already authoritative. As a process, counter-cartography struggles to resist being representational—mapping-as-method

Figure 17.2: Lucy A. Sames, Navigational Mapping, 2010

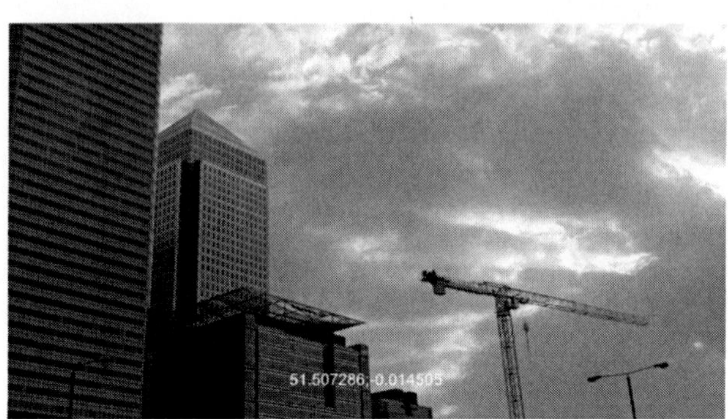

Video still: Capital Space

allows for the communication of such knowledge to be translated across many layers of working channels as dense and complex as their physical counterparts. It allows for the suspension of findings, approaches and positionings in a productive way. There is no centre-point, nor entrance or exit; instead, a limitless series of routes and ways-in emerge. This limitlessness informs the plurality of space and the structuring of place. Residues and future alike are able to rest together. Immersion allows for the questioning of what physically stands and the revelation of what is not categorically pronounced as territory. Through this immersion, economies that are non-exhaustive, those which inform and reform space over and over are presented, and juxtaposed against those which are already present.

BIBLIOGRAPHY

Britton, Lucy/Gouin, Julia/Haslam, Susannah (2010): Interview with Loraine Leeson, 14 May 2010.

Capital Space (2010), http://www.capitalspace.org

Deleuze, Gilles/Guattari Félix (2004): *A Thousand Plateaus: Capitalism and Schizophrenia*, trans. Brian Massumi, London and New York: Continuum.

Easterling, Keller (2005): *Enduring Innocence: Global Architectures and Its Political Masquerades*, Cambridge, MA: MIT Press.

Guattari, Félix/Rolnik, Suley (2008): *Molecular Revolution in Brazil*, Los Angeles, CA: Semiotext(e).

Haraway, Donna (1991): »Situated Knowledges: The Science Question in Feminism and the Privilege of Partial Perspective«. In: *Simians, Cyborgs and Women: The Reinvention of Nature*, London and New York: Routledge, p. 183–203.

Rogoff, Irit (2006): »What is a Theorist?«. http://www.kein.org/node/62 [accessed 10 February 2011].

POST-SCRIPT

Figure 17.3: Lucy A. Sames & KIOSK, Mapping Methodology: visualizing Capital Space, *2011*

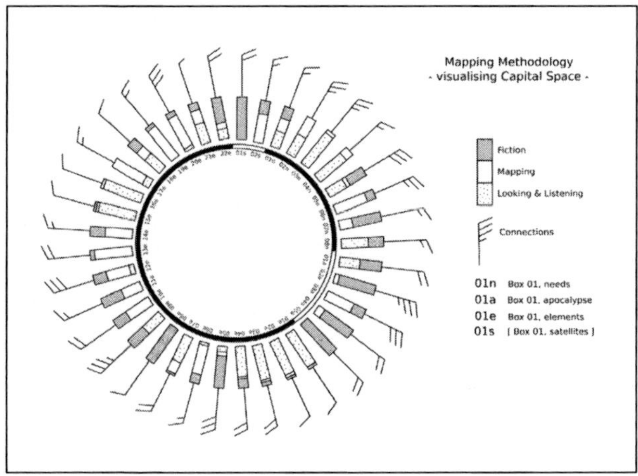

Drawing: KIOSKcollective

The Border Bookmobile

Intervention in an Age of Circulation Anxiety

Lee Rodney

I: Looking for the Border

Jim Lynch's novel *Border Songs* is set in northern Washington State along a sleepy, sparsely populated section of the US-Canada border. This scenic terrain of mountains and green floodplains stretches out to the Pacific coast and is home to a major drug trafficking route for one of British Columbia's major, if unofficial, exports: marijuana. The novel chronicles the lives of a close-knit community of people living on both sides of this border and their increasing suspicion of each other as US Customs and Border Patrol move in with new agents and surveillance gear after 9/11. The novel's main character is a newly minted US Border Patrol agent, an autistic young man with a keen sense of sight who spends most of his time on the job observing birds and wild life along the international boundary. Brandon Vanderkool's attentiveness to the natural world and its movements across this territory extends to his observations of the people he encounters crossing illegally into the US from Canada, who he sees rather sympathetically as stateless creatures fleeing emergencies elsewhere. A reluctant player in these border games, he observes the mundane activity of border policing as if in an otherworldly dream.

Border Songs is an incisive portrayal of the US-Canada border in so far as it draws out the complex politics of visibility and invisibility along this territory and the complications arising as new security mandates fall into place. However, the novel is unique in both its insight and subtlety. The sensationalist portrayal of both American land borders as inherently dangerous locations has gained traction over the last five years. Recent reality TV shows such as ABC's *Homeland Security USA*, The National Geographic Channel's *Border Wars*, and the Canadian Broadcasting Corporation's three-season series, *The Border*, have all sought to dramatize border patrol scenarios and build popular audiences for border policing. Many of these shows debuted at the same time as the Bush Administration's push to expand border security in 2005 by recruiting thousands of new agents yearly to meet targets set by the newly established Department of Homeland Security.

There has also been an emerging popular trend of border watching as a kind of spectator sport in the US which has manifest most notably in the Minutemen Project, established in 2004 in Arizona. Additionally, *The Smuggler's Inn*, a B&B on the northern border in Blaine, Washington bills itself as a kind of border tourism establishment with night vision equipment, binoculars and telescopes for guests eager to watch the more elusive Canadian border for suspicious activity. Bob Boule, the Inn's owner opened the establishment in 2002, somewhat ahead of network television's flirtation with border dramas, but the concept was popular from the outset. Guests often report nighttime visions of *illegals* on the Inn's property, with the hope of contributing to a takedown of an international smuggling ring. However, Boule reports that »usually it's just the Border Patrol walking around« (Mendoza 2009). *The Smuggler's Inn* draws upon quaint stereotypes of the prohibition era, but it also feeds into more powerful tropes of visuality that are written into contemporary discourse on borders. These various attempts to envision the border are linked to what Louise Amoore has termed »vigilant visualities,« an emergent »watchful politics« in America that encourages »looking out« preemptively »with an anticipatory gaze« (Amoore 2007).

Popular interest in border watching, whether on television, online or *on the line* stems from a wave of resurgent nationalism in the US that has been building since the mid-1990s. While 9/11 is cited as the event that irreversibly changed security policy and tightened US borders, both Peter Andreas and Nicholas Mirzoeff have suggested in various ways that the politics of fear that underpins current security regimes in Western nations emerged over a decade ago. Ideas of a borderless world began circulating shortly after the fall of the Berlin Wall in 1989. This idea also found voice in the techno-euphoria of the emergent World Wide Web which was buoyed up by the transnational enterprises of global capital. If this brave new world of flows was full of promise it also prompted unease: Mirzoeff suggests that a generalized form of »circulation anxiety« was at work in American culture prior to 9/11 which was fanned into flame with the attack on the Twin Towers and subsequent wars in Iraq and Afghanistan (Mirzoeff 2006: 12). Additionally, Peter Andreas chronicles the »border games« played by conservative politicians in the American Southwest during the 1990s who aimed to be tough on »illegal immigration« in order to win votes (Andreas 2009: 5).

But in the last decade there has also been a marked shift in the narrative about the US-Canada border, which for many years was known as the *world's longest undefended boundary*. This same territory is now seen as ›defenseless‹, and the Canadian border has been frequently referred to by American politicians as porous and threatening (Akelson/Kastner 2008: 6). Several American politicians have erroneously pointed to the US-Canada border as a ›gateway for terrorists‹ since 9/11, but recently the rhetoric has been stepped up: a report released by the US Government's Accountability Office in February 2011 concluded that only »50 kilometres along the more than 6,400 kilometres have reached an acceptable level of security« (CBC online news, 2 February 2011).

Part of the problem around the American perception of its northern border hinges on a paradox of invisibility which complicates the logic of the US homeland and the security programmes established in this framework since 2002. As there is little to immediately distinguish Canadian from American citizens and still less to distinguish Canadian from US territory along the 49th parallel, visible cues of identification fail to provide a quick snapshot of cultural difference.[1] The logic of visuality and identification that underwrites new security regimes falls apart on the territory of the northern border. The invisibility of Canada within the spectrum of American culture has long been established: for example, English-speaking Canadians are said to pass for Americans when living in the US (legally or not); Vietnam era draft dodgers were said to disappear into Canada. The slipperiness of Canadian culture is only reinforced by the underwhelming experience of driving across the border from the US into Canada where the only notable shifts on the landscape are metric-unit road signs (rather than imperial) and Tim Horton's drive-thrus (the Canadian equivalent of McDonald's). The relative invisibility of this northern border has prompted a reactionary sense of unease (sometimes verging on paranoia) about its porousness.

II: THE BORDER BOOKMOBILE
A framing device for partial and incomplete histories

Much of the confusion around the US-Canada border stems from the historical linkages between Canadian and American economies, which have long been intertwined: the automobile industry has been technically offshored in Canada for just over a century. Detroit's geographical location on the Canadian border placed it at a strategic economic advantage for most of the twentieth century: the major automobile manufacturers, Chyrsler, Ford and General Motors all set up shop on Canadian soil to obtain tariff-free access to markets around the British Commonwealth at the beginning of the twentieth century and in part Detroit's proximity to the international border enabled its meteoric rise (Colling/Morgan 1993). Windsor, Ontario (across the river) grew significantly as an American outpost for auto manufacturing and by the end of the twentieth century manufacturing techniques had become so reliant upon transnational supply chains that a car would techni-

---

1   One could easily dispute the finer points here, most notably important cultural and linguistic differences between English speaking Canada and the Quebecois and other Francophone populations in Eastern Canada and Manitoba.

cally cross the border between four and five times before it rolled off the assembly line on the Canadian side at Chrysler's assembly plant in Windsor. This history of manufacturing initially made Windsor-Detroit the world's most open border city, but the complications arising from the increasingly bifurcated, post-industrial geography are multiplying as border politics play out on the site of the largest urban area on the US-Canada Border.

Figure 18.1: The Border Bookmobile, *Storefront Residency for Social Innovation, Windsor, 5–10 July 2010*

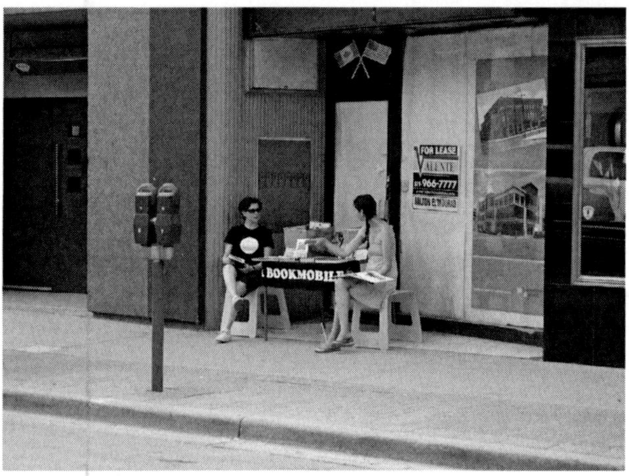

Photo: Michelle Soulliere

In 2009 I began a project, *The Border Bookmobile*, a travelling exhibition that tours the Windsor-Detroit region with a collection of books, artist projects, photographs and ephemera about the shared urban history of the two cities and other border cities around the world. The collection is housed in a 1993 Chrysler Voyager minivan. These vans were produced in the Chrysler Minivan Assembly Plant (the largest auto factory in Windsor) so the van acts a symbol of the economic cycles of the region and the vicissitudes of manufacturing and trade that constitute a local, transnational history. The Bookmobile is in part a memory project that seeks to chart the changing relationship between Detroit and Windsor as border cities in the industrial heartland of North America. But it is also a social platform and conversation piece, a catalyst to discuss borders within and between cities, and the production of space within borderlands in more heterogeneous and contested parts of the world.

The initial impetus for the project was to provide context for the changes that have taken place in the Detroit-Windsor region, changes that are directly linked to so-called thickening of the border after 9/11, but also to larger phenomena: transnationalism, de-industrialization, and shrinking cities: simply put, globalization's counter-narratives. The Bookmobile looks to border regions to critically and creatively map the spatial politics of twenty-first century global culture, but it also seeks to investigate the complex processes that mark these locales as contested or abject territories. Our research into the urban condition along this section of the US-Canada border builds upon recent research on Detroit: insight into its historical conditions, the violence of urban design in the mid-twentieth century and the ideas of planned obsolescence built into the foundations of the American automobile industry. While these are critical perspectives, Detroit's larger geographical position on an international border appears only as an obscure footnote in its twentieth century history. A transnational perspective on Detroit-Windsor history suggests that Fordist manufacturing was already moving offshore in the early part of the twentieth century, long before the height and eventual flight of global capital.

Figure 18.2: The Border Bookmobile, *Ambassador Park, 19 September 2010*

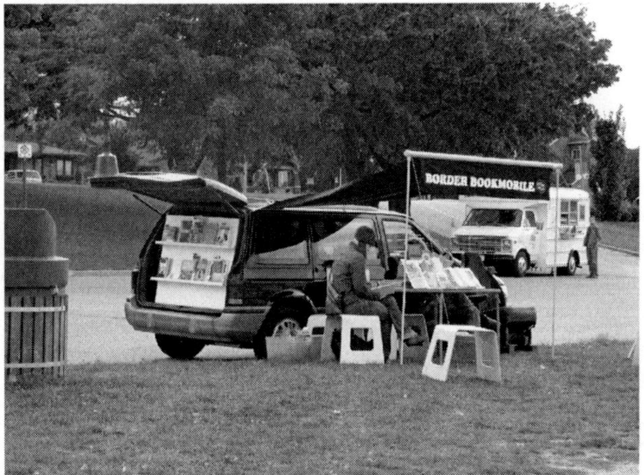

Photo: author

The Bookmobile seeks to archive and reposition local history within the framework of international borders, a situation that is often lost when histories are written along national lines. In pulling together a collection of local history books for the Bookmobile it emerged that there are two distinct sets of titles that indicate that Windsor's history is only tangentially involved in Detroit's and Detroit's history is entirely free of any reference to Windsor. Official history stops at the border, but longtime residents of both cities will suggest a very different interpretation of place, one that is often narrated by a sense that the two cities were, in the past, continuous and uninterrupted and that Windsor was one of many Detroit neighbourhoods rather than a border town of another country. To this end the van and its collection serves as a discussion platform to draw out the shifting relationship between the two cities. Visitors to the Bookmobile are interviewed about their impressions of their neighbouring city and whether their travels between the two places have been slowed down or altered in the last decade. Some also relate stories regarding border crossings in other places.

Both Detroit and Windsor share a tremendous sense of historical amnesia, as much of the early twentieth century architectural imprint has been lost in both places. Demolition has become a kind of strange panacea for the urban ills of the rust belt and the region's architectural history is rapidly disappearing. The Bookmobile's research seeks to reconstruct what has been taken out of view and to counter prevailing apathy about an urban condition that is increasingly bifurcated and disconnected.

III: TRANSNATIONAL SUPPLY CHAINS AND CIRCULATION ANXIETY IN THE HOMELAND

Border cities and border regions have become especially confusing places in the geography of globalization. In 1994 the North American Free Trade agreement was formalized as a series of transnational agreements on manufacturing and trade between Canada, Mexico and the US. While NAFTA was billed as part of a new world without borders, a classic piece of neoliberal policy that prioritized the movement of goods rather than people, the last decade has been particularly problematic for Western governments. The contradictory paradigms left over from 1989 and 2001 have proven incompatible: the supposedly borderless world of transnational trade and globalization does not mesh with newer paradigms of national security and safety.

In North America there has been a tendency to paper over the inherent contradiction between the free flowing border of transnational supply chains and that of the secure, impermeable border sealed off to both migrants and terrorists, who have ultimately been cast in the same threatening guise. The idea of the border as both open (for business) and closed (for workers) presents contradictions that have been only partly mitigated by new border policies that deploy clever terminology: *The Smart Border Accord* (2001) and the defunct *Security and Prosperity Partnership* (2005–2009), for example, suggest that it is possible to have it both ways. Similarly, biopolitical techniques and surveillance technologies have also worked to shift the concept of border security far beyond the physical location of international boundaries. Didier Bigo has suggested that the Möbius strip can be understood as a primary metaphor for state borders within globalization as internal checkpoints and external pre-clearance procedures, as well as the recurring characterization of immigrants as the ›enemy within‹, have worked to alter the idea of the border as a physical limit (Bigo 2005). However, in spite of the virtualization and expansion of security procedures in recent years, there has also been renewed emphasis on American land borders as important physical sites.

The recent emphasis on border security in American culture is fundamentally an ideological matter, one that masks questions of national identity behind the mantle of national security. In this context security operations can be seen as linguistic and performative phenomena as much as they are a function of the vast edifice that forms the Department of Homeland Security, which was the single largest reorganization of federal government since 1947 (Drache 2004: 12). Amy Kaplan has analyzed the importance of the semantic shift that results from the choice of the term homeland to refer to matters of national security, a term that has had little precedence in American history even during periods of world crisis (Kaplan 2003: 85). The critical turn that this concept introduces is a sense of nostalgia for an imagined home that is lost or inaccessible, a folksy and purist notion of an innocent past. Along with nostalgia the idea of the homeland introduces a measure of defensiveness: it is »something a larger power threatens to occupy or take away, and one has to fight to regain« (ibid.: 89). In this way the discourse of security serves to mask profound insecurity in North American relations and the introduction of resurgent nationalisms that have been played out around the site of the border. Kaplan suggests an inverse relation between American national identity and the scope of American power worldwide: with the ever expanding role of American imperialism through its role as a ›globalized police force‹ the perimeter around the space of the nation or homeland is seemingly more threatened (ibid.: 89).

Figure 18.3: The Border Bookmobile, *Storefront Residency for Social Innovation, Windsor, 5–10 July 2010*

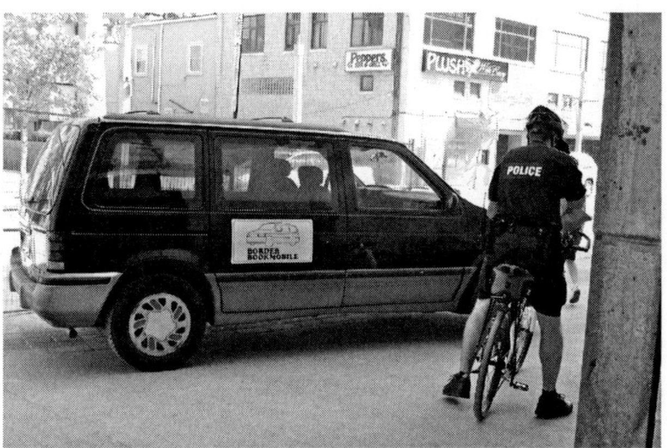

Photo: Michelle Soulliere

The theme of the home in relation to the War on Terror is also traced out by Nicholas Mirzoeff in his complex analysis of global visual culture produced during the Iraq war (Mirzoeff 2009). Whereas Kaplan examines what the *homeland* might mean in this context, Mirzoeff traces the distribution of domestic space in American culture and ways in which Americans watched and received news surrounding the invasion of Iraq. While much has been said about the spectacle created around the US invasion in 2003, Mirzoeff suggests that we must also look to the contemporary built environment, specifically the rapidly expanding suburbs and exurbs in order to understand popular protectionist impulses that had been building since the 1990s. Linking the arrival of the Sport Utility Vehicle and the popularity of suburban McMansions with the beginning of the War on Terror, Mirzoeff maps out the kinds of spaces built to accommodate a rising tide of ›circulation anxiety‹ in American culture. These increasingly fortified personal spaces became standard for many Americans as super-sized vehicles, homes and televisions became the new normal in the 1990s and early decades of the twenty-first century.

Suburbs have been linked to a form of military urbanism since their inception in the 1950s (Segrue 1996; Park 2005). Federal programmes promoting the dissolution of dense urban areas through the development of highways and sprawling metropolitan regions were undertaken as a means to protect against foreign military strikes after the bombing of Hiroshima and Nagasaki. Again, this footnote in urban history was linked to Detroit. As the ›Arsenal of Democracy‹ during WWII, when its factories were repurposed to produce munitions and war planes, the Eisenhower administration passed both the Federal Housing Act and the Federal Highways Act to speed the development of freeways and suburbs as new funding to inner city development was all but eclipsed. Detroit was the first large American city to undergo a long and seemingly irreversible transition to the suburbs and its automobile industries happily manufactured the vehicles to enable people to slowly unmake their cities.

Both Detroit and Windsor historically served as a template for twentieth century transportation patterns throughout North America. As automobile manufacturing and car culture linked the two cities, the border infrastructure emerged as a drive-through toll plaza, a kind of speed bump that served only as a mild inconvenience to people who worked in factories on both sides. The drive to drive was so strong in this border region that passenger ferries crossing the Detroit River were eliminated in 1942, and by 1990 the pedestrian walkway on the Ambassador Bridge—the last remaining method of crossing on foot—was shut down. These ideals of efficient circulation and constant movement were born with Fordism: in 1905 Henry Ford famously remarked that »the city is doomed [...] we shall solve the problem of the city by leaving the city« (Herron 1993). The flight from the city to suburbs and exurbs prophesied by Ford, and the city's eventual remaking as a tightly controlled, neo-liberal shopping space is illuminated by Jacques Rancière's characterization of contemporary space as the ›space of circulation‹, where one must not loiter, but rather constantly move, goaded by the policing slogan, ›Move along. There's nothing to see‹.

IV: MINIVANS AND THE SPACE OF CIRCULATION

The minivan plays a pivotal role in the economy of circulation in North America. As a late twentieth century concept vehicle, it corresponds in a number of ways to a moment in the late twentieth century when suburbanization had become the dominant model of spatial planning and land use in North America. With this second wave of suburbanization came affiliated concepts, which might also be linked to ›circulation anxiety‹: soccer moms and helicopter parents. Windsor's minivan plant produced the first of these vehicles in 1982 and it continues unscathed by the arrival of the SUV and the recent economic recession. While the minivan was manufactured in Windsor, it conceptually originated from the design studios of Detroit, which was one of the first big cities to abandon its dense urban core in favour of a sprawling suburban metropolis. While Detroit is often said to be shrinking, its population was more accurately moving, slowly and steadily away from the urban core to satellite cities and townships on the periphery (Park 2005). A similar pattern has ensued in the Windsor region on the Canadian side to the point where we are left with a loose and disjointed collection of developments that form a large international suburban donut.

Figure 18.4: The Border Bookmobile, *Assumption Park, 26 September 2010*

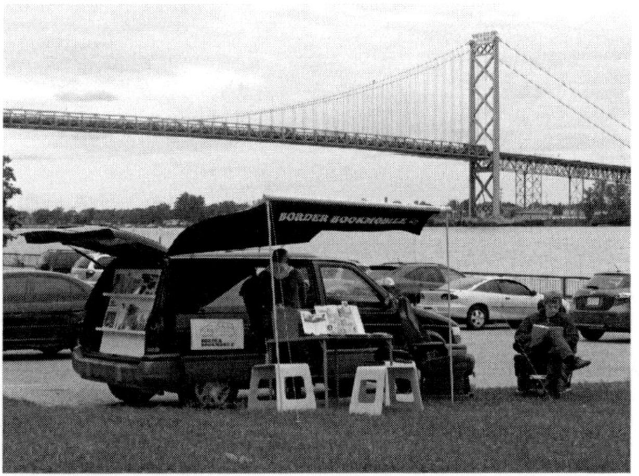

Photo: author

As the international crossing traverses the deteriorating urban core of the two cities, these once vibrant urban regions have been functionally reduced to thoroughfares that accommodate international and interurban traffic. Now the tightly controlled traffic zones that connect Windsor and Detroit privilege the movement of goods over the mobility of people. In the years immediately following 2001, the only thing that seemed to be moving were trucks—up to 9,000 of them daily, idling on the Canadian side waiting to gain access to the US. While the Möbius-like borders of global economies and transnational manufacturing logistics continue to be relatively unhampered by new security policy and the recent U.S recession, communities along the border are increasingly divided as security procedures increase crossing times. Here, relations of proximity and distance are determined by border infrastructure, traffic volume and wait times. This fragmented cultural geography is difficult to characterize or frame within the existing vocabularies of urbanism and nationalism.

Figure 18.5: The Border Bookmobile, *Open Corridor Festival, 29 September 2009*

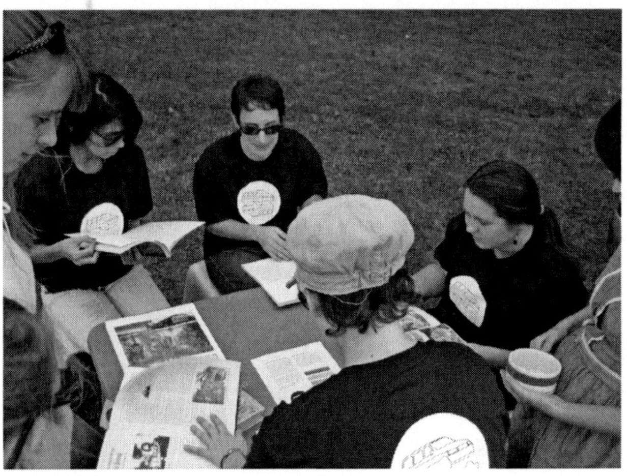

Photo: Julie Sando

The *Border Bookmobile* attempts to intervene in the tightly controlled spaces around the border, to encourage circulation (of ideas, of people) in an era of circulation anxiety. Mirzoeff's concept owes a debt to Jacques Rancière's reading of politics and the contradictory modes of circulation that are supported both by government and transnational capital. Public spaces in general, and borders in particular have become governed by what Rancière loosely but accurately termed ›the police‹, or rather, a policing function that aims to keep some things moving—goods, economies, while we busy ourselves more locally in consumption. What is lost in this distribution is politics because governments:

»[...] tend to shrink this public sphere, making it into its own private affair, and in so doing, relegating the inventions and sites of intervention of non-State actors to the private domain. Democracy, then, far from being the form of life of individuals dedicated to their private pleasure is a process of enlarging this sphere« (Rancière 2006: 55).

The minivan was once a vehicle for the spatial expansion of the American nuclear family, a vehicle that orbited the outskirts of the city in never ending loops between Costco, the elementary school and the hockey arena. It was first marketed during the Reagan era and aided in the atomization of the public sphere which was in the process of becoming reduced to relations of commuting, greater and greater distances, between the private home and the various spaces of leisure and consumption outside. The minivan's future remains uncertain as the SUV has taken its place in the North American driveway. However, minivans seem to be living a second life in the marginal spaces of American culture—there is no shortage of them on Detroit's inner city freeways and they are popular with Latino families in the Southwest where they eventually go south of the border filled with everything from mattresses and over-sized stuffed animals to old microwave ovens, all manner of consumer goods cast off in the cycle of newness.

If Rancière's ›space of circulation‹ is kept in motion by the idea that there is ›nothing to see‹ he is also suggesting that most of us are too busy to stop and look (Rancière 2001: 7). Mirzoeff advances Rancière's ›nothing to see‹ as another way of suggesting that we do not have the authority to interpret what we might be seen: »By being simply a citizen, one does not necessarily attain the full authority of the visual subject, the person who is allowed and required to look in all circumstances« (Mirzoeff 2006: 17). Contemporary border politics is complicated by mixed messages and conflicting notions of visibility and invisibility: from the ›vigilant visualities‹ of the Minutemen Civil Defense Corps and their obsessive search for the invisible trace of so-called illegals to the opacity of transnational trucking operations, a banal parade of invisible goods shuttered off in transport containers. This anti-spectacular border as a space of circulation remains a nonplace, the no-man's land of the frontier and a far cry from the media spectacle produced by major television networks.

In the midst of these conflicting ideas about borders, the *Border Bookmobile* acts as an exploration vehicle, a détournement of the minivan and the space of circulation that it participates in. Its aim is to open up other views to local history and other views to border politics than those put forward by Homeland Security and major television networks.

BIBLIOGRAPHY

Ackleson, Jason/Kastner, Justin (2008): »Routinizing Cooperation and Changing Narratives: The Security and Prosperity Partnership of North America«. *Journal of Borderlands Studies* 23(1), p. 13–30.

Amoore, Louise (2007): »Vigilant Visualities: The Watchful Politics of the War on Terror«. http://www.publicspace.org/en/text-library/eng/b033-vigilant-visualities-the-watchful-politics-of-the-war-on-terror [accessed 19 February 2011].

Andreas, Peter (2009): *Border Games: Policing the U.S.-Mexico Divide*, second edition, Ithaca, NY: Cornell University Press.

Bigo, Didier (2001): »Internal and External Security(ies): The Möbius Ribbon«. In: Mathias Albert, David Jacobson and Yosef Lapid (eds.), *Identities, Borders and Orders*, Minneapolis, MN: Minnesota University Press, p. 91–136.

CBC online news (2011): »Visas for cross-border travel not on radar«. http://www.cbc.ca/politics/story/2011/02/02/border-security-visas-cda-us.html [accessed 2 February 2011].

Colling, Herbert/Morgan, Carl (1993): *Pioneering the Auto Age*, Windsor, Ontario: Benchmark Publishing.

Drache, Daniel (2004): *Borders Matter: Homeland Security and the Search for North America*, Halifax, Nova Scotia: Fernwood Publishing.

Hallward, Peter (2003): Interview with Jacques Rancière, in *ANGELAKI Journal of the Theoretical Humanities* 8(2), p. 191–211.

Herron, Jerry (2003): *Afterculture: Detroit and the Humiliation of History*, Detroit, MI: Wayne State University Press.

Lynch, Jim (2009): *Border Songs*, New York: Alfred A. Knopf

Mirzoeff, Nicholas (2006): *Watching Babylon: The War in Iraq and Global Visual Culture*, London and New York: Routledge.

Mendoza, Moises (2009). »Exploring the border at Blaine: U.S.-Canada crossing offers its own tourist experience«. *Seattle PI*, 25 February 2009.

Park, Kyong/Vogel, Steven (2005): *Urban Ecology: Detroit and Beyond*, Hong Kong: Map Book Publishers.

Rancière, Jacques (2001): »Ten Theses on Politics«. *Theory & Event* 5(3).

—— (2006): *Hatred of Democracy*, trans. Steve Corcoran, New York: Verso.

Segrue, Thomas J. (1996): *The Origins of the Urban Crisis: Race and Inequality in Postwar Detroit*, Princeton, NJ: Princeton University Press.

Authors

Jorella Andrews is Head of the Visual Cultures Department at Goldsmiths, University of London, and on the editorial board of the journal *Third Text*. Her teaching and research is focused on the relations between philosophical inquiry, visuality, and art practice, with a particular emphasis on phenomenology and the work of Maurice Merleau-Ponty—her book on this topic, *Showing Off: A Philosophy of Image*, is forthcoming with I.B.Tauris. She is also interested in questions about the nature of learning within the dynamic, interdisciplinary field of visual culture. Her publications relevant to this topic include »Critical Materialities« in Angelika Nollert et al. (eds.) (2006), *Academy*, Berlin: Revolver, and »How to be counter-environmental: art, research and the techniques of discovery« in José Quaresma et al. (eds.) (2010), *Research in Art: A Forest, Many Paths*, Edição CIEBA, Faculty of Fine Arts, University of Lisbon.

Margot Bouman is an Assistant Professor at The New School, in New York City. Her research interests include rhetorical forms of visual culture, avant-garde television, video installation art, and the mediated production of the public sphere. Upcoming publications include an essay on televisuality, anamorphosis and transient spaces in *Television Theory Today* (Amsterdam University Press, autumn 2011). Bouman is working on two book projects: a historical examination of the unintended consequences of the avant-garde's foray into television and, with Aviva Dove-Viebahn, an anthology on art and televisuality. Bouman has a Ph.D. in Visual and Cultural Studies from the University of Rochester.

April Bojorquez is currently a Ph.D. student of Social Cultural Anthropology at the School of Human Evolution and Social Change at Arizona State University. Her areas of research include: maize foodways, identity and food production, and art as anthropology. She has a background in museum anthropology and has participated in the Smithsonian's Latino Museum Studies Programme and the US Embassy's Cultural Affairs Museum Internship Programme in Lima, Peru. In 2009, Bojorquez co-curated, with Casandra Hernandez, the national symposium *Exhibiting Ourselves: Representing*

Cultures in Museums in Cultural Centers, which explored new approaches to cultural representation in an increasingly multicultural society.

Lina Dokuzović is an artist and Ph.D. candidate at the Academy of Fine Arts Vienna. Her artwork and research, predominantly as a series of diagrammatical visualizations of theory, analyze the mechanisms of appropriation, privatization and militarization of structures, such as education, culture, the body and land. She is a board member of the Austrian Association of Women Artists (VBKÖ) and an artist-researcher on the *creating worlds* project of eipcp: the European Institute for Progressive Cultural Policies.

Eva Egermann is an artist based in Vienna. Working in various media and collectives as well as in the academic sphere, she has developed approaches that connect theory and research with artistic practices and the contemporary art field. In 2010, she co-organized, with Elke Krasny, the exhibition project *2 or 3 Things we've learned. Intersections of Art, Pedagogy and Protest.* She is currently a Ph.D. in practice student at the Academy of Fine Arts Vienna and involved in the *Model House—Mapping Transcultural Modernisms* project, investigating relations of urbanism, disability and colonialism.

João Florêncio has a background in music, film and philosophy and is currently a Ph.D. student in the Department of Visual Cultures at Goldsmiths, University of London, where he also works as an Associate Researcher of the *Performance Matters* research project. His research interests cover a diversity of scholarly bodies of work including, but not limited to, post-structuralist philosophy, speculative realism, complexity theory, ecohumanities, queer theory, performance studies and art theory. João has written for academic journals such as *Dance Theatre Journal, New Theatre Quarterly* and *Journal of the British Society for Phenomenology*, and several queer zines.

Eduard Freudmann is an artist, filmmaker and author, who researches and intervenes in the intersections of art and politics, power relations and social contexts, history-politics and media mechanisms, strategies of exclusion and the commodification of knowledge. He studied art in Vienna and Weimar and currently works on his Ph.D. at the Department for Contemporary History at the University of Vienna. Since 2007, he has been teaching at the Department for Post-Conceptual Art Practices at the Academy of Fine Arts Vienna, where he co-initiated *Plattform Geschichtspolitik*, an open collective of students, activists and teachers who critically reflect and publicly deal with the institution's participation in colonialism, (Austro-) fascism and Nazism.

Matthew Garcia is a Masters of Fine Arts candidate at the Herberger Institute for Design and the Arts at Arizona State University. As an intermedia artist, Garcia investigates the politics of American Western ecology, human rights and visual culture, with an emphasis on socially embedded art practice and digital media. In 2009, Garcia established Desert ArtLab, an initiative to create, promote, and explore the marriage of desert: art, science, ecology, history and community. He currently teaches at Arizona State University and Phoenix College.

KIOSKcollective is a group of research practitioners working collaboratively in the fields of relational geographies, critical spatial practices, micropolitics and contemporary art practice. KIOSK's research serves to develop an understanding of the multiplicities and multidisciplinarity within contemporary Visual Culture and explores these through diverse practice-led research methodologies. KIOSK formed through cross-disciplinary studies at Goldsmiths, University of London in June 2010, and is based in London, with outposts in Bogota and Berlin. www.kioskcollective.org

Elke Krasny, cultural theorist, curator and author; Senior Lecturer at the Academy of Fine Arts Vienna. She has lectured in Armenia, Austria, Canada, Croatia, the Czech Republic, Iceland, Italy, Germany, Slowenia and Switzerland. Her work on architecture, urban space, engaged art practices, cultural identity and gender is based on curatorial research resulting in exhibitions, walks or publications, including: *Penser Tout Haut. Faire l'Architecture*, Centre de Design de l'UQAM Montréal 2010, Dalhousie University Halifax 2011; *2 or 3 Things we've learned,* with Eva Egermann, Vienna 2010; *Walking Ijburg. City Telling*, Blue House, Ijburg 2009; *The Force Is in the Mind: The Making of Architecture*, edited with Architekturzentrum Wien, Birkhäuser 2008.

Krista Geneviève Lynes is Assistant Professor in Communication Studies at Concordia University. Her research examines the intersections of video art and documentary in making visible feminist political subjects and sites of struggle. Lynes holds a doctorate from the University of California, Santa Cruz's History of Consciousness programme. She is currently working on the aesthetics of ›groundedness‹ in representations of popular struggle and protest. She has published in the journals *Third Text* and *Signs*. Her book, tentatively entitled *Experimental Media, Transnational Circuits* is forthcoming with Palgrave MacMillan.

Ivana Marjanović, Ph.D. candidate at the Academy of Fine Arts Vienna; guest lecturer at Post-Conceptual Art Practices Class, Academy of Fine Arts Vienna; free-lance cultural producer in the field of contemporary arts and theory; co-founder of the Kontekst Gallery in Belgrade; member of Kontekst Collective; lives and works in Vienna and Belgrade.

Suzana Milevska is a theorist of visual art and culture based in Skopje, Macedonia. Currently she teaches art history and theory at the Faculty of Fine Arts, University Ss. Cyril and Methodius in Skopje. In 2004, she was a Fulbright Senior Research Scholar at the Library of Congress, Washington DC. She holds a Ph.D. in Visual Culture from Goldsmiths College, London. In 2010 she published her book *Gender Difference in the Balkans*, Saarbrücken: VDM Verlag, and edited *The Research Machine*, Ljubljana: P.A.R.A.S.I.T.E. Institute. Since 1992 she has curated international exhibitions, conferences and art research projects that engage in postcolonial and institutional critique in arts, visual culture, feminism and gender theory.

Peter Mörtenböck is Professor of Visual Culture at the Vienna University of Technology and visiting researcher in the Department of Visual Cultures at Goldsmiths, University of London, where he has initiated the *Networked Cultures* project (www.networkedcultures.org), a global research platform focusing on translocally connected spatial practices. His current work explores the potential of networked ecologies and collaborative forms of knowledge production vis-a-vis the dynamics of geopolitical conflict and urban transformation. His books include *Die virtuelle Dimension: Architektur, Subjektivität und Cyberspace* (Böhlau 2001), *Visuelle Kultur: Körper-Räume-Medien* (co-ed., Böhlau 2003), *Networked Cultures: Parallel Architectures and the Politics of Space* (co-ed., NAi Publishers 2008), and *Netzwerk Kultur: Die Kunst der Verbindung in einer globalisierten Welt* (transcript 2010), co-authored with Helge Mooshammer. His essays on contemporary art, architecture and visual culture have appeared in international journals such as *Grey Room*, *Architectural Research Quarterly* and *Third Text*.

Helge Mooshammer is director of the Austrian Science Fund (FWF) research projects *Other Markets* (www.othermarkets.org, 2010–2013) and *Relational Architecture* (2006–2009) at the School of Architecture and Urban Planning at Vienna University of Technology. In 2008 he was Research Fellow at the International Research Centre for Cultural Studies (IFK) Vienna and currently teaches at Goldsmiths, University of London. He holds a Ph.D. from Vienna University of Technology. His research is concerned with new forms of urban sociality arising from processes of transnationalization, transient and informal land use, and newly emerging regimes of governance. Publications include *Visuelle Kultur: Körper-Räume-Medien* (co-ed., Böhlau 2003), *Cruising: Architektur, Psychoanalyse und Queer Cultures* (Böhlau 2005), *Networked Cultures: Parallel Architectures and the Politics of Space* (co-ed., NAi Publishers 2008), *Netzwerk Kultur: Die Kunst der Verbindung in einer globalisierten Welt* (co-authored with Peter Mörtenböck, transcript 2010), and the forthcoming *Bauarten von Sexualität, Körper, Phantasmen: Architektur und Psychoanalyse* (co-ed., Scheidegger & Spiess 2012).

Irene Nierhaus is Professor of Aesthetics and Art Theory at the University of Bremen, Germany. She has been teaching at the Universities of Trier, Kassel and Vienna. Her research focuses on the relationship between visual and spatial cultures in architecture, the arts and media in the nineteenth and twentieth centuries and the present. She is the academic director of the Mariann-Steegmann-Institut »Kunst & Gender«. Selected publications: *Arch 6: Raum, Geschlecht, Architektur* (Sonderzahl 1999), *Räumen. Baupläne zwischen Raum, Visualität, Geschlecht und Architektur* (ed. with Felicitas Konecny, Edition selene 2002), *Urbanographies: Studien zwischen Architektur, Kunst und Theorie* (ed. with Elke Krasny, Reimer 2008), and *Landschaftlichkeit zwischen Kunst, Architektur und Theorie* (ed. with Josch Hoenes and Annette Urban, Reimer 2010).

Karin Reisinger works at the interface of architecture, art and theory. She received her diploma from the Vienna University of Technology and has pursued cultural studies at the University of Vienna. Recently, she has been working on her Ph.D. focusing on the visual culture of parks and war at the Institute of Art and Design, Vienna University of Technology. She is involved in *Economic Affairs*, a project about the spatial situation of sex work in Vienna and participates in the international research group Geocritical to elaborate critical concepts for a globalizing world. Recent works include a contribution to the exhibition *Unortnung VI*, 2010, and the essay »Bartleby, the Scrivener« in *trans* 18, 2011.

Lee Rodney is research director and custodian of the *Border Bookmobile*, and an interdisciplinary artist/curator interested in mobile spaces, transnationalism and alternative economies. She has has written on contemporary art, cultural theory, and visual culture in a range of books and publications including *Space and Culture, Parallax, Prefix Photo* and *PAJ: Performance Art Journal*. In 2008 she was a Fulbright Research Fellow at Arizona State University where she began a project investigating the fragmented cultural geography of border regions in North America and is currently writing a book from this research. She is Assistant Professor of Art History and Visual Culture at the University of Windsor (Canada).

Amila Sirbegovic, born in Brčko, Bosnia and Herzegovina; architect and Ph.D. candidate in the Visual Culture Programme at the Vienna University of Technology. Currently, she works in the Office for City Renewal (*Gebietsbetreuung Stadterneuerung*) in the seventeenth and eighteenth districts of Vienna on projects related to migration and urban development. She is co-founder of the interdisciplinary group *Was wohnst du?* (What do you inhabit?), which focuses on forms of habitation of the ›others‹ and on the connections between prejudice, culture and architecture.

Ernst van der Wal is a lecturer in Visual Studies at Stellenbosch University, South Africa. Working under the rubric of cultural studies, art theory and design activism, he investigates the embodiment and visualization of queer identity within post-apartheid South Africa. He is also currently busy with his doctoral thesis in which he focuses on queer/transgender photographic archives as sites of interchange and vehicles of visual transgression.

Dan S. Wang is a printer, writer, artist, and organizer who lives in Madison, Wisconsin. His recent texts have been published as catalogue essays for the Smart Museum of Art at the University of Chicago, the Milwaukee Art Museum, and the *Arrow Factory Triennial Book* (Beijing). He teaches printmaking at Columbia College and helped to co-found the experimental cultural space Mess Hall, both in Chicago. His new projects for 2011 include *The Journey West*, a collaboration with the media artist Stephanie Rothenberg that combines critical art tours of the US with the retailing of tourism in Beijing.

Stefanie Wuschitz is a visual artist, lecturer and researcher working on her doctorate in the Visual Culture Unit, Vienna University of Technology. She studied Media Arts (2006) and took her masters in NYU's ITP Programme at TISCH School of the Arts (2008). In 2009 she was Digital Art Fellow at Umeå University (Sweden) where she started the women artists collective *Mz Baltazar's Laboratory* (http://mzbaltazarslaboratory.org/). Wuschitz teaches at the University of Applied Arts and the Academy of Fine Arts in Vienna. In the last years she has presented her work in Berlin, London, Budapest, Damascus, Helsinki, Linz, New York, Brussels, Prague, Rotterdam and elsewhere (www.grenzartikel.com).

Nada Zerzer studied languages and architecture in Vienna and is now pursuing research in the fields of heteroglossia, public space and social constructions. She has published her work in Austria and Slovenia and has received several awards and scholarships. Zerzer is currently working on a doctoral thesis on visual heteroglossia in the Alpe Adria region of Austria, Italy and Slovenia in the Visual Culture Unit, Vienna University of Technology and in the Department of Linguistics, University of Vienna.